UNDERWATER DIVING

Basic Techniques

UNDERWATER
DIVING
Basic Techniques

Peter Dick
and
David Sisman

Pelham Books Limited
London

First published in Great Britain by
Pelham Books Limited
44 Bedford Square
London WC1B 3DP
1986

British Library Cataloguing in Publication Data

Sisman, David
Diving: Basic Techniques
1. Diving, Submarine
I. Title II. Dick, Peter
627'.72 GV840.S78

ISBN 0-7207-1664-0

While every care has been taken to verify facts
and methods described in this book, neither
the publishers nor the authors can accept
liability for any errors or omissions or for any
accidents or mishaps which may arise,
howsoever caused.

Diving: Basic Techniques
was edited, and designed by
Thames Head Limited,
Avening, Tetbury,
Gloucestershire,
Great Britain

Editorial and Marketing director
Martin Marix Evans

Design and Production director
David Playne

Art editor
Barry Chadwick

Editor
Gill Davies

Designers and illustrators
Jane Moody
Jacquie Govier
Philip Evans
David Ganderton

Photography
Kurt Amsler
Steve Birchall
Mike Busuttili
Gerald Clarke
David Sisman

Typeset in ITC Garamond and Europa Grotesk
on Scantext by Thames Head Limited

Printed by The Bath Press, Avon, Great Britain
and Hazell, Watson and Viney, Aylesbury,
Great Britain

Foreword

The sea covers most of our planet and to explore and experience its many wonders is a joy and a privilege. To dive, be it in the waters surrounding the British Isles or in any other part of the world, to be able to see the underwater world for ourselves, adds a new dimension to life and must count as one of our never-to-be-forgotten pleasures.

To take full advantage of such an opportunity requires understanding, training and practice. Diving is a physical sport and requires practical training in the water. *Underwater Diving: Basic Techniques* is designed to supplement this training and contains all the information that must be known by divers about to gain their first experience of the open water.

All well-written additions to our diving literature that give a better understanding of the skills and knowledge required, are to be welcomed.

As Chairman of the British Sub Aqua Club, which is the governing body for sports diving in the United Kingdom, and as a leading member of the World Underwater Federation, I am particularly pleased to welcome this excellent book. It has been written by two of the BSAC's leading instructors as an introduction to this sport for the novice diver.

This book will be a valuable aid in the diver education and training process — in clubs, schools and professional teaching organizations, both here and abroad.

Ian A.N. Irvine
Chairman, British Sub Aqua Club

Over the years there have been many books purporting to instruct readers in the skills of sub-aqua diving. Some have been inadequate to the task, while others have been too technical for the average reader.

The Sub-Aqua Association have long had a conception of the form that the ideal manual would take — easy to read, informative, profusely illustrated and offering genuinely useful and practical advice. So when we heard that Peter Dick and David Sisman were writing this book we hastened to meet them and to discuss their project. To our delight we discovered that they were producing the sort of book that the diving world has been waiting for.

This book complements the formal training provided by the diving instructor. It supplements the theory lessons and provides a unique reference to the practical techniques. It is very readable and easy to understand while providing all the necessary technical information. In every sport there are tricks of the trade which are performed unconsciously by the experienced but which must be discovered by the novice through trial and error. In this book the authors, through their wide experience, have included many tips which will greatly assist inexperienced divers in achieving competence in a short space of time. The Sub-Aqua Association recommends it to all divers as an excellent companion to their dive training.

Tony Hunt
Chairman, Sub-Aqua Association

Contents

8 **Underwater diving**

How to use this book
How to begin
Terminology, abbreviations
and symbols

12 **Approaches to training**

14 **Underwater skills**
Preparations to dive
Free swimming
Fitness

16 **Breath-hold or snorkel diving**
Choosing and fitting basic
equipment
Masks and flanges
Fins and snorkel tubes
Using basic equipment
Putting on a facemask
Methods of use
Leaking mask and clearing
Swimming with fins
Diving downwards
Pressure at depth
Ear clearing
Practice with basic equipment

25 **Aqualung training**
Aqualung function and operation
The regulator
Assembling and testing
the regulator
Fitting the regulator to
the cylinder
Aqualung assembly
Regulator function check
Ancillary equipment
Dressing
Basic skills
Into the water
Establishing a breathing rhythm
Leaking mask
Weighting technique
Buoyancy control
Entries and hand signals

37 **Elementary skills**
Removing and replacing the mouthpiece
Recovering the mouthpiece
Breathing without the mask
Clearing the mask of water
Ear clearing
Underwater movement
Coming to the surface
Dismantling the aqualung

42 **Advanced exercises**
Tackling problems
Doing two things at once
Removing the aqualung in the water
Exit from the water
Ditch and recovery
Sharing an aqualung
Finning on the back
Snorkelling with the aqualung
Running out of air

48 **Twin-hose regulator training**
Sensitivity to breathing
Removing and replacing a
twin-hose mouthpiece
Clearing twin-hose tubes of water

50 **Preparations for the first dive**
Buoyancy and buoyancy compensators
Pre-dive checks and assembly
Fitting the buoyancy compensator
Exercises and techniques
Buoyancy compensation
Controlled buoyant ascent
Assisted buoyant ascent
Breathing from the compensator bag
Maintenance of compensators

57 **Diving suits**
Wet suits and weighting procedures
Dry suits and suit seals
Dressing and general care of suit
Suit compensation and venting
Suit compensation procedure
Dry-suit buoyancy and weighting
Over-inflation
Blow up, inversion, and flooded suits

63 **Ancillary equipment**
Contents gauges
Depth gauges and knives

66 **The underwater environment**

68 **Man underwater**
Adapting to the environment
Environmental stresses
Cold and exposure

71 **Effects of pressure**
Units of measurement
Atmospheric pressure
Hydrostatic pressure

75 **Pressure and volume changes**
Boyle's Law

77 **Compression and expansion problems**
Effects on the body
Barotrauma
Barotrauma of descent
Barotrauma of ascent
Signs, symptoms and treatment
Vision and sound

85 **Diving physiology**
The release of energy
The mechanics of breathing
Lung capacity
The effect of exercise
The circulatory system
The diver's atmosphere
Gas partial pressures
Gas density and solubility
Oxygen, hypoxia and anoxia
Oxygen toxicity and dangers
Carbon dioxide
Nitrogen and nitrogen narcosis

96 **Decompression**
How our bodies absorb nitrogen
Elimination of nitrogen from
the body
Compression, decompression,
and recompression
Practical decompression
for beginners

100 **The open water**

102 **Conduct of a dive**
The dive plan
Preparation for the dive
Buoyancy check in a diving suit
The buddy system
Talk and check
Entering the water
Descent, ascent and
maximum depth
Visual contact
Separation drill
The ascent
On the surface
Picking up divers
Leaving the water
Post-dive actions
Debriefing and records

116 **Emergency ascents and rescues**

Methods of self-rescue
Ascents from depth
Negative buoyancy
Buoyant ascents
Diver's free ascent
Partial free ascent
Breathing from a BC

123 **Helping a companion**
A conscious victim
An unconscious victim
Deadweight lifts
Buoyancy rescues
Deep rescues
Victim has buoyancy
Victim has no buoyancy
Descent to a rescue
Rescues wearing a dry suit
On the surface
Landing the victim
Resuscitation
Basic life support

136 **Conversion tables**
138 **Glossary**
141 **Index**
144 **Acknowledgements**

Underwater diving

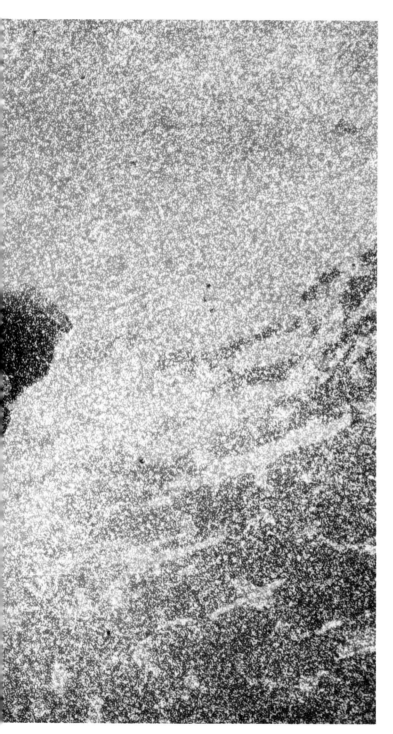

Introduction

Underwater Diving is presented in two volumes: *Basic Techniques* and *Advanced Diving.* This first volume introduces the complete beginner to the sport and takes the novice through all the basic training up to the following standards:

BSAC (British Sub Aqua Club) — Novice Diver
SAA (Sub Aqua Association) — Elementary Diver
PADI (Professional Association of Diving Instructors) — Basic Scuba Diver
CMAS (Confederation Mondiale des Activities Subaqua-tiques) — 1 Star Diver

The second volume deals with the many applied skills associated with diving and is intended for divers qualified up to:

BSAC — Advanced Diver
SAA — Dive Supervisor
PADI — Divemaster
CMAS — 3 Star Diver

Basic water skills and theory are essentially the same throughout the world of sports diving. All the organizations which train divers have their own methods of teaching the techniques but the basic principles are the same and can therefore be adapted to suit any training programme. Such differences as exist will be due to the varied conditions in which the diving is actually carried out.

Underwater diving in Europe is mostly taught and practised by clubs and schools. In the USA, however, it is more usual for beginners to be instructed by professionals who are attached to a diving store or a resort.

9

Underwater diving

How to use this book

The authors assume that the reader will be undergoing proper qualified instruction to include both practical lessons in the water and relevant theory lectures. It would be impossible to teach diving from a book only. Diving is an activity which has to be physically experienced; it can never be an armchair sport. But practical instruction time is very short and at a premium. This book aims to supplement such teaching.

Although the sections are arranged in a progressive order, the book can just as usefully be used for one lesson at a time. We would suggest that before every training session, novices under instruction read up the appropriate section in the book so that they will be prepared for the lesson to come. Forewarned is fore-armed; knowing what to expect will give confidence and make the lesson more readily understood. Then, sometime after the training session, they can read it again at leisure and cover any points they may have missed.

Volume One will contain all the information that must be known by any diver about to gain experience in open-water diving accompanied by an experienced dive leader.

For example, the principles of aqualung use and function are explained to the level of beginners' understanding, sufficient to enable them to use the equipment safely. *Volume Two* takes up this subject again and examines in detail different types of breathing apparatus.

Emergency ascents and rescues however, have been treated in full in *Volume One*. This is because by the time the novices are nearing the end of their training they will be diving with their companions in the open sea, and so this knowledge is vital. They **MUST** know how to make ascents and be capable of rescuing another diver.

Volume Two covers many subjects that are applicable to advanced diving, such as boat handling, tides, weather conditions, dive planning, safety and so on.

We trust that this arrangement will make it easier for the beginner to grasp the essentials of underwater diving, without being overwhelmed by unnecessary information.

How to begin

People are attracted to diving for many varied reasons. Some are excited by what they see on television; it is a fact that applications for membership of diving organizations always increase after an underwater film has been shown. Viewers see the divers in a strange and wonderful world enjoying sights only the privileged few can experience first hand. The implied element of adventure, of probing the unknown, lends a certain 'spice' to diving.

There is more to diving than merely learning to survive underwater, although diving just for its own sake, simply for pleasure, is all that most divers want. Amongst the many applications of diving are marine biology with its associated subject, underwater photography; nautical archaeology and the search for historic wrecks; research projects and so on. All these specialized interests can be enjoyed, provided that the diver can concentrate on the subject without worrying about the actual techniques of diving.

If you are attracted to diving, the first thing to think about is whether diving is a practical proposition for you. Normally, any healthy person can safely take up this sport but should have a medical examination to make sure. Diving training organizations all insist on this, as much for their sakes as yours.

The medical standard is not very demanding. Once this formality is over, sort out in your mind how you want to be trained — as trained you must be. The method chosen will depend on how much time is available in which to accomplish this. If time is at a premium because of some commitment, such as joining an expedition or going on holiday, there are recognized schools which will train you to Sports/Elementary Diver standard in a matter of weeks. Diving schools run courses at times to suit their trainees and will include open-water training sessions.

If you are going abroad on holiday to a place where there is good diving, you may prefer to learn at a local diving centre. Some countries are particularly well organized for this but of course the standards can and do vary. It is difficult to detect the good from the bad unless your choice is backed by personal recommendation or is approved by a national diving organization.

The remaining option is to join a diving club. There are many such clubs in almost every country, usually with a number of local branches. Clubs have regular weekly meetings at their local pools and do most of the diving at weekends and holidays. Although training will take much longer to complete because it is so spaced out, the novice is given much more time to become familiar with the equipment and the underwater environment. Additionally, clubs arrange specialized courses to cover such activities as instructor training courses, boat-handling and VHF radio courses, and offer a social side to their members.

Whichever method you choose, provided the tuition offered is of a recognized standard, the training is basically the same and differs only in detail. Obviously the schools tend to be more expensive than the clubs, but remember they are tailored to the individual's own requirements.

The whole aim of a basic training programme is to teach the new diver how to dive safely and how to avoid problems.

The techniques are designed to show the beginner how to cope with any emergency that might arise. For example, the novice is taught to deal with a flooded mask, or even with no mask at all, in order not to lose confidence should such a situation arise accidentally in deep water.

The finer points of exactly how these techniques are performed are not important − all that matters is that they should work.

For many reasons, most diving organizations have to impose a limit on the minimum age of their members. There are excellent clubs which cater for young enthusiasts and although they will be confined to learning snorkel or breath-hold training, these boys and girls soon develop into well-trained and knowledgeable young divers, ready to commence aqualung training as soon as they are about 15 or 16 years old.

Learning to dive is easy. Learning to survive underwater will require experience and confidence.

Terminology, abbreviations and symbols

In a book such as this, the use of many technical terms and symbols is unavoidable. The new diver will have to become familiar with a number of them that are in common use in diving. A problem arises in that not all the world has adopted the metric system. To assist those who have not, we have included both the metric and its equivalent, the U.S. Customary or the Imperial System. Also, a conversion table will be found on page 136.

Here are some words and abbreviations used in diving with a brief explanation of their meanings:

* Pressure is expressed as force per unit area of surface and is measured in ats or bar.

* Ambient pressure: the water or air pressure immediately surrounding the diver.

* Absolute pressure: total pressure of water at a particular depth (including atm pressure).

* Ats (atmosphere): atmospheric pressure (absolute); a unit of pressure − now superseded largely by the bar (= 1.02 bar).

* Atm: atmosphere

* Bar: a unit of pressure equal to 0.987 or 14.7 psi (plural is bar).

* psi: pounds per sq inch or (lb/in^2), also a unit of pressure.

* HP: high pressure (air)

* kg: kilograms, a unit of mass

* m: metres, a unit of length

* min: minute, a unit of time (also a unit of length or latitude).

* Temperate zones or latitudes: these are areas of similar diving conditions, particularly with regard to temperature. In the northern hemisphere they are the regions which lie between 30°-60° north approximately; in the southern hemisphere they lie between about 20°-40° south.

* Density is expressed as weight per unit volume; for example 1030 kg/m^3 or 64lb/ft^3.

* Capacity is expressed in litres (l) or cubic feet (ft^3).

* Rate of ascent is expressed as metres (or feet) per minute; for example, 15m/min (50ft/min).

Hopefully, within the context of the book these abbreviations and meanings will be acceptable and readily understood.

Approaches to training

Introduction

Breath-hold or snorkel diving is one step beyond swimming and provides the basic physical exercise and experience required for aqualung training (which is assumed to be the goal of those who are reading this book).

Aqualung divers consider mask, fins and snorkel as basic equipment. These can be used on their own to enable a diver to take a look at the underwater world – and their use, called breath-hold diving or snorkelling, is probably the route by which most candidates enter aqualung training.

The aqualung provides a continuous air supply, while the breath-hold diver must make do with a single inhalation before plunging downwards. A 'breath-hold dive' is of limited duration, though considerable depths can be reached by those who are well practised and fit.

This is, in fact, a highly developed sport for some. Man is a comparatively poor breath-hold diver when compared to whales, dolphins or seals, and dives lasting longer than two minutes are rare. The normal maximum depth even for highly-trained spear fishermen is about 30 metres (100 ft). This type of diving depends on using one's own abilities, unaided by any apparatus. The deepest breath-hold dive to date was to well over 100 metres (328 ft). Attempting to dive to such depths is unusual and inadvisable. Most divers are satisfied with a descent to about 10 metres (33 ft). Much could be written on this, but more normal breath-holding activities with shallow dives are the techniques that will be under discussion in this book.

Underwater skills

Preparations to dive

The obvious difference between swimming and diving is that the latter involves going under the surface of the water. All the same, free swimming will help develop a number of skills useful to the diver:

* Being aware of water; understanding the circumstances and the situations commonly encountered while in the water and learning how to deal with them.

* Water survival; staying and moving on the surface, keeping the head above water and obtaining air to breathe.

* Improved general fitness and stamina will also be important.

Potential candidates to a diving course who are poor swimmers will either lack the above skills altogether or will achieve only a poor performance.

Fortunately, within the friendly atmosphere of a diving group most beginners will find they improve quite quickly.

Free swimming

It is necessary to attain some proficiency in free swimming as there are two particular techniques which must be well established prior to using any equipment:

* Breath-hold ability while free swimming underwater.

* Buoyancy control; the amount of air held in the lungs.

Try the following three exercises and note how much you improve with practice:

1 Surface dive to retrieve items from the bottom in shallow water, no deeper than 2 metres (6½ ft). See page 22 for the techniques to use.

2 Float vertically in the water, then blow out and sink to the bottom (2 to 3 metres maximum). On touching bottom, push off and swim forward. The distance swum will increase with practice, but stay within the limits of your breath: do not force yourself to swim any further. This is very important (see also page 92).

3 Learn to float on the surface while stationary by keeping the lungs fully inflated. Take short quick breaths so as not to sink. The best attitude seems to be to lie with the ankles crossed and the legs bent, with the hands grasped behind the back or holding the thighs. Arching the back will lift the chest so that it comes almost clear of the water. Once fully proficient at this, it is possible to support 2 to 3 kilograms (4 to 7 lbs) of lead weight on top of the chest!

The knack with all these exercises, as well as with diving generally, is to relax and approach everything in a calm manner. Doing things in a rush indicates a lack of self assurance; this produces stress and subsequent failure time and again.

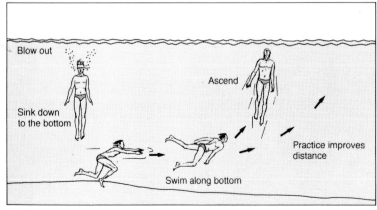

Sink and swim

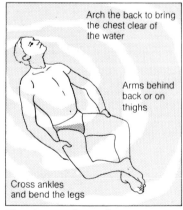

Floating on the surface

Fitness

In an active sport like diving a certain level of fitness is necessary for efficient bodily performance and to help the participant overcome danger. Physically fit divers are able to withstand fatigue for longer periods; they can tolerate stress and are less likely to suffer from decompression sickness. Most healthy people can meet the demands diving makes on them. It is not necessary to be 'superfit'.

Age or physical disability need not always exclude a person from diving. If he or she is medically fit to dive, the disabled or elderly person must simply impose certain limitations on the dive, regarding depth, distance to be swum and physical conditions such as water temperature. Divers should adapt the standard techniques to suit their particular disabilities. This is now becoming widely accepted in modern sports diving. The risk is no higher than with able-bodied or younger people since the essential art of diving is learning how to keep the risks within acceptable limits.

Medical fitness

A check must be made that there are no disqualifying diseases or deformities incompatible with diving. The medical examination should, in fact, encompass this.

Physical efficiency

The candidate must have sufficient energy output to cope with the heavy demands of diving, such as swimming against a tide, carrying equipment or rescuing a victim.

Mental and physical reflexes

The candidate must be able to absorb the training in order to respond properly to any diving emergency. No one knows how he or she will react in an emergency until put to the test, but usually there are some indications during early training. Instructors always look out for these reflex reactions.

The medical examination

To ensure safety, most diving organizations require members to have a medical examination, usually at commencement of training, then five-yearly up to the age of 30, and more frequently thereafter. It is not necessary to have the examination carried out by a specialist diving doctor, provided the general practitioner is given guidance as to which body systems should be examined. Diving organizations will usually provide the doctor with a summary of disqualifying and allowable factors, and will list specific cases which can be referred to specialist medical referees. The important areas of medical fitness include:

* Diseases of the respiratory system. Good lung function improves tolerance to exertion and lessens the chances of lung damage. A current X-ray will be required.

* Diseases of the heart and hypertension; the associated use of drugs such as Beta-blockers, Digoxin and antihypertensives.

* Diabetes/endocrine disorders.

* Chronic ear diseases: ear infections are a continual problem for divers; they can be persistent and hard to eliminate. However, if there is no rupture of the eardrum and the Valsalva manoeuvre can be performed (see page 79), only a chronic vestibular disease would be considered a disbarring factor.

* Epilepsy and some other diseases of the nervous system; psychiatric or personality disorders.

* Amputation or any deformity which excessively limits the ability to swim may disqualify the diver although a restricted-activity certificate (specifying the limitations of that particular person's diving activities) may be granted.

Other aspects to be considered are:

* Teeth: Attention should be paid to ensure fillings are sound. A tooth abcess can cause pain during descent. Loose-fitting dentures can be dislodged and obstruct the airways.

* Eyes: Many short-sighted divers find they do not need any kind of visual aids underwater as objects are magnified by about 25%. Masks can be fitted with prescription lenses if needed. Contact lenses may be washed out of the eyes if the mask floods but some are now available which minimize this risk.

* Pregnancy: We do not advise pregnant women to dive, due to the overall physiological reactions to pregnancy (such as reduced tolerance to exertion, and nausea) rather than to obstetric complications. Also high oxygen tensions may affect the foetus.

The diver may have to call upon considerable reserves of energy when faced with an underwater emergency. Divers have a personal responsibility to achieve and maintain a level of fitness — not only to themselves but also to their companion divers who may require assistance. Do not let yourself become a liability or a casualty!

Breath-hold or snorkel diving

Choosing and fitting basic equipment

The mask allows a clear view of the underwater world and fins provide propulsion, while a snorkel allows a diver to breathe when the face is submerged and looking down.

It will be necessary to know about the advantages and limitations of this basic equipment so as to be able to choose the designs best suited to your personal needs.

If possible try out a wide selection of the different types of mask, fins and snorkel that are available – and seek advice from more experienced divers before making a final choice.

Masks

The eye is designed to work in air; images are focused by the cornea and lens on to the retina. When the eye is in direct contact with the water it is unable to focus because light rays are bent when passing from water to air, blurring the vision. A mask simply interposes a layer of air between eye and water, restoring normal vision. However, the presence of the mask will cause the oblique light rays to be refracted yet again, and this will result in objects appearing closer and seemingly larger.

Refraction of light rays in air and water

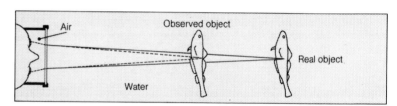

Objects observed underwater appear about 30% larger

Facepieces are made of tempered glass supported by soft rubber surrounds which enclose the eyes and the nose and make a radial seal against the face.

These rubber surrounds have a blinkering effect on the eye; the usual angle of vision is only about 75% which is far less than normal vision on land. Some designs use a

translucent silicon rubber which seems to improve this peripheral vision. Try wearing a mask when on land and see how your vision is tunnelled forward. In general, it is the distance between eye and facepiece which matters. The closer together these are, the wider the angle of view, with less 'blinkering'.

The nose is enclosed by the mask so air can easily be blown into the mask during a descent, to equalize pressures inside and out. This is necessary or, at depth, the air volume inside will be compressed and the mask would then be squeezed against the face by water pressure (see page 78).

Choosing a mask

Most stockists of sports diving equipment are divers themselves and can give help and advice, but here are a few guidelines to follow:

* Choose a simple straightforward design. The type with a kidney-shaped facepiece and rubber nose is as good as any.

* The mask should have a reasonable internal air volume. A very large volume makes the mask extra buoyant which will increase the chance of its lifting up and leaking; also such masks are heavy and take a lot of clearing. However, the inexperienced beginner should not choose one with too small a volume.

* Look at the edge on the rubber support flange which seals against the face. It should look wide and comfortable, not narrow and sharp.

* The strap, which holds the mask in place, should be strong. Ideally it should offer a wide area of support behind the head.

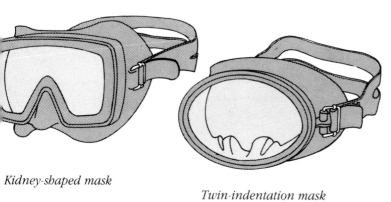

Kidney-shaped mask

Twin-indentation mask

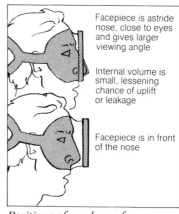

Facepiece is astride nose, close to eyes and gives larger viewing angle

Internal volume is small, lessening chance of uplift or leakage

Facepiece is in front of the nose

Positions of masks on face

A simple test

1 Brush the hair back from the forehead and hold the mask flange in place against the face. Does it seal comfortably against the face?

2 Take a slight nasal inhalation and see how it feels. If the mask seal fits correctly, it should be possible to release the hands; the mask will cling to the face so long as the inhalation is maintained.

3 During this inhalation, the mask will pull back on the face. If the mask is the kidney-shaped type, check if there is any restriction over the bridge of the nose; this may cause discomfort after a while.

Mask flanges

Masks are made for average facial shapes but not everyone is average!

* Choose a wide seal that makes good contact with the variations in facial contour shape. It must be comfortable to wear for a number of hours.

Sharp-edged seals hurt after a short time, especially where they pass over the upper lip.

* Leaking seals are often due to the retaining straps being too tight or too loose. The mask seals against the face by virtue of a slight internal air or an external water pressure, as the circumstances of the dive alter. Tighten the straps just so as to keep the mask firmly in place.

* Flanges sometimes leak near the temples, usually around the top of

the cheekbones where the face has a natural indentation.

Some divers have natural furrows running from the nostrils past the corners of the mouth. These are exaggerated when biting on the snorkel mouthpiece and the mask may leak then. Purse your lips around the mouthpieces. (See also page 33.)

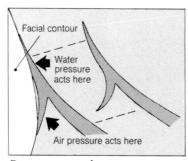

Facial contour

Water pressure acts here

Air pressure acts here

Pressure on seal

* If flanges leak this will usually be because the straps are not adjusted properly. These rubber seals are intended for average facial shapes, but of course no two people are exactly the same.

Does the seal leak air? Adjust the strap, fit the mask properly and see how it feels — is it the right overall size; not too small or too large?

Do you get a reasonable view through the front of the facepiece? Choose tempered glass facepieces as they are unlikely to break and do not readily mist up underwater.

When choosing a mask, or any other equipment, use a reputable dealer and pay a reasonable price. Cheap equipment soon fails and can, in fact, be dangerous. Good equipment will last for years.

Basic equipment

Fins

These appendages on the feet give a diver extra propulsion, enabling him or her to move around with relative ease in the water. They are called fins (not flippers).

Types of fin

There are two types used for normal diving purposes:

* The shoe design, which is usually made with a more flexible fin blade, is particularly suitable for the beginner. The shoe sole offers a barefooted diver some protection when walking in the shallows. These are ideal for pool use or to wear in warm water when diving-suit bootees would be unnecessary.

* With the pocket type, the foot slides into a rubber half-foot and is held in place by a strap around the heel. These fins are intended to fit over a bulky diving-suited foot and are of heavy design. They are more suited to the trained diver.

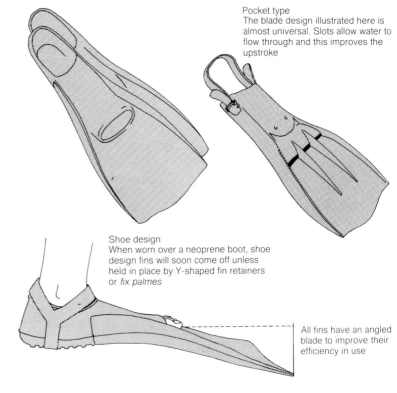

Pocket type
The blade design illustrated here is almost universal. Slots allow water to flow through and this improves the upstroke

Shoe design
When worn over a neoprene boot, shoe design fins will soon come off unless held in place by Y-shaped fin retainers or *fix palmes*

All fins have an angled blade to improve their efficiency in use

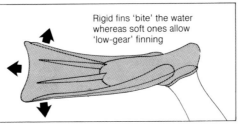

A good design will funnel from the fin tip all the energy that is put into the movement

Bad design will allow energy to be lost sideways from blade

Rigid fins 'bite' the water whereas soft ones allow 'low-gear' finning

Good fin design

Choosing a pair of fins

To drive the body forward through the water, the diver must move the fins up and down, so that the blade area bites into the water. The ability to do this depends in part on the training, but mostly on the development of the leg muscles. For this reason, flexible fin blades are more suitable for beginners. However, after some practice, it should soon be possible to graduate on to a heavy-bladed design, capable of giving greater forward drive.

The criterion for a good fin design is simple. It should funnel all the energy that is put into moving the fin blade up or down, off the blade tip in the opposite direction to create forward movement. If the fin is badly designed, energy may be lost from the side of the blade so that the foot is brought downwards in a falling-leaf effect, moving from side to side.

For the potential diver, the best fin is probably a semi-rigid type, with or without a shoe. Though difficult to use initially, the diver will eventually become accustomed to the fins and able to exploit their greater strength. Choose a rugged straightforward design that will survive some hard usage.

If the type selected is to be for open-water use (in the sea, for instance), remember to wear diving-suit bootees when trying on the fins.

Snorkel tubes

A snorkel is a lightweight rubber tube with a U-turn in its bottom and an attached mouthpiece. It is a simple piece of apparatus, yet an indispensible one, which allows the diver to breathe while looking downwards from the surface.

Choose a plain design, not less than 15mm ($\frac{5}{8}$ in) bore to ensure a good air flow. The snorkel should not be too long; approximately 30 to 35cm (12-14 in) between the mouthpiece and the open end is best.

Those intending to breath-hold dive only may try using a fairly short tube. But the weight of aqualung equipment will push the diver deeper into the water, even while on the surface, and so a little extra length is advantageous. Do not, however, use extra long snorkels, as when the chest is submerged the

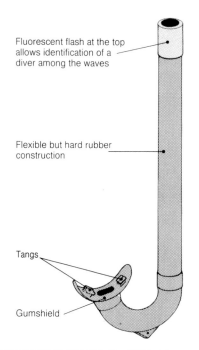

Fluorescent flash at the top allows identification of a diver among the waves

Flexible but hard rubber construction

Tangs

Gumshield

lungs must draw in air against water pressure. You will feel a distinct resistance to breathing because the extra length accentuates the resistance to air flow offered by the bore.

Snorkel tubes should never be integrated with the mask; have nothing to do with tubes that are permanently attached.

The word snorkel comes from the German *schnorkel*, a pipe used by U-boats during World War II to ventilate the boat whilst submerged.

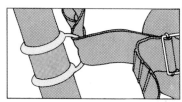

Snorkel mask attachment

Using basic equipment

The diving novice must become familiar with the pecularities and usage of basic equipment before progress can be made towards an aqualung training programme.

When first trying the equipment, choose a warm-water sheltered location (ideally a swimming pool, a gently sloping beach, or a jetty with a ladder) with normal, safe swimming conditions. Do not wear a diving suit at this stage in the training; it will only complicate matters.

Fitting the equipment
Wet the fins and slip them on the feet. If a heel strap is being used, adjust it to be comfortable. Keep the mask dry at this stage. It mists internally when underwater and in

order to avoid this, some divers advocate rubbing a raw potato or even tobacco juice around the inside of the facepiece before wetting it. The simplest way is to use spittle, rubbed around the inside of the glass and then rinsed out. This must be done with a dry mask; it does not work once the facepiece is wet. All divers may be observed following this small ritual before they enter the water.

Hold the mask's rubber retaining strap away from the support flange. Brush the hair back from the forehead with one hand, then bring up the mask to the face, sealing it firmly over eyes and nose. A simple inhalation will confirm if it is seating properly without bad leaks. Pull the

mask's retaining strap into position behind the head.

Slip the snorkel tube up under the mask-retaining strap. It may be fitted to whichever side suits, although aqualung divers will find using the left side better, so they can avoid the regulator mouthpiece tube (see page 29) which usually comes over the right shoulder.

Pull the snorkel forward so it rests on the flange; if it is left resting against a bare cheekbone it will soon become uncomfortable. The breath-hold diver may attach it to the support strap with a small grommet-like device. The aqualung diver should keep the snorkel tube readily available elsewhere.

The facemask

Putting on a facemask

Points to watch

Adjust the mask retaining strap about the crown of the head. Pressure on the forehead or upper lip will indicate that it is too high or too low. If it is left in this position, the mask will leak and will be quickly displaced. Adjust the tension of the strap until it feels quite comfortable.

When positioning the snorkel, make sure that you pull the tube well forward on to the mask flange; otherwise it will press into the cheek which will soon start to hurt.

The angle of the snorkel will allow it to stay vertical while the diver remains on the surface looking forward and down.

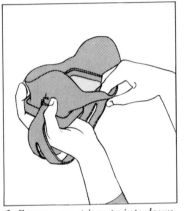

1 Ensure nosepiece points down. Bring the retaining strap forward over the front of the facepiece

2 One hand holds hair clear of forehead while the other hand brings mask up to the face

3 Draw the retaining strap over crown of head. Hold mask firmly against the face

Methods of use

Stand in water which is about a metre deep; stay adjacent to the side of the swimming pool.

Having adjusted the snorkel tube as shown, slip the mouthpiece into place. The rubber projections go between the teeth; the gumshield inside the lips and in front of the teeth. Do not bite heavily on the mouthpiece; it will stay in place if lightly held. Purse the lips around the mouthpiece but not so tightly that you pucker them.

Breathing while looking down

Check that the mask is in place, hold on to the side of the pool and put the head underwater. The initial reaction is to hold the breath, but after a moment try a tentative inhalation. Air comes readily if there is no water in the tube and soon you will be breathing quite happily.

Water in the snorkel tube

Water can enter into the snorkel if its end is allowed to dip under the surface. While the diver is swimming around, the snorkel will have to be routinely cleared.

The instant an inhalation starts it is possible to tell if there is water in the tube. After a while the diver will become very aware of breathing technique at this point and will learn how to avoid drawing water directly into the mouth. Initially, some will probably be swallowed.

It can be cleared by a short sharp blow through the mouth. Not all the water will necessarily be expelled, so the next breath should be made with caution. Make a slow inhalation, which would still allow air to be taken in past any water that has been left in the snorkel bend.

Once another breath has been taken, the remaining water can then be blown out.

Practise ducking underwater and filling the snorkel (you will hear the water enter), then come up to the surface and clear it. Tip head back before surfacing so that the snorkel's open end is pointing down. Exhale to displace any water. When on the surface, still exhaling, bring head forward so the open end is clear of the water. (Note how easy it is to blow while the tube end is still under the surface; the right time to start blowing is when the nape of the neck reaches the surface. Until then, hold your breath!)

Leaking mask and clearing

Even if you have chosen a mask that fits well, it may leak due to a poor seal between flange and face. Water is sometimes drawn in, as most beginners have a tendency towards nasal inhalation.

The retaining strap may be too tight, and this will distort the seal, causing the mask to leak.

Gripping the snorkel mouthpiece too tightly will distort the face so that the mask no longer fits snugly. This causes leaks. Just purse the lips around the snorkel and the problem disappears.

Mask clearing

When breath-hold diving, the simplest way to clear any water that may have entered the mask is to tread water and lift the bottom edge of the mask away from the face. If the mask should flood underwater, it may be cleared by the technique illustrated in the diagrams below: start exhaling through the nose and at the same time tilt the head back. This will prevent the water running up into your nose.

1 Holding the mask by its rim, lift it off the face to allow water to fill it from the bottom

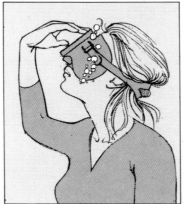

2 Place your fingers on the rim of the mask and tilt head back to look up towards the surface

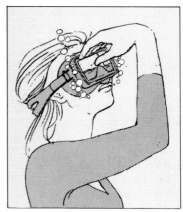

3 Press your fingers against the glass. Blow out through the nose to expel water from the mask

Swimming with fins

Good surface swimmers take to fins quite readily, as they have the correct movements well established and so use the fins efficiently. The right action involves a combination of body angle and leg movement. Other beginners do reasonably well and require only to have their style tidied up a little. The following points will help develop their style.

* The most inefficient fin action is to 'bicycle'. The legs are used in a pedalling motion with a lot of bending, and the fin blade will tend to slide through the water instead of biting into it.

* The most tiring stroke is to keep the legs stiff and straight so that the blades of the fin fully bite the water.

* The most efficient fin action lies between the two, but it will vary according to individual ability.

* Start by finning forward while keeping the legs stiff. This action strengthens the leg muscles. However it is so tiring it soon gives way to a natural amount of leg bending, an approximation of the action

Finning

required so all that is needed then is some expert advice to tidy it up. Essentially, this involves learning to put power into the downstroke, making the fin bite the water. This produces a good forward thrust. The upstroke will take care of itself and help maintain the motion.

The arms are never used when finning, except to help in turning or angling the body. Keep them by your sides or held behind the back.

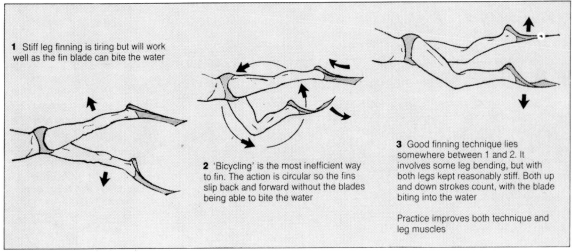

1 Stiff leg finning is tiring but will work well as the fin blade can bite the water

2 'Bicycling' is the most inefficient way to fin. The action is circular so the fins slip back and forward without the blades being able to bite the water

3 Good finning technique lies somewhere between 1 and 2. It involves some leg bending, but with both legs kept reasonably stiff. Both up and down strokes count, with the blade biting into the water

Practice improves both technique and leg muscles

Finning actions

Diving downwards

Having mastered the use of mask, fins and snorkel, many beginners will be entirely satisfied just to swim about on the surface, taking an overhead view of the underwater world. Others will wish to dive down, so they can really feel they are becoming a part of the underwater environment.

The surface dive
While finning on the surface, try to spot some suitable bottom feature to aim for when diving down. When almost overhead, do the following:

* Fold sharply at the waist. Swing the legs vertically upwards, clear of the water and closed together. Their weight in air provides the weight and downwards thrust required to push the diver under the surface.

* Wait until this momentum starts slowing down before giving a single, or maybe two fin flicks to complete the descent. With a little practice, this is all that is required to reach 3 to 4 metres (10-13 ft).

* Do not start finning too early. You will feel the legs go underwater but wait a moment until the fin blades have followed. Make a stroke too soon and you merely thrash the air or water surface. Waiting however, enables the fins to be a good half-metre down before a stroke becomes necessary.

The art of surface diving (and all underwater movement) is in saving energy. Glide as much as possible and make sparing use of the fins. Movements should be effortlessly smooth and controlled.

Surfacing drill
To make a vertical ascent to the surface, the breath-hold diver should fin upward, keeping a sharp lookout above for obstructions and to avoid colliding with surface swimmers. Hold an arm up to protect the head and turn around 360° to ensure that it is safe to surface. Be ready to stay down or immediately dive again. When the surface has been reached, a short sharp blow will clear the snorkel tube.

Control and mobility
The breath-hold diver should develop underwater mobility to counteract his weightlessness, disorientation and lack of stability. Practise performing forward and backward rolls – in depths of no more than 3 metres (10 ft) to avoid risk of lung expansion damage.

22

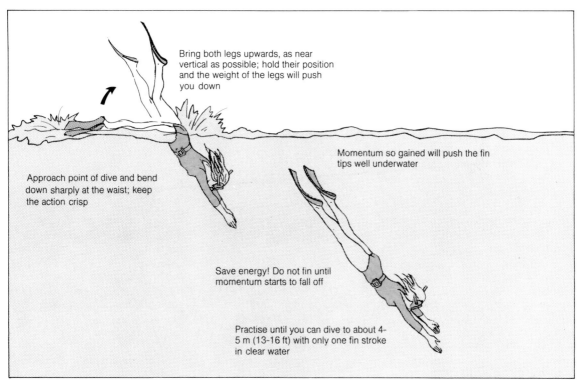

Bring both legs upwards, as near vertical as possible; hold their position and the weight of the legs will push you down

Momentum so gained will push the fin tips well underwater

Approach point of dive and bend down sharply at the waist; keep the action crisp

Save energy! Do not fin until momentum starts to fall off

Practise until you can dive to about 4– 5 m (13-16 ft) with only one fin stroke in clear water

The surface dive

Pressure at depth

A breath-hold diver must be aware of the effects that pressure will have on the body.

Experiment by pulling yourself down the ladder at the deep end of the swimming pool. Two effects of pressure will be noticed:

* The mask presses on to the face as water pressure increases. Humming may alleviate this (see page 78).

* Pressure is also felt on the eardrums. Grip hold of the nose, using the mask's rubber nose or by inserting fingers into its indentations. Blow against this restriction and notice the relief of the pressure on

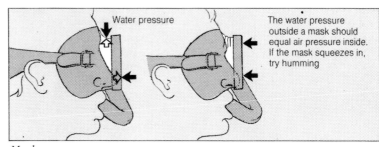

Water pressure

The water pressure outside a mask should equal air pressure inside. If the mask squeezes in, try humming

Mask squeeze

the ears, accompanied by a characteristic screeching noise as air is pushed up into the ear. For a full explanation of this process (known as ear clearing), and why it must be repeated during a descent to any depth see pages 24 and 79.

Make sure that you never dive with a cold or catarrh. It is all too easy for the diver to end up with a bad sinus headache or to have mucus forced into the ears by the increasing pressure at depth — both of which will cause discomfort or pain.

Ear clearing

The usual method involves forcing air pressure from the back of the mouth along the Eustachian tube (see page 78). This offsets the increasing water pressure from the other side of the eardrum.

Block off the nostrils by gripping the mask's rubber nose or inserting a forefinger and thumb in the indentations provided.

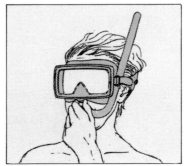

In order to clear the ears, grip hold of the rubber nose of the mask with one hand and blow against the restriction

Make a positive effort and blow against this restriction. Often there is a characteristic squeaking or popping noise as air moves along the Eustachian tube. Sometimes nothing is heard, but the flexing of the eardrums is felt. Blow only as hard as when normally blowing one's nose into a handkerchief.

Descend further and 'clear' the ears as and when required, as soon as the build-up of pressure is felt. Some divers do this automatically whether they feel anything or not.

Never tolerate partial clearing or the clearing of one ear only. If you feel you have a problem, you must come to the surface straight away and consult the instructor.

If difficulty is experienced due to mask design or the physical size of regulator mouthpiece, use both index fingers

Clear the ears continually on every descent. Do this first when just under the surface, and then regularly on the way down.

Take good care of your ears; never clear with force. Descend and ascend slowly.

WARNING Closely follow all the instructor's directions regarding ear clearing. Do not make repeated attempts at descending in an effort to clear an obstinate ear. Any definite pain associated with the ears (as opposed to 'feeling' them) indicates an unacceptable imbalance of pressures and the chance of injury due to a 'squeeze' effect. To try and force the issue simply aggravates the situation, and can lead to more serious problems.

Report any pain felt, typically over one eye, or behind the cheekbone. This involves the 'sinuses' (see page 00), bony cavities within the skull with narrow entrances into the upper respiratory system. Any pain shows that the pressure-equalizing airflow into the cavity is being impaired in some way, and so must not be ignored.

Practice with basic equipment

Breath-hold diving not only allows future aqualung divers to become used to basic equipment, but also acclimatizes them to the water.

For instance, there is a chilling effect felt after a time in the water. A short expanded neoprene jacket may be used to counter this, but a weightbelt must be worn, as the jacket is buoyant and diving down could prove very awkward. Alter-

natively, a T-shirt or similar top may be worn, anything that will prevent body heat being lost to the water. However, there are two techniques which will be of great use when aqualung diving; both can be developed while breath-hold diving.

Good finning technique
This develops the leg muscles and the ability to produce an extra turn of speed when required.

Breath-hold capability
Being able to hold the breath for a reasonable period can often help the experienced aqualung diver to cope with many small problems. Otherwise the urgency to breathe might tip the scales against the diver in a difficult situation. Try to swim considerable distances, making frequent surface dives and swimming underwater. The right skills and abilities soon develop naturally.

Aqualung training

Introduction

This section deals with the early training period. It is best carried out in the safety of a covered swimming pool which offers consistent water temperature and visibility. It could equally well take place in a suitable sheltered outdoor location; a purpose-built tank, the shallow water of a bay, or in any other body of more open, but essentially safe, water. Later on, training can take place in more general open-water conditions like the open sea. We assume that the reader is a beginner who has never been underwater before with an aqualung.

An awareness of the underwater world will develop as training progresses, along with general confidence and competence. The various exercises are listed in a progressive manner and at the correct level of understanding. It is recommended that this initial period of training be carried out under the guidance of a qualified instructor.

The novice who is medically fit to dive should be encouraged to go underwater as quickly as possible, both to try out the apparatus and to gain experience and confidence. None the less the first dive must still be preceded by some explanations, equipment checks and warnings of the possible dangers.

Aqualung function and operation

Divers must make use of apparatus to stay and breathe successfully underwater and the air supply must be portable. They have therefore to be trained both in the use of the apparatus concerned, and in how to survive in an alien environment.

The breathing apparatus a diver uses was originally known as the 'aqualung' (Trademark of La Spirotechnique, US Divers).

Nowadays the North American word scuba (self-contained underwater breathing apparatus) is more generally used. The word 'scuba' in fact refers to a family of underwater breathing apparatus, of which the 'aqualung' is one. An aqualung set comprises three parts:

1 A cylinder or tank, containing a quantity of air under high pressure. Air is drawn from this container by way of an on/off tap.

2 A regulator or demand valve is fitted to the cylinder's on/off tap. This valve meters air to the submerged diver on demand (by inhalation) and at the same pressure as the surrounding water. It also allows him to exhale freely.

3 Harnessing holds the aqualung unit in place on the diver's back.

Cylinders and harness

Cylinders hold a large volume of air at high pressure — typically 200 bar (about 200 times atmospheric pressure or 3000 psi). High-pressure air obviously represents a potential hazard, but there will be nothing to worry about if learning to dive under qualified tuition; the apparatus used will be designed to handle air pressure safely. Follow the simple procedures here, listen to and question the instructor, apply some common sense and all will be well.

Cylinders vary considerably in size and shape and may be made from either steel or aluminium alloy. Different countries have their own authorities to determine the specifications for manufacture and the regulations for their use. The most important cylinder characteristics are their capacity for air storage and their weight. Such information is found stamped into the metal around the cylinder shoulder, along with working pressure, test pressure and the dates when the tests were made. Study these marks and ask the instructor to explain them, as they will provide information vital to the planning of a dive.

The cylinder is the largest and heaviest part of the diving aparatus and is worn on the back. During training, a single cylinder will be used. More advanced divers, who require more air for deeper, longer dives, sometimes use a twin-cylinder arrangement, joined by a high-pressure manifold. A harness holds the cylinder in place on the diver's back. It usually consists of two adjustable shoulder straps and a waist strap with a quick-release buckle. On some types the straps attach to metal rings fixed around the cylinder, on other versions they anchor to a 'back pack' which fits the contours of the diver's back.

Prior to use, cylinders are 'charged' with air to their working pressure by using a special high-pressure compressor or by decanting from larger and higher-pressure cylinders (see *Volume Two*). The purity of the air from these sources must be to specific standards as it will be breathed. After diving, the empty cylinder is returned to the compressor room or equipment store for re-charging ready for further use.

The regulator

How a regulator works — a single hose two-stage balanced piston

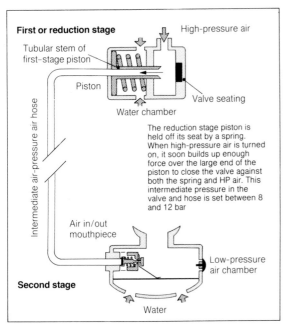

First or reduction stage

- Tubular stem of first-stage piston
- High-pressure air
- Piston
- Valve seating
- Water chamber
- Intermediate air-pressure air hose
- Air in/out mouthpiece
- Low-pressure air chamber

Second stage

Water

The reduction stage piston is held off its seat by a spring. When high-pressure air is turned on, it soon builds up enough force over the large end of the piston to close the valve against both the spring and HP air. This intermediate pressure in the valve and hose is set between 8 and 12 bar

Static or neutral state

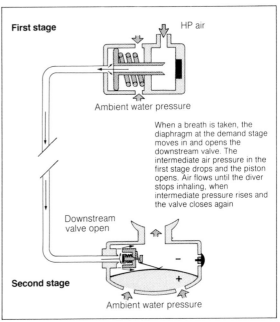

First stage

- HP air
- Ambient water pressure
- Downstream valve open
- Ambient water pressure

Second stage

When a breath is taken, the diaphragm at the demand stage moves in and opens the downstream valve. The intermediate air pressure in the first stage drops and the piston opens. Air flows until the diver stops inhaling, when intermediate pressure rises and the valve closes again

Inhalation

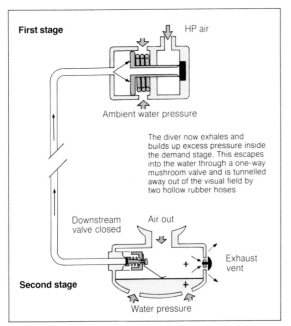

First stage

- HP air
- Ambient water pressure
- Downstream valve closed
- Air out
- Exhaust vent

Second stage

Water pressure

The diver now exhales and builds up excess pressure inside the demand stage. This escapes into the water through a one-way mushroom valve and is tunnelled away out of the visual field by two hollow rubber hoses

Exhalation

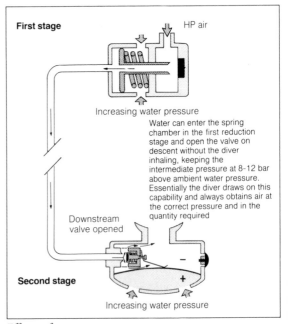

First stage

- HP air
- Increasing water pressure
- Downstream valve opened

Second stage

Increasing water pressure

Water can enter the spring chamber in the first reduction stage and open the valve on descent without the diver inhaling, keeping the intermediate pressure at 8-12 bar above ambient water pressure. Essentially the diver draws on this capability and always obtains air at the correct pressure and in the quantity required

Effects of water pressure

The regulator

It is impossible to breathe the high-pressure air directly from the cylinder, so the pressure is first reduced inside a regulator. This is the 'nerve centre' of the aqualung and is divided into two basic parts called the first and second stages.

The first stage clamps on to the cylinder and reduces its high-pressure air (typically 200 bar; 3000 psi) to medium pressure, about 7 bar above ambient pressure. The second stage is itself divided into two parts. The outer part is open to the water; the inner part is dry and contains a valve. When this valve is opened, air from the cylinder can flow freely into this dry compartment. The two parts are separated by means of a flexible pressure-sensitive diaphragm.

When the diver puts in the regulator mouthpiece, he or she is connected to the dry compartment. The diver's inhalation causes suction which pulls the diaphragm inwards, opens the valve, and lets in more air. The valve will close only when this suction stops — in other words, when the diver feels he or she has sufficient air and so stops inhaling.

The deeper the dive, the greater the surrounding water pressure. This pressure and inhalation causes the diaphragm to bow inwards, which opens the valve to allow air to enter the dry compartment, until the pressure in it is equal to that of the water acting on the open part of the regulator. When a balance of pressure has been achieved and the diver feels he or she has sufficient air, the valve closes.

When exhaling, the diver blows back into the air compartment. This causes the diaphragm to bow outwards, well away from the valve. The pressure of the excess air in the dry compartment opens a simple, one-way 'mushroom' valve, made of rubber and facing outwards; the excess air escapes into the water. When exhalation is complete, the pressures equalize and the valve closes. When the diver inhales again, the mushroom valve is pulled down firmly on to its seating.

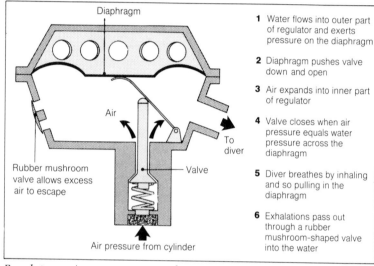

1 Water flows into outer part of regulator and exerts pressure on the diaphragm

2 Diaphragm pushes valve down and open

3 Air expands into inner part of regulator

4 Valve closes when air pressure equals water pressure across the diaphragm

5 Diver breathes by inhaling and so pulling in the diaphragm

6 Exhalations pass out through a rubber mushroom-shaped valve into the water

Regulator action; cross-section of a simplified model

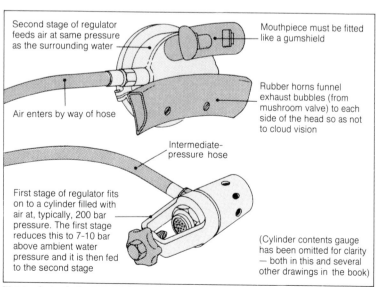

Second stage of regulator feeds air at same pressure as the surrounding water

Mouthpiece must be fitted like a gumshield

Air enters by way of hose

Rubber horns funnel exhaust bubbles (from mushroom valve) to each side of the head so as not to cloud vision

Intermediate-pressure hose

First stage of regulator fits on to a cylinder filled with air at, typically, 200 bar pressure. The first stage reduces this to 7-10 bar above ambient water pressure and it is then fed to the second stage

(Cylinder contents gauge has been omitted for clarity — both in this and several other drawings in the book)

Typical single-hose regulator arrangement

The regulator

Assembling and testing the regulator

To prepare the aqualung for use, this sequence of pre-dive checks must be carried out prior to every dive throughout the individual's diving career.

How to inspect and prepare the equipment

Inspect the cylinder after it has been charged with air and before use. Chipped paint is of cosmetic consequence only: look instead for dents or gouges in the metal, or any other irregularities, and make sure the on/off tap is not bent or leaking. Bring any potential problems to the attention of the instructor.

Check the air pressure in the cylinder. Use a 'test gauge' or the cylinder contents pressure gauge: the beginner will be shown how to do this. Check this pressure with the instructor to be certain it is enough to cover the planned dive.

Never take anyone else's word regarding cylinder pressure. Always make a personal check so that you are not taking unnecessary risks.

The novice's first lesson in diving will always include instruction on how to look after the equipment he or she will be using.

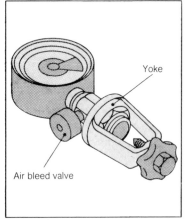

Test gauge

Fitting the regulator to the cylinder

1 Stand the cylinder upright; unravel the harnessing and make a careful check of all the buckles and all the fastenings.

2 Inspect the circular neoprene O-ring (set in the on/off tap of the cylinder) for damage. It should not be scored, pinched or flattened. Wipe it clean.

3 Make a visual check of the regulator for defects. It is assumed that a single-hose regulator will be used for training. Take a close look at the integrity of the hose, particularly where the flexible part enters the metal ferrules at each end.

4 Inspect the 'yoke', and see that the locating screw set in it moves freely. At the same time remove the 'dust cap'. (This fits within the yoke and is held in place by the locating screw. It sits on the circular metal seating and prevents dust or water entering the internal mechanism of the regulator).

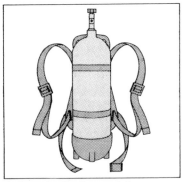

1 Stand cylinder upright

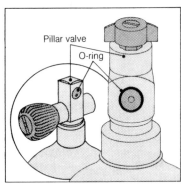

2 Inspect neoprene O-ring

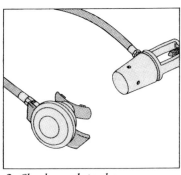

3 Check regulator hose

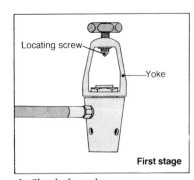

4 Check the yoke

5 Within the yoke, inspect the circular, metal seating surface (which will make a seal against the O-ring) for score marks and so on.

6 Inside this metal seat, inspect the 'sintered bronze filter' for clogging and/or cracking. The bronze beads do not have to be bright and shiny, just reasonably clean and without any trace of deposits from previous use. Bring any doubts you may have about the equipment to the attention of the instructor.

7 Loosen the locating screw on the yoke, slip the yoke over the top of the on/off tap, making sure that the single hose is on the correct side, so that the mouthpiece will be the right way up. Most (but not all) single-hose regulators pass over the right shoulder.

8 Bring the regulator's circular metal seating surface up to the O-ring. Make certain this metal seat locates well within the groove containing the O-ring. Do up the screw lightly, locating it into the notch set at the back of the on/off tap.

9 Slightly rotate the body of the regulator on the seating, to ensure a good seal. Then angle the single hose marginally upwards, so that it will pass freely over one shoulder (usually the right-hand one) and brings the mouthpiece into its correct position in front of the mouth. Some hoses cannot be angled upwards. It is important to prevent the hose angling downwards below shoulder level as this causes the mouthpiece to fit awkwardly.

10 Tighten down the locating screw to complete the required pressure-tight seal between regulator and cylinder on/off tap. Do not overtighten; hand-tight is sufficient.

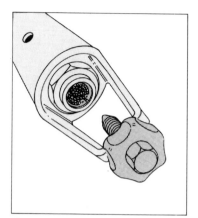

5 Inspect the O-ring seal

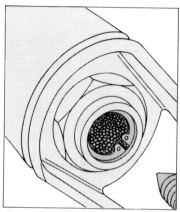

6 Thoroughly check filter

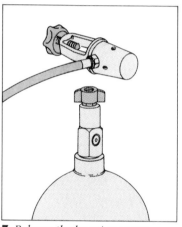

7 Release the locating screw

8 Connect regulator to O-ring

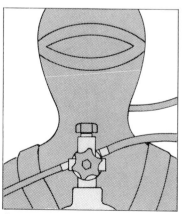

9 Rotate regulator to ensure seal

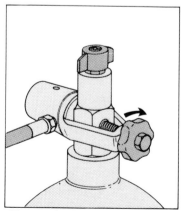

10 Hand tighten locating screw

Fitting the aqualung

Aqualung assembly

Check the high-pressure seal and the cylinder contents. Having fitted the regulator to the cylinder, turn on the air supply from the cylinder by slowly opening the on/off tap anticlockwise. This allows high-pressure air (normally around 200 bar) to flow into regulator.

DO NOT bend over the tap during this operation. Do it at arm's length and with the face turned away. In the unlikely event that the seal is badly connected, the O-ring may blow out with a loud bang. If this should happen, the air will rush out with a most dramatic whoosh. It is nothing to worry about, however, just a waste of air! Avoid looking directly at the gauge whilst turning on the air. The sudden pressure has been known to shatter the glass. In fact these events are rare, so do not be nervous; it is just a simple case of taking sensible precautions.

An O-ring may blow a few seconds after turning on the tap. If it does, close the tap and then disconnect the regulator. Check the O-ring for damage and replace it if necessary. Also, have another look at the circular seating surface on the regulator. If it leaks air when the tap is turned on, remove the regulator, reseat it and try again.

It is good practice to depress the regulator purge button when first turning on air pressure, releasing it as soon as air is flowing. This helps prolong the life of regulator internal seating surfaces. The on/off tap may be fully opened, to about eight turns. It will not unscrew completely from the pillar valve.

With the air turned on, check the cylinder by looking at the pressure gauge. Make sure the cylinder contains enough air for the intended dive. Pressure gauges may be calibrated in either 'bar', psi (pounds per square inch) or in 'ats' (atmospheres). Typically, a 1,841 litre (65 cu ft) cylinder, when fully charged to a working pressure of, say, 200 bar would show 204 bar (or 3,000 psi or 207 ats) on the pressure gauge. This gauge should always be shown to the instructor for the first one or two training sessions. Thereafter, the instructor should ensure novice divers check their own cylinder pressures.

Leave the on/off tap in the open position. Do not leave the cylinder where it can be knocked over. It is safest if laid down flat.

Regulator function check

If they are maintained properly and overhauled by professionals at the end of each diving season, regulators are usually reliable pieces of apparatus. However, they are only mechanical devices and the pre-dive inspection must check that:

* The parts are working properly.

* The regulator will supply, on demand, enough air to fulfil the diver's requirements.

Therefore, prior to each and every use, the following routine should be carried out:

1 Put the rubber mouthpiece in the mouth, pinch the nose shut and demand air from the regulator by inhaling and then exhaling. First use a long slow breathing cycle, simulating a near-normal breathing pattern. Next try a short, fast cycle, creating a sudden demand for air to simulate the worst type of pattern, as encountered under conditions of heavy work or undue stress. There should be no resistance to inhalation or exhalation. Draw the instructor's attention to any problem in breathing from the regulator.

2 Now turn cylinder tap off clockwise, and breathe all the air from the regulator. Create a suction and see if any air leaks into the regulator by way of the diaphragm or the mushroom exhaust valve. Turn the cylinder air back on again. This time fully open the on/off tap and then close it half a turn. Then there is no mistaking that the tap is on, as it can be rotated with ease. If left fully open against its end stop, someone else, thinking it is jammed shut, may try to force it.

Note: Certain on/off taps, particularly the balanced type, give no visual clue that they are open or closed. Remember, when the aqualung is in position on the back, it is good practice to have a companion check that it is turned on.

The aqualung is now ready for use.

Having been shown the correct sequence for assembling and testing the aqualung, every diver must take the responsibility for making certain that the apparatus used is in good working order before he or she enters the water.

Ancillary equipment

The aqualung is used in conjunction with basic equipment; that is mask and fins, with a snorkel carried at all times. A weightbelt with a quick-release is also worn.

Weights are required in order to offset any tendency to float. Using them enables a diver to sink with ease by simply blowing out air from his or her lungs.

The amount of weight carried will be chosen by the instructor during the early training period. It will be selected to suit the diver's personal requirements, taking into account the buoyancy of the suit, if one is worn, and the natural buoyancy of the individual.

The intricacies of weighting will be discussed in greater detail later in the book (see pages 33 and 50).

Dressing

We shall discuss here the usual sequence for fitting the equipment before entering the water. If, however, this is the initial training lesson, then it may be easier if the equipment (which is very heavy) is fitted from the poolside − after the novice has entered shallow water. The procedure is as follows:

* Adjust the fin straps, wet the fins and fit them.

* Untangle the aqualung harness, lift the set up, or have someone lift it for you, and slip both arms through the shoulder straps. Notice the weight of the cylinder when worn in the air, as opposed to in the water.

* Once in position, make certain that all the straps are adjusted for comfort and that the waist strap is properly fastened.

* Fit the weightbelt, making sure that it will not catch on any piece of equipment should it have to be released in the water. The weightbelt should always be put on last, over all other harness, as it is the first item which will be removed in an emergency.

* Rub spittle around the inside glass surface of the mask whilst it is dry, rinse out and fit it. Stow the snorkel in a convenient position. During pool training it is usually tucked under both the waist harness and weightbelt straps, or even inside the swimming costume. Unless firmly held, it will slip out.

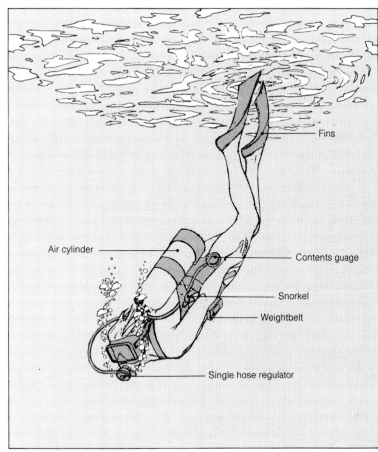

A novice diver fully kitted for training

Air cylinder

Fins

Contents guage

Snorkel

Weightbelt

Single hose regulator

Into the water

Basic skills

All divers must master certain basic techniques which will help to instil confidence in the apparatus being used. Training is carried out in 2 to 3 metres (6-10 ft) of water while sitting or kneeling on the bottom. (Movement introduces a different dimension and so should not be practised until the later exercises.) Proficiency and confidence are important. Eventually there should be no sign of stress or agitation while performing any of the techniques covered in this section. Only when all the elementary skills can be performed with confidence should the beginner be allowed to undertake more advanced training.

Into the water

The time has come to make a dive and try out the aqualung. The term 'dive' means here the act of going underwater and returning to the surface again.

For this first immersion only, entry to the water should be by a ladder. Enter the water without equipment. Stand in shallow water at the poolside and don equipment there.

This first dive, when the water closes over your head, is a moment that you will always remember. It must be made under controlled conditions, preferably in a swimming pool, but in any case it should certainly take place in warm, sheltered, clear waters, in a depth of not more than 1 to 1½ metres (3-5 ft). Second and subsequent dives can be made in slightly deeper water.

If such a venue is adopted, there need be only one warning:

> DO NOT hold your breath at any time, particularly when returning to the surface. Breathe normally and there will be no problems

If pressure is felt on the eardrums, signal to the instructor (see page 34). Otherwise continue as follows:

* Purse the lips lightly around the mouthpiece, without puckering them, to make a good seal.

* Relax the jaw muscles or they will soon begin to ache.

* Be aware that you are breathing from a mechanical device. It will be necessary to create a suction to open the valve and allow air to flow. Concentrate on breathing through the mouth. Avoid nasal breathing while underwater. If bubbles can be seen escaping past the mask seal or the mask feels as if it is being sucked inward on to the face, this indicates that you have started breathing through the nose.

Once breathing properly through the mouth, you will find the aqualung easy to use. Some finning should be attempted, using the arms for turning only.

The beginner has to come to terms with breathing from a mechanical device. It is surprising how easy the action becomes so that soon the diver can forget about it and concentrate on other facets of the dive.

Establishing a breathing rhythm

Establishing a breathing rhythm is important. Heavier work loads such as hard finning or anxiety over some predicament, can disrupt or possibly break the rhythm completely. If this happens a diver may quickly lose control of the situation and be in possible danger. To develop the technique, kneel or sit on the bottom, or hold on to something solid. Now establish (or re-establish) a good breathing rhythm, making well-spaced exhalations. Throughout your diving career, you must always establish a breathing rhythm prior to every new action or movement. Once well practised, this takes only seconds. If the breathing rhythm is being affected during the course of an action, stop all movement, assume a stable position (holding on to something if possible) while re-establishing the breathing rhythm. Then continue.

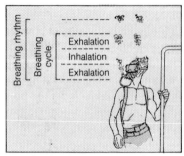

Establish a breathing rhythm

Leaking mask

'My mask leaks and my jaw aches!'
This complaint is commonly heard
when the novice diver first wears a
mask in water. The tendency is to
grip the mouthpiece too hard,
which soon leads to an aching jaw.
Moreover, this action accentuates
the furrows on the face running up
under the mask rim, allowing it
to leak. Instead try to purse lips
around the mouthpiece, and relax!

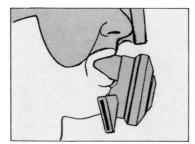

Do not bite mouthpiece too hard

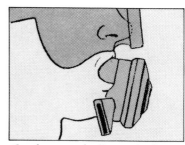

Gently purse the lips and relax

Weighting technique

Like breathing, buoyancy control
soon becomes second nature but, if
there is an overriding tendency to
rise (positive buoyancy), this indicates that not enough lead weights
are being carried.

'Weighting', as divers call it, is
intended to overcome any natural
positive buoyancy and so make the
diver neutrally buoyant in the water.
In this state a small controlled
change in lung volume will allow
complete control over buoyancy
and movement.

The instructor will probably make
the beginners perform a buoyancy
check on a first dive. They will be
asked to lie face-down in the shallows, with their arms and legs fully
extended. If they are correctly
'weighted' (by means of the lead
weights on the weightbelt) they will
sink on exhalation and just start to
rise on inhalation.

Initially, the amount of weighting is
decided by the instructor, but trainees must soon learn to adjust their
own weights. For training in 2 to 3
metres (6-10 ft), adjust weighting
to achieve neutral buoyancy at a
depth of about 1 metre (3 ft).

As a rough guide, a diver not wearing a diving suit would require
about 2 to 4 kilograms (4½-9 lb)
weighting for neutral buoyancy.

Weighting check (in deeper water)

When the diver thinks the correct
weighting has been achieved, it is a
good idea to try this simple check. It
should be carried out every time
you enter the water.

1 Stay still, breathe lightly and float
vertically just under the surface. If
the tendency is to sink, this means
you are too negative.

2 Blow out gently and start to sink.
If this descent is difficult, you are
too positive.

3 After 1 metre (3 ft) the descent
should be caught and terminated by
a single stroke of the fins. Negative
buoyancy makes this difficult so this
manoeuvre gives an indication of
your buoyancy state.

4 If you are correctly weighted, you
will discover that you can stay
suspended in mid-water, striking a
balance between exhaling (to sink)
and light finning (to rise).

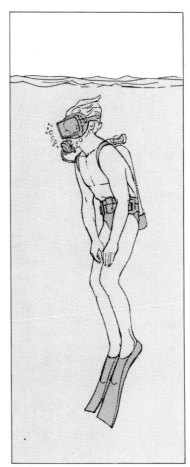

Buoyancy check

Into the water

Buoyancy control

Try some gentle finning in mid-water, with a matched breathing cycle. To sink, make a controlled momentary change to this cycle, and exhale. Readapt the cycle to suit this new mode of action, and again to terminate it once the new level is reached.

Control over buoyancy ensures a freedom of underwater movement.

To achieve this, beginners must acquire the knack of balancing the amount of air held in the lungs with the buoyancy state required. Think of the lungs as buoyancy reservoirs.

When you are on the bottom, incline the body forward and make a sharp full exhalation. You will notice that there is a time lag before settling down under this induced

shift toward negative buoyancy. Now take a slow full inhalation. This time you will observe that there is a similar but longer time lag before you start to move up. This will give you ample time in which to exhale again and keep your buoyancy well under control. You will soon learn to recognize just how closely the breathing cycle and the buoyancy are linked.

Hand signals — basic signals used in training

Communication between divers underwater is very limited. There can be no verbal conversation so hand signals are used instead. At this level of training, a few basic signals will need to be remembered and practised.

The instructor will enquire if you are all right after every exercise that is completed or at regular intervals. Answer with the appropriate reply.

Note that it is often difficult to attract another diver's attention unless you are close to the diver concerned and directly in front of his or her faceplate.

Make signals forcefully, with some movement of the arm so as to emphasize the hand. Make them to one side of the body, above shoulder level. Never make the signals in front of the body where they can all

too easily disappear against a backdrop of harnessing or equipment.

Repeat the signals until answered. If no answer is given, move in closer and try again. It is important to move nearer to your companion because then, not only will the signals be more likely to be noticed but you will also be in a much better position to give help — should this be required.

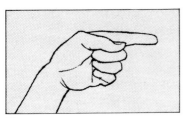

You, or me
Indicating person referred to

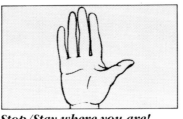

Stop/Stay where you are!
In the USA this also means 'help'

Stop!
US version

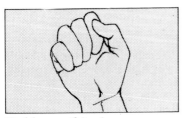

Hold everything!
US version

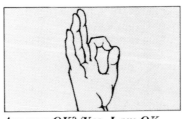

Are you OK?/Yes, I am OK
A question or affirmative answer

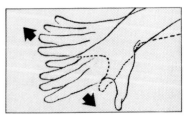

Something is wrong
Point to the cause of the trouble

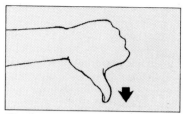

Go down
An instruction to descend

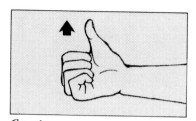

Go up
An instruction to ascend

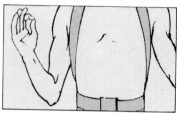

All hand signals must be made to the side of the body

Entries

There are a number of ways for entering the water, depending on the nature of the water's edge. An entry directly into deep water may be made by the diver rolling in backwards or by his stepping out, depending on whether entry is from a boat, jetty or swimming-pool edge. Whatever the method of entry, the following advice should be remembered:

* Make certain you are fully aware of water depth. Poor water clarity can hide a lot, including dangerous obstacles. In a lax moment mistakes are all too easy — and divers have been known to break both ankles by jumping into shallow water!

* For the initial aqualung lesson it is recommended that the diver enter the water via a ladder. For subsequent dives, however, it is a good idea to practise the various methods of entry that are relevant to open-water diving.

The three most useful methods are described here. These are the forward stride, the backward roll, and the silent entry.

Stabilize the equipment

The shock of a sudden entry can displace equipment, so always follow this procedure:

* Put the flat of one hand over the mask glass to avoid it being broken and lessen the risk of the mask being knocked off.

* Incline the head slightly forward so that if the cylinder rides up it does not hit the base of the skull.

* Grip the shoulder harnessing with one hand and pull it tight. This action should prevent the cylinder moving around.

These precautions are taken before making any of the following entries:

The forward stride entry

This is the usual method of entry into a pool or from a jetty or a hard boat which has a freeboard of up to 2 metres ($6\frac{1}{2}$ ft).

First stabilize the equipment and then face outwards. Point one fin tip outward and down. Push off lightly with the other. Point both fin tips downwards and overlap them. Never try to enter the water with flat fins, especially from a height, or you may twist or hurt the ankles. In reality the weight of the cylinder makes the diver incline forwards.

Backward fall

Backward falls are the most convenient way to enter the water from a boat which has a low freeboard, such as an inflatable. All the diver has to do is to let the body fall backwards over the boat's side. Because such boats have no sides underwater, the diver will fall clear once in the water. Swimming pools, on the other hand, have sides which extend underwater, so a slightly modified drill will be necessary:

First stabilize the equipment. Turn your back to the water and squat down so that the heels are just over the edge of the pool. Fall over backwards, making sure there is no one in the water directly below you. Just after the point of balance is past, straighten the legs and push outwards to clear the edge.

Once in the water, surface and confirm a safe entry to those on land or on the boat with the 'I am all right' hand signal.

WARNING Never make forward somersaults into the water. Exhibitionists occasionally try this and it is very dangerous. Masks have been smashed in an awkward entry, equipment lost, and one or two divers have been hit on the back of the head by their cylinders, which can ride up during a somersault. By far the safest way is to sit down and slide into the water; the silent entry.

The silent entry

The silent entry should be made only from a well-defined edge no more than ½ metre (20 in) above the level of the water, and, as the name suggests, this entry is possibly the quietest way of slipping into the water. It will cause the least disturbance to any underwater life you may wish to observe.

* First, sit down on the edge with both legs in the water.

* Then, with the weight of the body supported on one hand, twist the body outwards.

* Turn until the body faces the side and then quietly lower yourself into the water below.

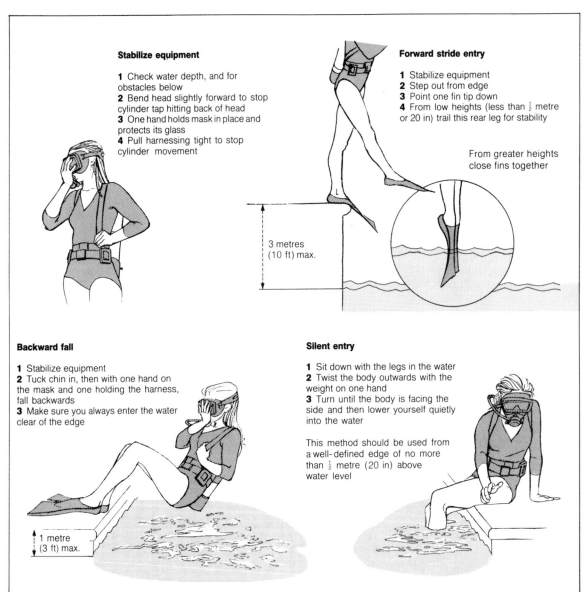

Stabilize equipment

1 Check water depth, and for obstacles below
2 Bend head slightly forward to stop cylinder tap hitting back of head
3 One hand holds mask in place and protects its glass
4 Pull harnessing tight to stop cylinder movement

Forward stride entry

1 Stabilize equipment
2 Step out from edge
3 Point one fin tip down
4 From low heights (less than ½ metre or 20 in) trail this rear leg for stability

From greater heights close fins together

3 metres (10 ft) max.

Backward fall

1 Stabilize equipment
2 Tuck chin in, then with one hand on the mask and one holding the harness, fall backwards
3 Make sure you always enter the water clear of the edge

1 metre (3 ft) max.

Silent entry

1 Sit down with the legs in the water
2 Twist the body outwards with the weight on one hand
3 Turn until the body is facing the side and then lower yourself quietly into the water

This method should be used from a well-defined edge of no more than ½ metre (20 in) above water level

Standard entries

Elementary skills

Removing and replacing the mouthpiece

The act of taking the mouthpiece out underwater will prove quite easy. Replacing it again is slightly more difficult, as it is then filled with water which must be cleared before the diver breathes again.

Remove the mouthpiece slowly and hold the breath. The action of the regulator ensures that the air pressure within the mouth is equal to water pressure outside, so no water will enter unless it is sucked in, even if the mouth is open.

Replace the mouthpiece by sliding it in from one side and then positioning it centrally in the mouth. (Its general shape usually precludes the mouthpiece from being pushed in

Do not attempt to put mouthpiece in from the front

Slide mouthpiece in from the side

from the front, as this action would necessitate opening your mouth rather wide.)

When using single-hose regulators, a single blow should be sufficient to clear the water from the mouthpiece and so allow breathing to recommence.

Alternatively, the 'purge button' on the front of the regulator may be pushed to clear the water if you do not have any breath left!

You will soon learn to trust your own ability to clear the water and breathe again. Then try to hold your breath and keep the mouthpiece out for longer periods.

Recovering the mouthpiece

If a single-hose regulator mouthpiece is dropped or knocked from the mouth, it can swing away, out of sight and behind the body. Recovering it will be a simple confidence-building exercise.

* Take out the mouthpiece and let it drop free behind the shoulder.

* Remember which shoulder was involved! Lean over to that side and back a little. This will make the regulator hose hang down free of the cylinder.

* Bring the appropriate arm in tight against the body and then move it backwards by feel, until it is well past the cylinder.

* Bring it outwards and around, bending the elbow as the arm comes forward. The regulator hose will end up nestling in the crook of

the arm. Replace the mouthpiece, clear it, and start breathing.

Occasionally the hose may become hooked up somewhere on the cylinder and cannot be caught by this method. This is no cause for alarm. Simply feel behind your head, locate the cylinder on/off tap with the regulator body attached to

it, and then pick up the flexible hose at this point, pulling it outwards and free as necessary.

After one or two practice runs on dry land you will find you can perform both of these techniques with confidence. All that is required is to be able to hold the breath for a short period of time.

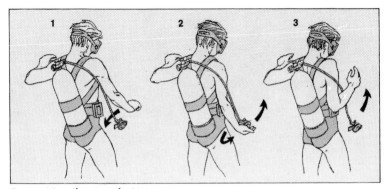

Recovering the mouthpiece

Elementary skills

Breathing without the mask

The mask can be accidentally knocked off a diver's face while underwater — it may be kicked by a companion's fins or snagged in a confined space. The diver should know how to deal with this unexpected situation so that he or she will be able to regain the surface without difficulty.

Once this skill has been mastered during training, losing a mask will hold no more terrors.

Once the mask is removed, air pressure inside the nose will equal water pressure outside and no water should enter. However, there can

be a slight reflex inhalation as cold water first hits the face.

The knack of breathing without a mask lies in knowing when to apply a slight and controlled positive exhalation pressure to the end of the nostrils, to maintain the air water interface in this position.

First, concentrate on breathing through the mouth. Slow the rate of breathing down until it has almost stopped. (This will eliminate the chance of nasal inhalation when the mask is first taken off.) Remove the mask slowly, using both hands to unhinge the lower seal. Then allow

it to flood up as the upper flange is pulled clear and the mask is lifted off. Take about six breaths with the mask removed, then refit it. This skill will enable you to swim, or even to surface, if your mask should be lost or broken.

Some people find that water entering the nostrils is a persistent problem. If this happens, pinch the end of the nostrils once the mask is removed. Then, blow gently against this restriction and allow some bubbles to escape. Slow the exhalation down and stop just as the fingers are removed. Repeat if necessary; you will soon acquire the knack.

Clearing the mask of water

Air can be blown into the mask, displacing any water inside it. To stop this air escaping past the upper mask seal, this is closed up against the forehead by pressing the upper mask rim. The flat of one hand can be used; or the tips of all the fingers of one hand; use two hands if this proves easier. Do not rely on just one or two fingers, as these may prove ineffective points of pressure.

Kneel on the bottom. Now take a full breath and flood the mask.

Press the upper rim against the forehead and start exhaling slowly through the nose.

At the same time bend backwards from the waist, but not too far. Incline the head backwards from the neck (about 25°) and look up towards the surface. This brings the water inside the mask back against the lower flange.

If you lean back before starting to exhale, water will most likely go up

the nose so remember to exhale first. Once looking upward, exhale the remaining air through the nose. This should expel the water out past the lower mask seal.

If any water is left in the mask, repeat the exercise.

Clearing the mask of water is a way of life while diving and it is a technique which must be mastered so as to be almost automatic before diving in open water.

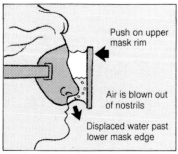

The basic mask-clearing action

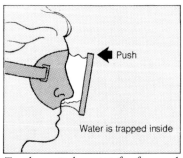

Tendency to lean too far forward

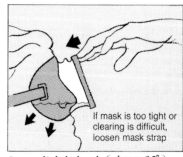

Lean slightly back (about 35°)

Ear clearing

During a descent, pressure may be felt on the eardrums. This must be countered by a process known as 'ear clearing' (equalizing pressure on both sides of the eardrums).

1 To 'clear' the ears, air pressure is forced along the Eustachian tube from the back of the mouth.

2 Air pressure in the middle ear then equals water pressure in the outer ear. Pressures are thus balanced either side of the eardrum.

3 Pain indicates that there is an inbalance of pressures.

4 'Feeling' the ears is the cue to clear them, so do so straight away.

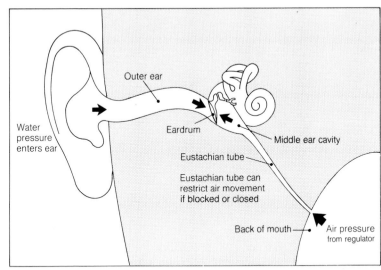

Outer ear

Water pressure enters ear

Eardrum

Middle ear cavity

Eustachian tube

Eustachian tube can restrict air movement if blocked or closed

Back of mouth

Air pressure from regulator

Pressure on the ear

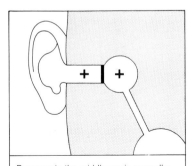

Pressure in the middle ear is normally the same as in the throat and outer ear canal. There is no imbalance of pressure on the drum

Ear in normal state

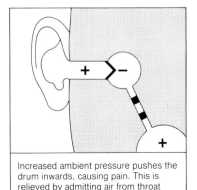

Increased ambient pressure pushes the drum inwards, causing pain. This is relieved by admitting air from throat via Eustachian tube — if it is not blocked

External pressure on ear

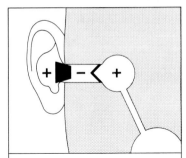

Ear plugs seal off the outer ear canal; an increase in pressure in the middle ear could cause the drum to bulge outward and suffer damage

Reversed ear

Underwater movement

Inefficient underwater movement wastes a lot of energy and can disrupt the breathing rhythm. Efficient movement capitalizes on buoyancy control and on a good breathing rhythm. (It is assumed that during the following exercises the diver is weighted for neutral buoyancy.)

Vertical descents
Stay vertical on the surface. Blow out, hold this for a moment, and sink. The downward momentum will build up surprisingly quickly, and the breathing rhythm is quickly re-established. One flick of the fins retards the motion. Use this method

whenever possible as it involves no outlay of any energy.

Try finning downward from the surface — either head-first or in an angled descent. Notice the extra energy required, first to direct the body's angle downwards and then

Underwater mobility

to break free of the surface and to start the descent.

Any change in direction, in order to go up or down, is achieved by a subtle change in the buoyancy, and an angling of the fin thrust.

Horizontal movement

Finning uses energy so avoid it if possible. Try these two techniques; practise whichever suits you.

* Sustain a steady forward cruising motion by flicking the tips of both

fins together from the ankles. In between fin flicks simply glide along so as to save energy.

* Try gliding down diagonally. Spread the fins and arms for stability and control of water drag, and then

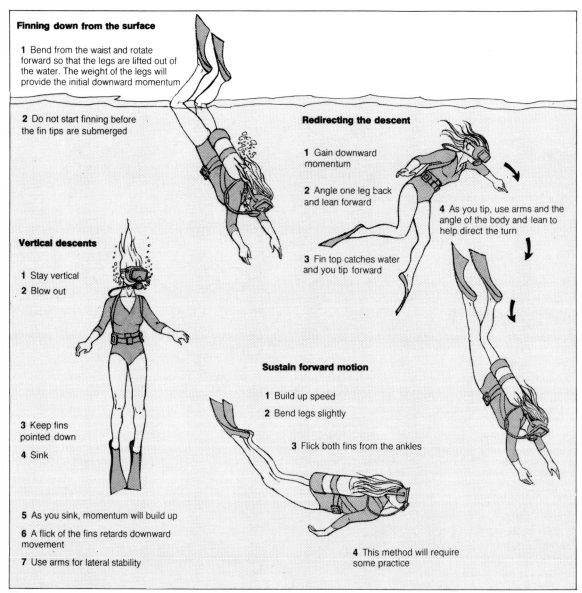

Finning down from the surface

1 Bend from the waist and rotate forward so that the legs are lifted out of the water. The weight of the legs will provide the initial downward momentum

2 Do not start finning before the fin tips are submerged

Vertical descents

1 Stay vertical

2 Blow out

3 Keep fins pointed down

4 Sink

5 As you sink, momentum will build up

6 A flick of the fins retards downward movement

7 Use arms for lateral stability

Redirecting the descent

1 Gain downward momentum

2 Angle one leg back and lean forward

3 Fin top catches water and you tip forward

4 As you tip, use arms and the angle of the body and lean to help direct the turn

Sustain forward motion

1 Build up speed

2 Bend legs slightly

3 Flick both fins from the ankles

4 This method will require some practice

Underwater movement

exhale. The resultant glide will be 'free of charge'. It may be useful to have competitions to see who can glide the greatest distance.

Lateral stability and turning

Finning is very efficient when compared with the leg actions that are used, without fins, for surface swimming. Normally, when divers swim underwater, their arms are used only to change direction. However, in the following exercise the arms will also be used to provide lateral stability.

Try making forward and backward somersaults in a tight ball without finning. Spread the arms a little and pull yourself around by using the arms alone. Ideally you should turn in one plane, without rolling sideways. This is really an exercise in buoyancy control as well as underwater orientation and mobility. The ability to spin quickly and efficiently can prove useful on occasions.

Do be aware however, that if this is practised when wearing an aqualung, and if the breath is held when moving vertically, there is a danger of the expanding air causing damage to the lungs. (This problem will be discussed in greater detail on pages 81.)

Coming to the surface

The basic rules for any ascent are quite simple:

* Ascend slowly, looking up and holding one hand above the head to avoid any overhead obstacle. As a rule of thumb, rise no faster than your own small exhaust bubbles.

* The maximum safe rate of ascent is 15 metres (50 ft) per minute. Throughout the ascent it is essential that the diver breathes normally without any hint of breath-holding.

* Normally, in order to mimic the conditions of open-water diving, trainees will be encouraged, once they have surfaced, to fin back to the place where they will make their exit from the water. This is because in the real-life situation they will probably surface some distance from the boat or shore.

* On first reaching the surface, give the 'I am all right' hand signal to those watching.

* Keep the mouthpiece in place at all times; never be tempted to remove it until after a safe landfall has been made.

(See also *Snorkelling with the aqualung* on page 46 and *Surfacing drill* on page 22 .)

Dismantling the aqualung

When you finally leave the water, you will notice how the returned weight of the apparatus in the air restricts ease of movement.

After diving has finished, the regulator must be disconnected from the cylinder to be ready for transportation and storage, or so that the cylinder can be refilled.

Whenever possible, wash off the entire aqualung set with fresh water soon after leaving the water and, before dismantling, be certain to rinse the inside of the regulator mouthpiece. Do be careful, however, not to allow any water to enter the hose via the first stage or into the orifice on the pillar valve. Otherwise this water might eventually find its way into the cylinder.

Make a note of how much air is left in the cylinder from the pressure gauge, then close the on/off tap.

Bleed all the air from the regulator. Do this either by pressing the purge button or by breathing it dry so as to exhaust the medium-pressure hose. Check that the pressure gauge now reads zero.

Remove the regulator and immediately replace the dust cap over the first-stage air inlet so as to avoid any dirt or water entering.

Have the cylinder recharged ready for reuse. Store it upright, away from heat and in a safe place where it cannot be knocked over.

Debrief

In the debrief that follows every dive, those divers who have made their first submersion usually claim that they have been thrilled by the experience. Their initial apprehensions forgotten, there is a great sense of accomplishment.

There is obviously an enormous amount to learn and discover, and much to enjoy. This can be achieved only by way of a well-organized training programme.

Advanced exercises

Introduction

These exercises will increase confidence in apparatus and personal ability. They provide the basis for open-water diving, and introduce companion divers and surface support, showing the part these play in the safe conduct of a dive. Each exercise has a practical use, and variations of these should be tried under differing conditions in order to give the diver a broader-based experience. Exercises should be practised under controlled environmental conditions, in most cases preferably without wearing a diving suit. The venue should be chosen accordingly. Ideally use a swimming pool with a maximum water depth of 3 to 4 metres (10-13 ft).

Tackling problems

The basic exercises should be practised in order to have experience of the most common problems encountered in diving. This practice should, of course, take place in a safe and controlled manner and with the help and supervision of a qualified instructor.

The more complicated exercises which follow may go a little wrong on occasions. To tackle and solve such problems involves skill — both in doing two or more things at once, and in tackling the difficulties in a priority order. At this level, the order of importance will be:

* Obtaining air to breathe.

* Establishing a breathing rhythm.

* Controlling buoyancy: do you wish to sink, rise or stay still?

* Tackling any other problems.

A sound training programme equips individuals to cope with straightforward problems quickly and efficiently. Always tackle the simple problems as rapidly as possible; underwater situations have a habit of becoming complicated surprisingly quickly.

When some exercise has not gone as smoothly or as satisfactorily as it should, it may often be necessary to be able to hold the breath a little longer to achieve a good result. Have you practised well enough to do this?

After a training session, consider all the situations that occurred and your personal performance in tackling them. If mistakes were made, was it a matter of technique? Or, was the order in which they were dealt with at fault? Always evaluate carefully what has happened while it is still fresh in your mind.

Doing two things at once

When two actions are required at once, the mind tends to concentrate on one and ignore the other. In particular, buoyancy is often forgotten in early training.

Try to remove and replace the mouthpiece at the same time as finning just off the bottom. The trick is to concentrate on finning; otherwise leg action will probably stop and you will start to sink as soon as the mouthpiece is touched.

Practise and develop a procedure for clearing the mask of water while finning in mid-water. Do the following as a continuous action: roll over to one side; press one hand against what is now the upper part of the mask rim; exhale through the nose to clear the water; roll back, and keep finning.

Mask clearing while finning in mid-water
1 Press a hand on one side of the facemask.

2 Turn so this side is uppermost. Water is now at bottom of the mask.

3 Exhale slowly while turning.

4 End face-up momentarily, to clear out last drop of water.

5 Rotate back and keep finning.

Mask clearing and finning simultaneously

Removing the aqualung in the water

The cylinder can prove a bulky appendage on occasions, particularly when trying to leave the open water at some awkward location. It is often wiser to pass the aqualung up to those waiting ashore or in a boat. Alternatively, it might be necessary to exchange cylinders without surfacing – during a long decompression stop, for instance.

During training, aqualung removal is first practised under stable conditions on the bottom. There are two methods. Try them both, taking comfort in the fact that they allow the mouthpiece to be left in place!

Overhead method
The traditional method, developed originally for twin-hose regulators, works just as well with the single-hose regulators.

Unfasten any waist straps and, if possible, loosen the shoulder harnessing. Leave the weightbelt in place. (This rule will be common to all methods.)

Place the thumbs under the outer edge of the shoulder straps, slide them back, and firmly grip the straps as close to the cylinder as possible. The elbows are now in a raised position, with the straps loose about the shoulders.

Lean forward and pull the straps so that the cylinder slides up the back and over the head. Once over the head, straighten the arms, so that the elbows do not trap the straps as the cylinder floats free.

Hold the cylinder in front of the body for a while, compensate for the shift in personal buoyancy, then replace it in the same way.

The drawback of this method is that when the cylinder passes over the head, the diver runs the risk of concussion! Be very careful not to hit your head.

Coat method
The use of a single-hose regulator allows a simplified method to be used. This is also the method that would be adopted before transferring into a boat at the end of a normal dive. First undo the waist strap, then loosen the shoulder strap on the opposite side to the demand valve, and shrug it off. Now remove the other, in much the same way as taking off a coat. It is necessary to remember which shoulder the regulator hose passes over, so as to co-ordinate the action properly. Do it the wrong way around, and the regulator hose will end up wound around the neck!

Practise the chosen method whilst kneeling on the pool bottom. Once proficient, try it in mid-water, at least 1 metre (3 ft) under the surface. (See also *Doing two things at once* on page 42.)

This will give an idea of what may be entailed in removing the aqualung prior to entering a boat, as divers often find it necessary to stay under the surface in order to keep clear of wave action.

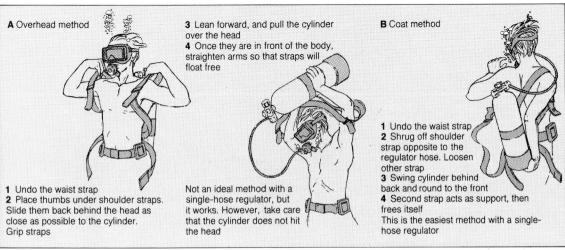

A Overhead method
1 Undo the waist strap
2 Place thumbs under shoulder straps. Slide them back behind the head as close as possible to the cylinder. Grip straps

3 Lean forward, and pull the cylinder over the head
4 Once they are in front of the body, straighten arms so that straps will float free

Not an ideal method with a single-hose regulator, but it works. However, take care that the cylinder does not hit the head

B Coat method
1 Undo the waist strap
2 Shrug off shoulder strap opposite to the regulator hose. Loosen other strap
3 Swing cylinder behind back and round to the front
4 Second strap acts as support, then frees itself
This is the easiest method with a single-hose regulator

Methods of removing the aqualung in the water

Advanced exercises

Exit from the water

As a 'finale', remove all the equipment whilst still in the water. First, undo the weightbelt with one hand and pass this up to a companion on the poolside or in a boat. Be sure not to let go of the weightbelt until it has been firmly grasped by your companion. Then undo the aqualung waist strap and the shoulder straps — as in the 'coat' method, described on the previous page. Remember to disconnect the direct feed if wearing a buoyancy compensator and, finally, don't forget to let go of the mouthpiece!

Now you can make your own exit from the water.

Ditch and recovery

Practised as a continuation of the aqualung-removal exercise, this is intended to build confidence in personal ability.

Remove the aqualung on the bottom by whichever of the three methods is suitable.

Place the aqualung on the bottom and bring buoyancy back under control while still breathing from the mouthpiece. Avoid taking very deep breaths, breathing out if there is any tendency to float up and away from the cylinder. With one hand grasping hold of the pillar valve, re-establish a steady breathing rhythm while you are still resting on the bottom.

With the other hand, carefully remove the weightbelt and drape it across the cylinder.

Now rise to the surface, as follows:

* Place the mouthpiece on the bottom and immediately begin to exhale. Most divers will find that they start to rise naturally; very few experience difficulty with this.

* Look up and keep exhaling all the way to the surface, which is at most only 3 metres (10 ft) away.

DO NOT be tempted to hold the breath. This is very important.

You must maintain this exhalation because the air in the diver's lungs is at pressure and will expand during an ascent. This expansion could cause an air embolism (a bubble of air which creates an obstruction in a blood vessel).

See also *Effects of pressure* (page 71) and *Emergency ascents and rescues* (page 118 - 122).

On the surface, wait for a few moments and recover composure. Then dive down again in a long sloping glide, wasting as little energy as possible (see page 22). On approaching the aqualung, remember the sequence of actions:

1 Grasp the aqualung, preferably by the pillar valve. Do not let go of it.

2 Quickly recover the mouthpiece, clear it, and obtain air to breathe.

3 Remember buoyancy control as the tendency is now to float up. Then, in whichever order suits the situation:

* Blow out to sink and stay adjacent to the aqualung on the bottom.

* Pick up the weightbelt and drape it across the back. When breathing has been stabilized and the shift in buoyancy controlled, fasten the weightbelt buckle.

4 Sort out the cylinder harnessing and refit the cylinder by the same method that you used to remove it. Be careful to avoid putting an arm through inside the bend in the regulator hose.

The complexity of this operation is self-evident. But it embodies various techniques which have all been practised before. The skill

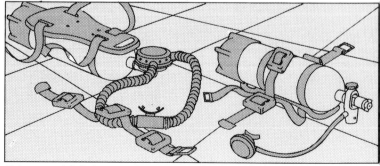

Using a weightbelt to anchor an aqualung on the bottom

comes in co-ordinating the actions while at the same time controlling the buoyancy.

As a further exercise in control, in case it should ever have to be done 'for real' in murky waters, practise the following:

* First remove the mask, then take off your fins and, finally, remove the rest of the equipment.

* Replace the facemask only when all the other pieces of equipment have been refitted.

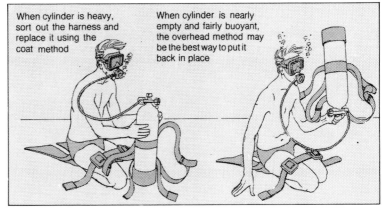

When cylinder is heavy, sort out the harness and replace it using the coat method

When cylinder is nearly empty and fairly buoyant, the overhead method may be the best way to put it back in place

Ditch and recovery

Sharing an aqualung

Should a diver be deprived of an air supply, he or she may need to share an aqualung mouthpiece with a companion. This is possible provided that they adopt a combined breathing rhythm and hold fast to each other.

This is an emergency technique, and is usually the first exercise which involves trainees having to work in direct co-ordination with a companion. In this lesson it is assumed that both the divers will be wearing single-hose regulators. Try it as follows:

* Decide who is going to be the victim and who the rescuer.

* Underwater, approach each other in direct visual contact. The victim gives the 'I am out of air' hand signal to start the exercise and then removes his or her mouthpiece.

* The rescuer closes in fast. Each takes hold of the other's shoulder straps and they kneel diagonally facing each other on the bottom. If using a hose which passes over the

right shoulder, the rescuer should be positioned on the victim's right-hand side.

* The rescuer offers the mouthpiece to the victim, who takes it and slides it into the side of his or her own mouth. The victim must first clear the mouthpiece of water by breathing out and then should take two breaths before the rescuer takes back the mouthpiece.

* The rescuer takes two breaths in turn, and then passes it over to the

victim again. Do not snatch breaths; keep them of reasonable length, adequate for the breath-holding period that must follow. The rescuer should never release his hold on the mouthpiece. The victim holds it to his or her mouth only whilst actually breathing from it. The rescuer should not purge the regulator when passing it to the victim, who should be able to do this if necessary. Once a good breathing rhythm is established, practise moving horizontally along the bottom, keeping close together.

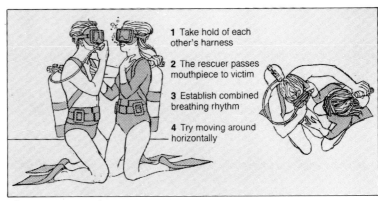

1 Take hold of each other's harness

2 The rescuer passes mouthpiece to victim

3 Establish combined breathing rhythm

4 Try moving around horizontally

Sharing an aqualung

Advanced exercises

At the instructor's discretion, a 'shared ascent' back to the surface may also be tried. Ascent speed must be very slow, about 7 to 8 metres (23-26 ft) per minute at maximum (see pages 77 and 112).

While performing this ascent, the participant not in possession of the mouthpiece must be careful to exhale gently and continuously, (remembering the dangers of breath-holding on ascent), so each diver comes to the end of his breath at about the time the mouthpiece is handed back. A combined breathing rhythm, established before leaving the bottom, and a slow ascent speed, will contribute to the safe practice of this technique.

The same exercise can be practised with a twin-hose regulator. Its greater sensitivity allows the victim to be lifted slightly upwards while transferring the mouthpiece, which then clears itself automatically of water.

A similar effect can be obtained by pressing the purge button on a single-hose regulator.

Finning on the back

Divers often have to fin on the surface to their point of exit from the water. When their air supply is finished they must breathe from the open air.

This can prove difficult as the cylinder weighs a lot when on the sur face, and if the diver assumes a face-down attitude, he or she will be pushed downwards, leaving the mouth barely level with the surface.

In this situation, take advantage of the buoyancy of the empty cylinder by finning on the back. Practise the technique so as to appreciate, and learn to deal with, the difficulties in maintaining a desired direction while looking the wrong way.

You should soon learn to cope with this. An inflated 'buoyancy compensator' often proves very useful.

Be sure to keep the snorkel tube pointing upwards to avoid water entering

The cylinder will be almost weightless underwater

Do not stop finning or you will sink

Finning on the back

Snorkelling with the aqualung

The use of a snorkel on the surface allows divers to breathe in a face-down attitude. They can see where they are going and will be able to maintain a near-normal finning action over reasonable distances. In favourable conditions, it is common practice for the diver to snorkel out to a remote dive site, and back again.

The trainee must pay attention to two things during practice:

1 The need to effect a smooth change-over from regulator to snorkel, or vice versa

2 The maintenance of adequate forward momentum once snorkelling. If the diver should slow down, the weight of the cylinder in air will push him or her downwards, so that the end of the snorkel disappears under the surface! This is quite a common fault.

In order to improve the necessary technique, the novice diver should practice the exercise described on the next page.

Try this technique:

* While still on the bottom, remove snorkel from its storage position. Fit it under the mask strap so it is ready for use, and start ascending.

* Just under the surface, start swimming forward, so as to be moving horizontally when the surface is finally broken. Having established an adequate forward momentum, remove the regulator mouthpiece and slip in the snorkel. A short sharp blow clears it of water.

* Take the first breath cautiously, in case some water is still in the tube. Either clear this, or breathe past it, but continue moving forward. The head must be angled downwards at about 30° to the surface while finn-

ing. This ensures the snorkel stays vertical. Already low in the water, the snorkel top can dip beneath the surface if too far forward or back.

The first breath from the snorkel comes as a shock, after the comparatively easy breathing when using the regulator.

This increased breathing resistance is due to the restrictive bore of the tube and because the chest is well down in the water and must expand against a higher water pressure. The trick with this exercise is to keep swimming. Slow down or stop and you will sink.

Try changing back from snorkel to regulator. Once it is cleared of water, air is available immediately.

Start the descent by assuming a vertical attitude and exhaling.

Snorkelling with the aqualung is often the first exercise to be tried on the surface. After the stability of kneeling on the bottom, the added difficulties introduced by the weight of the cylinder in air are soon apparent.

Towards the end of the training session, come to the surface and float vertically. Avoid any impulse to take out the regulator mouthpiece. It is still impossible to breathe naturally as you will settle a good 5 cms (2 ins) deeper than if surface swimming, due to the weight of the equipment. The general rule is to have either the snorkel or regulator mouthpiece in place at all times.

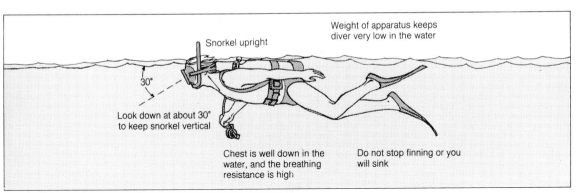

Snorkelling with an aqualung

Running out of air

Part of the pre-dive check is to ensure that there is ample air for the dive on hand. Occasionally, however, a trainee overbreathes and runs out of air while underwater. Normally the instructor will watch out for this, but may allow the diver to experience and learn to recognize the feeling associated with an emptying cylinder. A restriction will

be imposed on the breathing and the regulator feels tight when an inhalation is made. Do not worry; simply change the breathing cycle to cope. Introduce a long drawn-out inhalation phase and longer exhalation. Limit the amount of work (finning) to conserve energy and the demand for air. If air is demanded faster than it can be sup-

plied through the regulator, none will be delivered at all, due to the inadequate back-up pressure in the cylinder. If the cylinder pressure gauge registers in the red reserve sector this usually indicates the dive must terminate and an ascent must be started. Do not wait until a resistance to breathing is felt; you will need some air for the ascent.

Twin-hose regulator training

Introduction

Twin-hose regulators are now rather outdated and have been largely supplanted by the single-hose type. However, they are still preferred by some divers, especially as they have certain useful characteristics, notably with regard to their sensitivity to breathing.

It is therefore important to understand how these twin-hose regulators function in case you ever dive with a companion who uses this type of equipment.

Sensitivity to breathing

The depth of the regulator diaphragm determines the pressure of the air delivered to the lungs. Their relative positions are therefore of importance. Try the following:

* Look vertically upwards while using a single-hose regulator. A slight resistance to breathing will be felt. This is because the diaphragm (in the mouthpiece) is shallower than the lungs and is supplying air at a slightly lower pressure. In more normal positions, such as when swimming horizontally, the diaphragm and the lungs are on about the same level and no resistance is felt.

Twin-hose regulators are positioned on top of the aqualung cylinder, placing them a little below the nape of the neck. They have large diameter diaphragms, which gives them a particular sensitivity regarding air flow and this is helped by their position relative to the diver's lungs. Try them out in the following positions:

* Head down; there is a slight resistance to breathing.

* Roll on to back so the diaphragm is down; air gushes into the mouth.

In a normal horizontal swimming position, no resistance to breathing is felt. However, with some twin-hose regulators, the suction that is required to first 'crack' the valve open, is higher than with single-hose regulators.

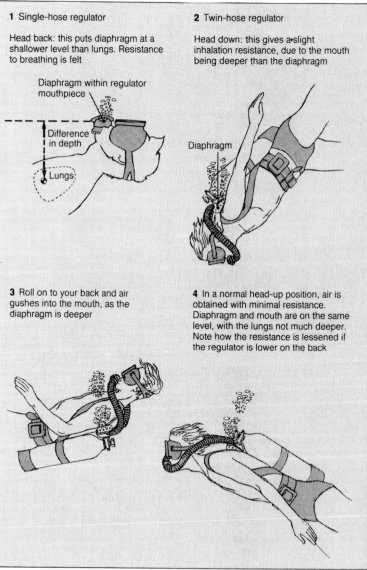

1 Single-hose regulator

Head back: this puts diaphragm at a shallower level than lungs. Resistance to breathing is felt

Diaphragm within regulator mouthpiece

Difference in depth

Lungs

2 Twin-hose regulator

Head down: this gives a slight inhalation resistance, due to the mouth being deeper than the diaphragm

Diaphragm

3 Roll on to your back and air gushes into the mouth, as the diaphragm is deeper

4 In a normal head-up position, air is obtained with minimal resistance. Diaphragm and mouth are on the same level, with the lungs not much deeper. Note how the resistance is lessened if the regulator is lower on the back

Breathing resistance

Removing and replacing a twin-hose mouthpiece

1 Remove mouthpiece and raise it. As the mouthpiece reaches shallower water, the air gushes out, clearing all the water with it.

2 The mouthpiece should be downwards and the head up. Insert mouthpiece gumshield in one side of the mouth and then start breathing immediately.

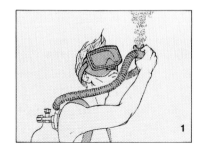
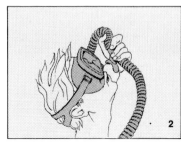

Clearing twin-hose tubes of water

While assembling and testing the aqualung, take a close look at the twin-hose regulator. Note that there is an exhaust hose which returns to the wet side of the diaphragm (see pages 27). Check which shoulder this passes over; usually it is the left-hand one.

Normally one-way valves are fitted in each hose on either side of the mouthpiece to avoid flooding. For this exercise, it is better to use hoses without any one-way valves built into their mouthpieces, so that the hoses can flood completely.

Enter the water and lie on the bottom; now establish a good breathing rhythm.

1 Remove the mouthpiece and flood up the hoses.

2 Roll on to your back. Hold the mouthpiece slightly above your head and air will gush from the mouthpiece because it is shallower than the diaphragm.

3 Look upwards and bring the mouthpiece down, sliding it into the mouth (see page 37) so that the air flow continues to displace the water. Start breathing normally.

Alternatively, replace the hoses while still flooded and lie on your side so that the return (left-hand) hose is lowest. Pinch the upper hose shut with one hand and blow hard into the mouthpiece. This will displace almost all the water out through the exhaust valve and breathing can recommence.

If there is a small amount of water in the hoses, it is possible to continue rolling (exhaust hose lowest) until you are on your back. The water then ends up at the exhaust valve, and the extra air flow that is available in this position will blow it out.

Try all the variations of this exercise until you are confident.

(A full description of the mechanics of the twin-hose regulator will be found in *Volume Two.*)

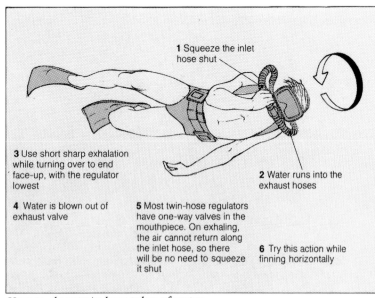

1 Squeeze the inlet hose shut

2 Water runs into the exhaust hoses

3 Use short sharp exhalation while turning over to end face-up, with the regulator lowest

4 Water is blown out of exhaust valve

5 Most twin-hose regulators have one-way valves in the mouthpiece. On exhaling, the air cannot return along the inlet hose, so there will be no need to squeeze it shut

6 Try this action while finning horizontally

How to clear twin-hose tubes of water

Preparations for the first dive

Introduction

The move from sheltered training conditions to open water, whether fresh water or the sea, can be a physical and psychological jolt for the trainee. Usually the water will be colder, the visibility poor and a diving suit will normally be required.

The information and the exercises described in this section provide a general picture of what is involved when diving in open water. In particular, the equipment that must be worn and some of the specialized techniques involved will be examined in detail.

Buoyancy

More complex equipment will be required than when training in a swimming pool. This makes it necessary to rethink the buoyancy situation and to consider it under three distinct headings:

Weighting
This is the name given to the correct choice of weights to be carried for a particular dive. The factors affecting this choice are:

* The type of equipment used.

* The depth and the duration of the dive concerned.

Depth will always be a prominent consideration.

Control of buoyancy
It has been shown that personal buoyancy will be affected by the compression of the suit and the reduced weight of any air which is left in the cylinder.

Good weighting allows these shifts to be kept under control, so that all that is required is a subtle change in the volume of air held in the lungs. This will happen while breathing normally and the diver is usually unaware of the process.

Correction of buoyancy
Excess negative buoyancy can be an embarrassment to the diver, while controlled positive buoyancy can always be put to good use. If nothing else, at least it will ensure an ascent back to the surface!

If for some reason negative buoyancy cannot easily be controlled by changes in lung volume, a definite correction can be made by using a 'buoyancy compensator'.

Remember that no such effective control will be available for excessive positive buoyancy.

Buoyancy compensators

Everybody who goes to sea in a small boat should wear a life-jacket which will provide buoyancy support on the surface and helps keep the face clear of the water if the wearer falls overboard.

The diver needs this facility too, but also requires a means of adjusting buoyancy while underwater, so as to be able to stay neutral at depth or to return to the surface if necessary (see also page 55).

Under the general classification of buoyancy aids are purpose-built life-jackets which provide all these requirements and are called buoyancy compensators (BCs). They are essential items of equipment and should be worn on every single dive, regardless of the type of diving suit that is worn.

Basically, a buoyancy compensator is a flexible bag worn about the upper half of the body. Air may be blown into the bag, or vented, to provide buoyancy as and when this is required.

(For fuller details on buoyancy control, see *Volume Two.*)

There are two types of buoyancy compensator available; one fits over the head; the other is worn as a waistcoat. (The former is the type most commonly used and is the one discussed in detail here.)

These two different types of compensator both vary in the total volume that they are able to supply for inflation, but both of them are capable of providing the following requirements:

* Buoyancy compensation when at depth, to counter any unwanted negative tendencies.

* A means of making a controlled buoyant ascent from depth.

* A potential breathing source in emergencies.

* Ample bag volume for a face-up support on the surface (the life-jacket role).

Inflation

The three possible methods are:

1 Oral; by an inflation tube (for use on the surface).

2 Emergency inflation cylinder; this is a small high-pressure cylinder of air which is able to inflate the bag very quickly.

3 Direct-feed system; this is an advisable extra which is fed from the main cylinder via the intermediate pressure side of the regulator. It will inflate the bag slowly.

The oral inflation tube is flexible and enters the top of the bag. Air can be blown in to the bag via the tube. This air naturally migrates upwards and can be breathed if necessary (see page 56). To inflate the bag, or to breathe from it, a push button in the tube mouthpiece is depressed to give direct access to the interior. On most mouthpieces, the action of releasing the button not only closes off the bag but also opens access to a simple, one-way, mushroom exhaust valve. If breathing from the bag, the exhalations may be passed directly into the water while still keeping the mouthpiece in place.

On the overhead type of compensator the emergency cylinder is stowed horizontally across the back of the lower part of the bag; or vertically on the waistcoat or dry-suit types, to suit the design concerned. The screw connection has a one-way valve to stop any water inside the bag entering the cylinder when empty. Check the cylinder for internal water after every dive as sometimes the on/off tap may have been forgotten and left open.

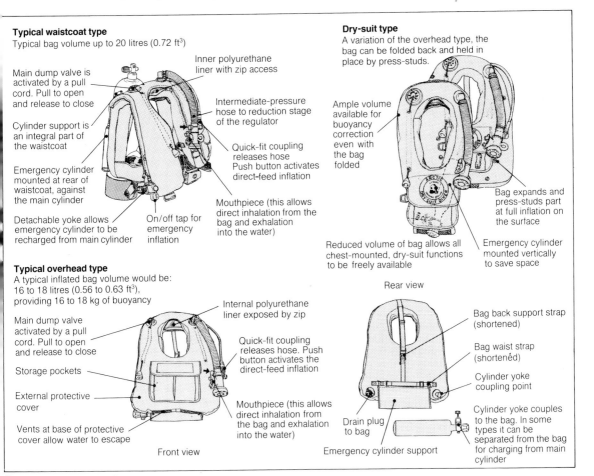

Typical waistcoat type
Typical bag volume up to 20 litres (0.72 ft³)

Main dump valve is activated by a pull cord. Pull to open and release to close

Cylinder support is an integral part of the waistcoat

Emergency cylinder mounted at rear of waistcoat, against the main cylinder

Detachable yoke allows emergency cylinder to be recharged from main cylinder

Inner polyurethane liner with zip access

Intermediate-pressure hose to reduction stage of the regulator

Quick-fit coupling releases hose Push button activates direct-feed inflation

On/off tap for emergency inflation

Mouthpiece (this allows direct inhalation from the bag and exhalation into the water)

Dry-suit type
A variation of the overhead type, the bag can be folded back and held in place by press-studs.

Ample volume available for buoyancy correction even with the bag folded

Bag expands and press-studs part at full inflation on the surface

Reduced volume of bag allows all chest-mounted, dry-suit functions to be freely available

Emergency cylinder mounted vertically to save space

Rear view

Typical overhead type
A typical inflated bag volume would be: 16 to 18 litres (0.56 to 0.63 ft³), providing 16 to 18 kg of buoyancy

Main dump valve activated by a pull cord. Pull to open and release to close

Storage pockets

External protective cover

Vents at base of protective cover allow water to escape

Internal polyurethane liner exposed by zip

Quick-fit coupling releases hose. Push button activates the direct-feed inflation

Mouthpiece (this allows direct inhalation from the bag and exhalation into the water)

Front view

Drain plug to bag

Emergency cylinder support

Bag back support strap (shortened)

Bag waist strap (shortened)

Cylinder yoke coupling point

Cylinder yoke couples to the bag. In some types it can be separated from the bag for charging from main cylinder

Buoyancy compensators

Buoyancy compensators

The direct-feed hose draws air from the intermediate-pressure side of the regulator reduction stage. This tube attaches to the compensator by a quick-fit coupling on the mouthpiece of the oral inflation tube. Air enters when a push button on the mouthpiece is depressed.

Deflation

Two methods can be used to deflate the compensator:

* A large diameter 'dump valve' on the upper part of the bag is usually activated by a push button or a pull cord. This quickly vents all or part of the air. It also acts as an overpressure valve, opening automatically

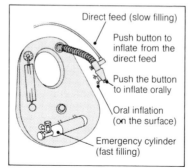

Compensator inflation

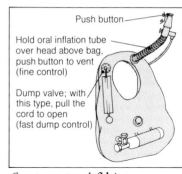

Compensator deflation

on excessive inflation to release air and stop the bag from bursting.

* The oral inflation tube has a venting capacity to allow fine control of

the amount of air in the bag. The tube must be held higher than the bag and the button in its end pushed so that air can escape through the mouthpiece.

Pre-dive checks and assembly

Fully inflate the compensator bag, using the oral inflation tube, until the dump valve is overpressured and blows off. Check if there are any obvious leaks.

Check the integrity of all harnessing and buckles.

Emergency cylinders are normally charged from a diver's main cylinder by means of a yoke attachment similar to that on a regulator.

These small-capacity emergency cylinders should be tested in the same way as the main cylinder. Provided this is done, the user need have no worries when charging them with high-pressure air.

Charge the cylinder before each and every dive from the full main aqualung cylinder (typically a pressure of 200 bar). Never charge from a low-pressure source, such as a partially-filled main cylinder which will give only a reduced pressure to

the emergency cylinder. Connect it to the main cylinder by way of the adaptor and close the bleed valve.

Open the small cylinder tap, then 'crack' open the main one, so as to slowly leak air in to it without the temperature rising too much. ('Crack' means to open an on/off tap in a very slow, controlled way.) You will hear the hiss of air and know when it is complete. The small cylinder will feel warm. This happens when any cylinder is charged with high-pressure air. Close both cylinders' on/off taps.

Vent the charging adaptor and remove the small cylinder. Venting makes a loud sharp noise, so be ready for this.

Emergency cylinders are typically 0.2 litres water capacity and 200 bar working pressure. This gives a free air volume of 0.2 x 200 (or 40) litres, which is almost 9 gallons. Thus an 18 litre compensator bag

can be filled just twice from one emergency cylinder when on the surface. As this cylinder is charged from the main cylinder, lower pressures are to be expected.

The fully-charged emergency cylinder may now be fitted on to the compensator bag.

Visually inspect the direct-feed hose connected to the regulator. Ensure the integrity of the quick-fit coupling.

When checking the action of the regulator, make sure the aqualung cylinder is turned on and test the action of the direct feed, using the push button provided.

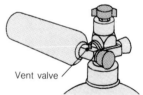

Filling an emergency cylinder

Fitting the buoyancy compensator

Put on the buoyancy compensator immediately after having donned the diving suit; it goes on under all other equipment. Adjust harnessing for a comfortable loose fit.

The waistcoat-type compensator is an integral part of the cylinder harnessing and so will be automatically fitted at the same time. With other types of compensator, don the cylinder after the compensator, keeping its edges free of the aqualung shoulder harnessing. Adjust the support harness between the legs for comfort and to prevent the bag riding up too high.

The weightbelt is best fitted once all equipment is in place and over all other harnessing. Never fit it under the compensator support strap. Otherwise, if released, it would end up dangling between the legs! The weightbelt must be able to drop clear in an emergency.

Adjustable buoyancy compensators will keep the head above water even if the diver is unconscious. Wave slap will be a problem if the diver is too low in the water, so choose one with enough volume to suit the diver's equipment and still keep his head above water.

Heavy equipment such as excess lead weight and the heavier type or twin cylinders, will cause the diver to float deeper by a few centimetres, leaving him or her more vulnerable to wave slap.

Inflate the buoyancy compensator on the surface, to use as a life-jacket.

Fully inflate
When out of air, or in an emergency, inflate the bag fully to bring the mouth clear of the water. The bag holds the head rigidly, making it difficult to turn and look sideways.

Partly inflate
Partial inflation leaves the mouth nearer the water level, but allows more head movement. If air is available, leave regulator mouthpiece in position and inflate with emergency cylinder or direct feed.

If using a fully inflated buoyancy compensator, simply lie on your back and fin.

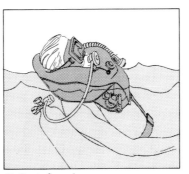

Make sure strap is not too loose or, when inflated, the bag will ride up about the head and throat

Adjust support harness loosely under legs for comfort

Adjust lateral support strap behind back

Fitting buoyancy compensator

Fully inflated

Partially inflated

Exercises and techniques

Accustom yourself to the feel of the compensator in the water. Then, on the water's surface, inflate the bag orally and float. Deflate it. Do this slowly at first, using the oral inflation tube (held above the head and opened); then faster by means of the main dump valve. Inflate the bag using the direct-feed system. Note that it fills slowly.

At the end of the training session, inflate the compensator bag by means of the small emergency cylinder. Note this time that it fills very quickly.

Close the on/off tap immediately. If the tap is left open, any water in the compensator bag will be forced inside during a subsequent descent later in the training session. Unless removed, this water would in time corrode the cylinder.

Always use the direct feed for bag inflation to adjust buoyancy. Reserve the small cylinder solely for emergency situations

Buoyancy compensation

For this exercise, readjust personal weighting to be slightly negative, and descend to the bottom, in two to three metres (6-10 ft) maximum.

Feel for the location of the main dump valve or its pull cord, and make sure the oral inflation tube is readily to hand. Do this at the start of every dive, in case they have been caught up or covered by other equipment.

Sitting cross-legged or kneeling on the bottom, slowly inflate the bag with the direct-feed system. On lifting off the bottom, pull the main dump valve and vent all the buoyancy to settle down again.

After one or two tries, trim the air buoyancy in the bag and float vertically in mid-water, free of the bottom. It is easier than it sounds!

If positive buoyancy starts to take over and you begin to rise, arrest

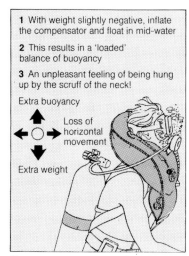

1 With weight slightly negative, inflate the compensator and float in mid-water

2 This results in a 'loaded' balance of buoyancy

3 An unpleasant feeling of being hung up by the scruff of the neck!

Extra buoyancy

Loss of horizontal movement

Extra weight

Buoyancy compensation

this ascent by venting air from the oral inflation tube. Try to do this while maintaining your location in mid-water.

Note the disadvantages of floating in mid-water:

* When the air gathers in the top of the bag the feeling of being strung up from the neck can prove very uncomfortable.

* The balance of buoyancy is loaded. Extra weight is offset by extra air in the bag. Movement is more restricted when turning.

The results of overweighting
With too much compensation, the diver will be in a nearly vertical position and swimming is inefficient.

If weighting is neutral, the required compensation is minimized; the diver will be nearly horizontal and swimming is efficient.

The diver will very soon recognize the wisdom of first weighting to achieve neutral buoyancy, and then using the buoyancy compensator (by direct feed or oral injection) to adjust for small negative buoyancy tendencies during the dive.

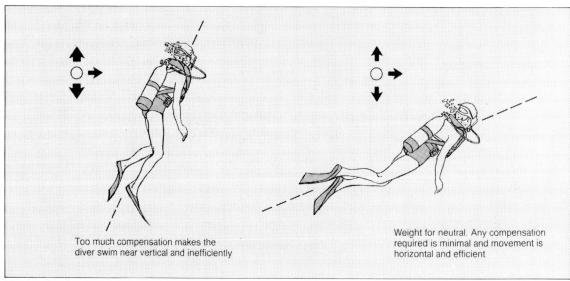

Too much compensation makes the diver swim near vertical and inefficiently

Weight for neutral. Any compensation required is minimal and movement is horizontal and efficient

The result of overweighting

Buoyancy control

Controlled buoyant ascent

This is a technique for self-rescue in an emergency. Weight for neutral buoyancy and descend to the bottom, in a maximum depth of 2 to 3 metres (6-10 ft).

* Bring the oral inflation tube to hand and ready for use.

* Crack open the emergency cylinder and slowly inflate the bag to achieve a controlled lift-off from the bottom. Close the cylinder tap.

(Remember the term 'crack' means to open an on/off tap slowly in case too much air gushes out.)

* The ascent starts slowly but will soon pick up speed. The main point of this exercise is to learn to control this speed by venting air from the oral inflation tube held above the head. Come up as slowly as possible. In emergencies 7 to 8 metres (23-26 ft) a minute, half the normal ascent rate, is the ideal maximum. This may be difficult to maintain in such circumstances. If speed starts building up uncontrollably, vent by means of the main dump.

* Look up while ascending and make sure you breathe in and out normally at all times.

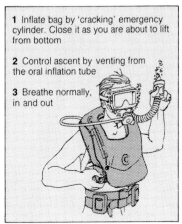

1 Inflate bag by 'cracking' emergency cylinder. Close it as you are about to lift from bottom

2 Control ascent by venting from the oral inflation tube

3 Breathe normally, in and out

Controlled buoyant ascent

Assisted buoyant ascent

This is an emergency technique for rescuing a companion. Weight normally and go to the bottom in 2 to 3 metres (6-10 ft) maximum.

For practice purposes, the proposed 'victim' must be conversant with the required exercises and be an experienced diver. That is, the person chosen must be capable of controlling his or her own situation, should the ascent start getting out of hand.

* Approach the victim and take a firm hold of him by gripping the yoke of the buoyancy compensator. Then crack open the victim's emergency cylinder and slowly inflate the compensator bag.

* As the victim begins to rise, close the cylinder tap. Then control the ascent by venting from the oral inflation tube as before.

Having tried this exercise, you will be aware of two points:

1 It is necessary to work out the initial angle of approach beforehand, to be within reach of both cylinder tap and oral vent tube.

2 As the victim is more buoyant than the rescuer, there is a tendency to separate, so keep close together, with the rescuer holding on firmly.

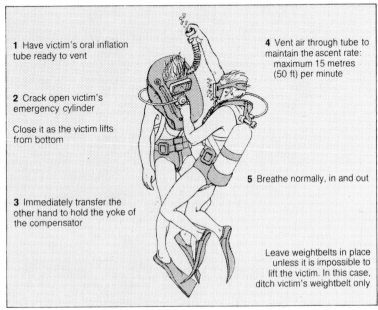

1 Have victim's oral inflation tube ready to vent

2 Crack open victim's emergency cylinder

Close it as the victim lifts from bottom

3 Immediately transfer the other hand to hold the yoke of the compensator

4 Vent air through tube to maintain the ascent rate: maximum 15 metres (50 ft) per minute

5 Breathe normally, in and out

Leave weightbelts in place unless it is impossible to lift the victim. In this case, ditch victim's weightbelt only

Making an assisted buoyant ascent

Breathing from the compensator bag

This is a method of self-rescue, but one to be used only if no other air supply is available. It requires a strict sequence of actions and a cool head in an emergency. In view of this, and in order to attain a clear idea of what is involved, some practice is necessary.

Air is obtained by way of the oral inflation tube mouthpiece, and two types are available:

1 The push-button type is intended for surface inflation. Its use underwater is complicated; the button must be pushed before inhaling, then closed prior to exhaling, with the surplus air sometimes dribbled away past the corner of the mouth or nasally past the mask seal.

2 An improved purpose-designed version is activated by pushing a button. The diver then inhales past a one-way valve and exhales into the water past another, in a continuous action. This type is easier to use and is recommended as a standard attachment to all the buoyancy compensators.

The air can be breathed as it is compressed to the same pressure as the water surrounding the flexible compensator bag, which acts as a 'counterlung'. Attempt these progressive exercises only under the supervision of an instructor.

Breathing technique
Learn to introduce a minimal amount of air into the compensator bag — enough for one or possibly two breaths, but not enough to lift the body off the bottom.

With air in the bag, raise the oral tube above the head. When the bag is compressed on descent, water seeps into it on every dive and gathers in the semi-rigid tube. Raising the mouthpiece allows this water to drain from the tube.

Lean back and look up. Lower the oral-tube mouthpiece until it is just shallow of the mouth. Press the oral-tube end button and air will bubble out. Practise this action.

This time remove the regulator mouthpiece and put some more air into the bag with the emergency cylinder. With the other hand, slip the oral-tube mouthpiece into the mouth and press the button to obtain air.

Breathing from the compensator

Take one, possibly two breaths, then replace the regulator, clear it of water and start breathing again.

When proficient in the breathing action, practise taking multiple breaths from the bag, topping it up with more air when necessary, by:

* Using the direct-feed system to simulate what happens when the regulator is faulty but there is air in the cylinder.

* Cracking the emergency cylinder, to simulate a situation when no air is available from any other source.

DO NOT attempt an ascent or vertical movement with these exercises.

Maintenance of compensators

Most modern buoyancy compensators have a double-bag system. That is, a tough attrition-proof exterior, with a clear polyamide separate bag inside to contain the air. Fittings are of the screw type to hold both bags together. Prior to the first dive and under qualified guidance, be certain that all screw threads are silicone-greased, to allow for easy removal when the polyamide bag finally requires changing.

Periodically fully inflate the bag and check for leaks. Carefully study the joints and flexible hose for signs of perishing and give attention to the one-way valve where the emergency cylinder attaches; it may be corroded and open only with difficulty. More regularly, check the main dump valve for leaks and test its venting capability from a fully inflated bag. It may have a sticky action or be slack in its response. If in doubt over any point, seek qualified advice. A compensator is only as good as its ability to function properly; that is, it must hold air and give assistance when required.

Diving suits

Introduction

Without adequate protection, the diver's water-softened skin will be exposed to abrasive contact with rocks. More importantly, the body will lose heat to the surrounding colder water and will certainly require adequate thermal protection. A diving suit may prove an effective survival aid during long immersions and will offer protection against both cold and injury. Sports divers generally wear a conventional wet or dry suit.

Wet suits are made of expanded foam neoprene. Water is allowed to leak into the suit at the neck and cuffs and be warmed by body heat. The foam neoprene then slows down the heat loss to the surrounding colder water.

Dry suits trap an insulating layer of air about the body. They come in two designs:

1 Membrane suits are made of thin rubber or synthetic material and warm underclothing is needed.

2 Neoprene suits are made of foam neoprene. Less underclothing is needed as the suit material gives a degree of thermal protection.

Skin suits, as they are called, offer little or no thermal protection and guard the diver only against abrasive contact. They are used mainly in warmer waters. The name is of commercial origin and the suits fit in a tight streamlined manner. Similar (but less smart) protection is given by a fairly tight-fitting sweater and a pair of old jeans!

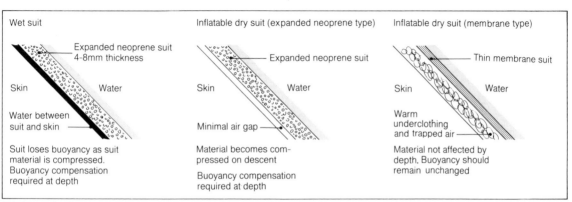

Diving suits in common use

Wet suits

These are made of expanded foam neoprene and come in many varieties and combinations. For diving in colder waters, it is best to choose 'long john' trousers, which include an integral singlet top, and a long-sleeved jacket with an attached hood. Bootees with built-in hard soles are recommended and gloves should be worn. In much colder water, try fingerless mittens. The suit should fit closely but not tightly, to allow freedom of movement without restricting the arms, legs, chest or neck. When worn in the water, suits are usually entirely

comfortable, but before diving, or afterwards on the boat ride home, tightness about the neck may lead to an uncomfortable reaction particularly in warm weather.

In warm waters it is sometimes enough to wear only the jacket part, but always use a hood. There can be a considerable heat loss from the head as the skull lacks the insulative properties of the rest of the body. However, beware! Cold water conditions are often encountered even in the warmer areas of the world. Warm water on the surface often

changes to much colder water at lower depths. Always use adequate protection. Never risk being caught unprepared!

The thickness of the foam neoprene matters on two counts. It offers thermal protection and provides buoyancy. Buoyancy decreases as the foam is compressed during descent; the diver becomes slightly more negative, but buoyancy is regained on ascent. With thicker materials, the rate of change of this buoyancy balance could cause the diver some problems, either on the

Wet and dry suits

bottom or during the latter stages of the ascent. A material thickness of about ¼ inch (6mm) probably offers adequate thermal protection and controllable buoyancy variations. With a material that is only very slightly thicker, surface buoyancy is appreciably higher.

Those who claim they require very thick wet suits have a personal problem to come to terms with. Perhaps they are susceptible to cold due to a lack of physical fitness, or they simply expect to stay in the water too long. Remember, diving suits simply prolong the diver's in-water survival time and it is very important to make arrangements which will allow the diving to fall within a sensible time window. Also do not overlook the loss of thermal protection due to suit compression at depth. Theoretically, by about 30 metres (98 ft), the suit has only a quarter of its surface thickness.

In the colder water at depth, divers can survive quite well for limited periods, but they will suffer should they have to stay in the water on the surface for an extended period after the dive.

Wet-suit weighting procedures

The wet suit should be the type first tried by a trainee; its buoyancy control is simple compared with a dry suit. It is usually best to consider the weighting for two different depth ranges, as well as taking into account personal buoyancy characteristics and the equipment being worn. If in doubt, consult an experienced companion.

For shallow dives, up to 20 metres (66 ft), weighting is arranged so as to be neutral on the surface and should remain controllable over the whole depth range. For deeper dives, beyond 20 metres, to compensate for buoyancy loss at depth, less weight is carried. The diver must arrange to be marginally positive at the start of the dive on the surface; this requires experience.

If too negative, the diver becomes over-negative on first reaching maximum depth because of the full weight of air still in the cylinders and the reduction of the suit's own buoyancy due to compression. If too positive, however, the diver becomes over-positive during the final stages of the ascent, when the suit buoyancy returns because the weight of air in the cylinders has by then been reduced (air weight having been breathed).

As a general rule, a sensible weighting procedure that works well in the shallows will allow adequate buoyancy control when diving to depths of up to 20 metres (66 ft). This should be ample for the initial open-water dives. However, when diving any deeper than 20 metres (66 ft), it will be necessary to take some extra care over the weighting.

Most divers appear happy to start out slightly negative on the bottom, as they can always use the buoyancy compensator. But control over positive buoyancy at the end of the dive is lost once the air has been breathed. So it is suggested that divers should ascend while there is still ample air (weight) in the cylinder. Never wait till it is nearly empty, particularly when large capacity single or twin cylinders are being used.

Trainees must seek the guidance of more experienced companions on the proposed weighting for their first open-water dives. On subsequent dives, weighting will already have been decided and adjusted.

Dry suits

The thought of a dry dive appeals to everyone and the layer of insulating air, particularly in a neoprene type of dry suit, can certainly make it a warm comfortable experience. For very cold water diving, such suits are vital.

However, trainees must be warned that diving in dry suits involves special techniques which need to be well understood and practised. Divers should progress on to dry suits only after a number of open-water dives in a wet suit. This gives them experience of the buoyancy variations to be expected over the length and depth of a submersion. Even so, when they progress on to the dry suit, they should first practise under supervision in a sheltered shallow location. The watertight integrity of a dry suit is ensured by seals at the neck, wrists and (sometimes) the ankles. Suits should always have a hood which is free flooding and not pressure resistant in any way. A sealed hood will cause a reversed ear problem (which is explained more fully on page 79).

Dressing and general care of suit

With the membrane type of suit, the seals are made of thin soft rubber. They are quite tight-fitting and can be easily torn. With the neoprene type, the seals are made of thin neoprene instead and they will be relatively loose.

Leaking seals are a constant problem and a few tricks will have to be practised. (Some ways to deal with the problems are described below.)

Entry into modern suits is usually by way of a watertight zip across the shoulders. Old-style dry suits were often two-piece or the front-entry type. Use French chalk to ensure the hands slip easily through the seals. Use beeswax to lubricate the zip. Avoid some household silicon sprays as they may attack the supporting synthetic rubber. Always wash suit after use, allow to dry and do any simple repairs immediately.

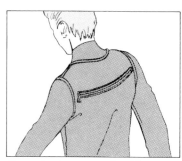

Dry-suit zip across shoulders

Suit seals

With a dry suit, happiness is a truly dry dive. However, both neck and wrist seals have a habit of leaking when they are badly seated or are put under any tension.

Neck seals

Put the seal under tension by bending the head forward on the chest.

1 The suit neck seal can pull away from the nape of the neck unless the seal is a snug fit.

Very tight neck seals restrict the neck and can lead to a carotid reflex (see *Volume Two*).

2 The thin rubber seals on membrane suits should be pulled down to loosen them and to accommodate any neck movement. This is usually effective.

3 Seals on neoprene-type dry suits are made of thin neoprene and are naturally loose. A seal is effected by folding the neoprene inwards.

4 Leaks can occur through wrist seals, due to natural furrows formed by the wrist tendons. Pull the seal back to introduce some looseness, though it may still leak if it is put under tension by hand movement.

With dry-suit wrist seals, fold the neoprene inwards.

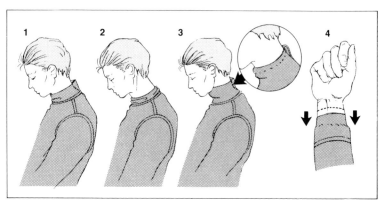

Leaking suit seals

Suit compensation and venting

The air space inside the suit must be pressure compensated during descent or the diver will suffer from a 'squeeze' effect. The air blown in to achieve this expands during the ascent and must then be vented or else the diver will become grossly overbuoyant. Therefore all dry suits will be provided with both compensation and venting valves, in much the same way as an adjustable buoyancy compensator.

Air for compensation is supplied by a direct-feed system, drawing air from the intermediate side of the regulator. This usually enters the suit on the left side of the chest through a hand-operated valve.

Suit buoyancy

Venting is achieved by means of a large diameter overpressure (main dump) valve set. This is positioned on either the right-hand side of the chest or on the upper right arm and is either hand adjustable or lightly sprung. In this way only a little more air volume than is necessary need be retained within the suit. Some valves are fitted with a pull cord that allows instant dumping of all the air in the suit.

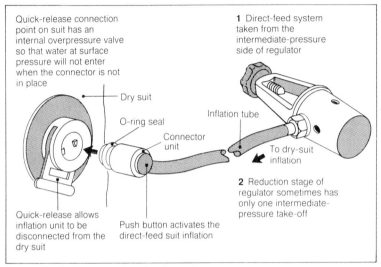

Quick-release connection point on suit has an internal overpressure valve so that water at surface pressure will not enter when the connector is not in place

Dry suit

O-ring seal

Connector unit

Inflation tube

1 Direct-feed system taken from the intermediate-pressure side of regulator

To dry-suit inflation

2 Reduction stage of regulator sometimes has only one intermediate-pressure take-off

Quick-release allows inflation unit to be disconnected from the dry suit

Push button activates the direct-feed suit inflation

Direct-feed compensation for dry suits

Chest-mounted direct feed

Arm-mounted main dump valve

Chest-mounted dump valve

Dump valve can be adjustable, or activated by a pull cord. It may be chest-mounted, or on the upper or forearm

Dry-suit deflation dump valves

Suit compensation procedure

This will be required on descent to offset increasing water pressure.

The standard inflation device is a direct-feed system from the low-pressure side of the regulator (see above). It is similar to that on the buoyancy compensator.

Blow minimal air into the suit at depth to alleviate any feeling of pressure, without unduly increasing buoyancy.

ALWAYS try to use suit inflation to make adjustments for comfort; use the buoyancy compensator for corrections in buoyancy. (In reality some of the air will always go towards correcting buoyancy. Provided the diver is not excessively negative, this is permissible, as the air blown in can still be considered minimal.) Vent this air as it expands on ascent, using the dump valve situated on the chest or arm. When a comfortable level of air has been introduced, expansion will be minimal. Only one or two ventings will then be necessary.

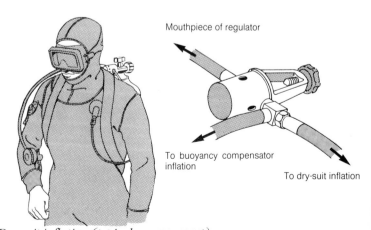

Mouthpiece of regulator

To buoyancy compensator inflation

To dry-suit inflation

Dry-suit inflation (typical arrangement)

Dry-suit buoyancy

Dry suits have variable buoyancy characteristics due to the air volume trapped inside. Therefore it is best if trainee divers start training in a wet suit and graduate to dry suits only after some experience has been gained in the buoyancy variations to be expected throughout a dive.

A neoprene-type dry suit has an integral buoyancy due to its foam neoprene construction; it is also fairly snug fitting. During a dive it behaves much like a wet suit and air is required only for compensation purposes, with little temptation to blow in extra air in order to adjust for buoyancy loss.

The membrane type has no integral buoyancy and there is a great temptation to blow in extra air.

What is more, it has a relatively large internal volume which is necessary to accommodate the extra undergarments required to offset its lack of thermal protection. For the inexperienced diver, this can easily lead to difficulties with buoyancy.

Because these suits present more complex problems, full training in their use is recommended.

Dry-suit weighting

This depends partly on the material from which the suit is made, and partly on the amount of underclothing worn as thermal protection. This extra layer increases the internal volume of the suit which may trap a buoyant air volume.

Foam neoprene type
Buoyant and yet warm material; requires minimal underclothing.

Membrane type
Non-buoyant, with little thermal protection; requires extra underclothing, particularly when diving in colder waters.

Both types discussed here should require approximately the same weighting in order to achieve neutral buoyancy on the surface in average water temperatures.

If divers are seen to carry inordinately large amounts of lead weight, particularly with the membrane-type of suits, matters may be partly explained by an excess of underclothing. But this can also be a reflection of personal buoyancy characteristics and the experience of the diver in controlling them.

IMPORTANT: Be sure to wear a buoyancy compensator at all times, to control any undesirable shifts towards negative buoyancy.

An excess of air may become trapped in the suit while dressing. Before donning the cylinder, practise crouching in a ball, then gently insert two fingers into the neck seal to vent the surplus.

Over-inflation

If there has been sufficient early practice in the shallows, only incompetence or an accident will cause the suit to over-inflate at depth. Be aware of these following points:

* All air inflation devices should be fail-safe. For example, there are buttons which must be depressed to open, but which close when released. Any tap arrangement which could be accidentally left or knocked open is best avoided.

Run a regular check on the action of the dump valve in dry conditions. Fully inflate the suit and ensure that the dump will vent when overpressured or when it is activated by hand.

Maintain air inflation and dump valves in good mechanical order. Check that dump-valve pull cords are not about to break.

In the water be certain that the dump valve is available and is not restricted in any way by equipment. If pull cords are used, be sure they are readily to hand.

Underwater situations are never simple so, to be ready for awkward moments, practise venting air through a cuff seal. Hold one hand up and gently ease back the seal to tease the air into escaping. A little water will dribble back; be heavy handed and there will be an inrush! It is inadvisable to practise this in mid-water as the resultant buoyancy loss will retard or hinder an ascent.

Blow up

Some traumatic incident could conceivably leave a diver floating on the surface with an over-inflated suit, possibly face-down and unconscious. 'Blow up' is the term given to this situation by 'hard-hat' divers. Practice venting a companion's dry suit on the surface. Use your body weight to reposition the victim head-up and vent the air through the cuffs or neck seal. Then quickly inflate the buoyancy compensator.

This will make certain that the victim floats face-up.

Inversion

When the diver is in a head-down position, any air inside the suit rushes up to the feet. A little carelessness or over-inflation and it is all too easy for the diver to end up floating upside-down.

Clearly this is a situation to avoid, particularly when diving at depth, so always practise the following:

* Use minimal suit inflation; just enough for comfort only.

* Do not use inflation when head-down, otherwise the extra air may tip the balance and you will find you start to rise.

* When working in a head-down position, trim for slight negative buoyancy if convenient.

* Be sensitive to the problem. If excess air starts to gather, quickly fin head-up and vent as necessary.

Always ensuring that there is suitable supervision, practise the following exercises:

* Float feet-up, and inflate the buoyancy compensator, using the emergency cylinder. Note how this will help you to regain a head-up vertical stance.

* Watch a companion practise the above exercise and so become familiar with the sequence of actions and the timing. (There will be a short pause before inversion.) Assistance may be given to companions in this situation by pulling their feet downwards.

Be careful not to lose your mouthpiece during practice. It is difficult to recapture and to clear while you are upside-down.

Both automatic overpressure valves which are set at ankle level, and suits that terminate in ankle seals, will allow air to escape while the diver is inverted.

Ankle weights may have an application in working dives. However, for everyday diving, a good weighting and buoyancy control procedure is by far the best technique to employ.

The problem of inversion is not new. Hard-hat salvage divers used suits that were laced at the back of the legs. In this way the potential volume of suits could be limited.

Flooded suit

A ripped cuff, a puncture or some such accident will allow water to enter and the suit loses whatever buoyancy it had due to the air trapped inside.

Suits of expanded neoprene retain some buoyancy because of the nature of their material, although this buoyancy will decrease with the suit's compression at depth.

Membrane suits are usually much looser fitting to allow for warm underclothing. Any change in buoyancy will be very noticeable.

Once flooded, the suit becomes a negatively buoyant drag on movement. Those who have been unwise enough to have used suit inflation to provide a large part of any buoyancy correction would be at an added disadvantage. The wisdom of wearing a buoyancy compensator against such emergencies will be immediately appreciated. Without one it could prove very difficult to ascend, even from shallow depths. Divers who have known this misfortune have described it as a most unpleasant experience, and one they would rather not repeat!

Try flooding a dry suit, under supervision, in the shallows or a pool. This will give some intimation of what is involved. Imagine it occurring during a dive, or worse, during a descent. Decide what action you would take to regain control over buoyancy and to ensure an ascent.

Ancillary equipment

Contents gauges

The term contents gauge is perhaps misleading, for a contents gauge is not like the petrol gauge in a car, which shows how full a tank is. What these gauges actually show is the pressure of air remaining in the cylinder. This pressure is a direct indication of the amount of air it contains. If a cylinder is normally charged to, say, 200 bar and shows 103 bar on the gauge, it can be assumed to be only about half full. Contents gauges deal with high pressures, usually having a full 0 to 250 bar scale deflection.

The reason these are called contents gauges is to distinguish them from depth gauges, many of which work on the same principle. Internally, they consist of a 'Bourdon tube', a flattened tube of copper, sealed at one end and curved in shape. Air pressure entering the tube tries to straighten it and this deflection is transmitted by gearing to register on a pointer. The whole case is flooded in silicone oil to make it proof against water pressure and lubricate the mechanism.

The contents gauge is connected to a high-pressure flexible tube, which screws into the high-pressure side of the regulator reduction stage. The reduction stage port is marked 'HP' on most regulators to avoid the risk of attaching the wrong hose. Both dry-suit and compensator intermediate pressure take-off points are found on the same body.

Look after contents gauges. Do not knock them about or put the hose under any unnecessary tension. Check the gauge reading against other gauges occasionally, and see if the gauge reads true. Periodically inspect the hose, especially where it enters the swage fittings at its end. If in doubt, change them for new ones; the cost will be well justified.

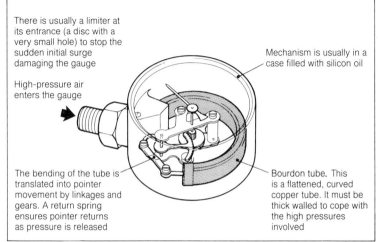

There is usually a limiter at its entrance (a disc with a very small hole) to stop the sudden initial surge damaging the gauge

High-pressure air enters the gauge

Mechanism is usually in a case filled with silicon oil

The bending of the tube is translated into pointer movement by linkages and gears. A return spring ensures pointer returns as pressure is released

Bourdon tube. This is a flattened, curved copper tube. It must be thick walled to cope with the high pressures involved

High-pressure cylinder contents gauge

Depth gauges

These are pressure gauges which are calibrated in either metres or feet to indicate depth and are required only to cope with 7 or 8 bar (70 or 80 metres) above atmospheric pressure. Remember, these indicate gauge pressure, not absolute pressure, and read 0 on the surface. There are two types:

Bourdon gauges

Compared with the contents gauge Bourdon tube, the tubes used in depth gauges have a much thinner wall. In the earliest designs, water

was allowed to enter the end of the tube and straighten it out. However, the presence of salt water soon led to internal deposits and inaccurate readings. Modern gauges are now arranged rather more efficiently.

The Bourdon tube is sealed inside the gauge case and is surrounded by silicone oil, so it has no direct contact with the water outside. Further, it has all air evacuated from it during manufacture, making its accuracy independent of temperature changes in the water. The

gauge case is semiflexible and, as liquids transmit pressure, depth changes affect the tube, thus making it curl inwards. This deflection, although opposite to that in the contents gauge, is registered in exactly the same way, through a gear mechanism.

Diaphragm gauges

This is an older style of depth gauge, but is still in use. The interior contains air and the bottom of the gauge case is a corrugated metal diaphragm, which deflects inwards

63

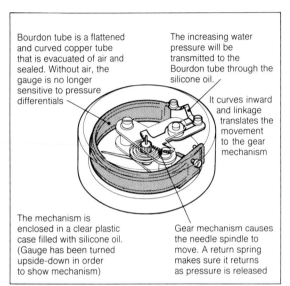

Bourdon tube is a flattened and curved copper tube that is evacuated of air and sealed. Without air, the gauge is no longer sensitive to pressure differentials

The increasing water pressure will be transmitted to the Bourdon tube through the silicone oil.

It curves inward and linkage translates the movement to the gear mechanism

The mechanism is enclosed in a clear plastic case filled with silicone oil. (Gauge has been turned upside-down in order to show mechanism)

Gear mechanism causes the needle spindle to move. A return spring makes sure it returns as pressure is released

Depth gauge (Bourdon gauge)

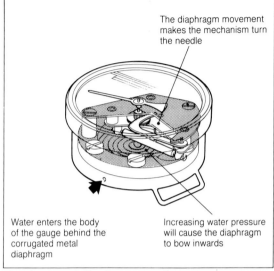

The diaphragm movement makes the mechanism turn the needle

Water enters the body of the gauge behind the corrugated metal diaphragm

Increasing water pressure will cause the diaphragm to bow inwards

Depth gauge (diaphragm type)

or outwards with changing water pressure. This deflection is then transmitted to a pointer.

Bourdon-tube gauges give a linear readout (that is, the depth divisions are equally spaced around the dial). Diaphragm gauges are non-linear, and are accurate up to around 15 metres (50 ft), then giving way to widening spacings for equal depth changes from there on. These are particularly useful for decompression stops. Their advantage is that they are purely mechanical, with the internal workings readily available.

Inaccuracies

Transportation may cause problems. Air travel will mean that the equipment is exposed to reduced atmospheric pressure so that the depth gauge pointers will be pulled backwards, perhaps damaging the mechanism. Special pressure-proof cases, sealed with 0-rings, are available and these enable gauges to be safely transported by air.

Diving at altitude (in a mountain lake, for instance) will have similar effects, as will temperature changes on non-compensated designs. One

or two models have an adjustable scale, with a pointer which can be zeroed prior to use. With a diaphragm gauge, it is possible to unscrew the case seal and equalize both atmospheric pressure and temperature differentials immediately prior to a dive or to prepare the equipment for air travel.

Calibrate the depth gauge against known depths, ideally in a purpose-built test rig. There may be a sticky movement in one sector of the pointer movement, or in different sectors during descent and ascent.

Knives

Knives should be solid, heavy and strong and will usually be worn strapped to the calf of the leg along with the snorkel tube. A small knife can also be carried on the arm so it is readily accessible, especially if diving in restricted areas. All knives should have well-sharpened edges but, for safety reasons and to pre-

vent damage to dry suits, their points should be blunt. Normally one edge will be serrated, for sawing rope and so on.

Nylon line and modern synthetic fibres are incredibly strong and very slippery — so normal knives will be unsuitable for cutting through

them. The best knife to use on tangle nets has proved to be the small blunt-ended type, such as is found in the equipment of rescue dinghies and the exposure suits worn by submariners and airmen. A special type of scissor which is capable of cutting these lines is also now available.

Signals

Hand signals — Diver to diver and diver to surface

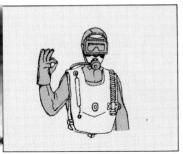

Make clear signals

I have no more air *also USA*

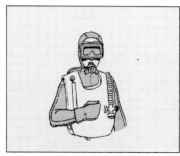

I am low on air *also USA*

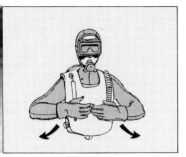

I am out of breath

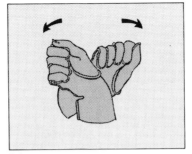

Distress

I am on reserve

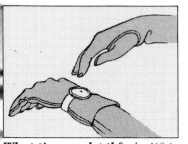

What time or depth? *also USA*

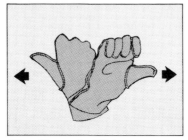

Direction *also USA*

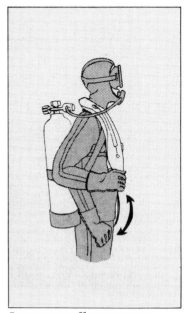

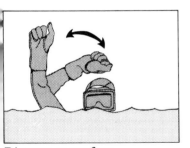

Distress at surface

OK at surface

I cannot pull my reserve

The underwater environment

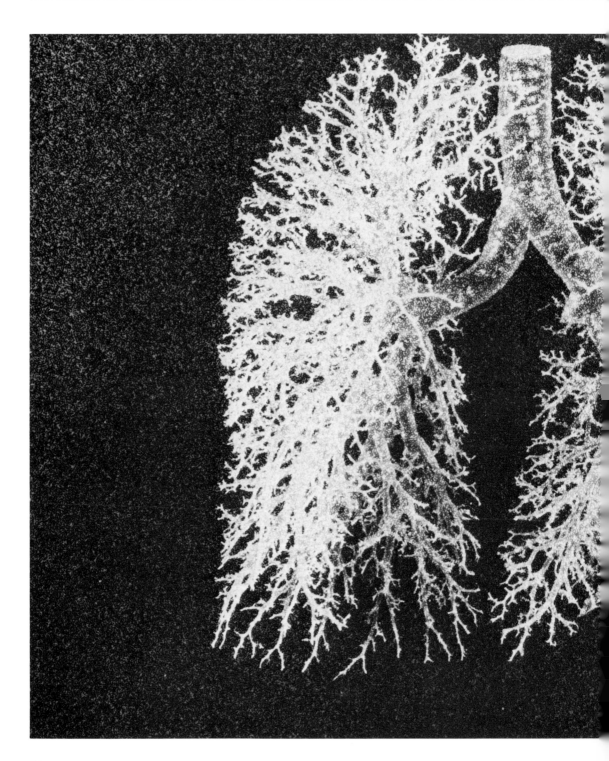

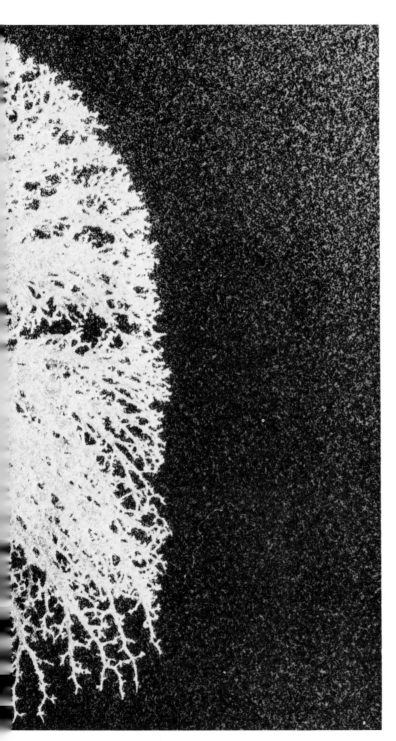

Introduction

Anyone who enters the underwater environment accepts there is an element of risk which for many adds to the excitement. Diving appeals to the adventurous free spirit, but it also demands a willing acceptance of its disciplines.

At first sight this may appear to be a contradiction, but it need not be so. Good divers will be aware of their own and their companions' capabilities. They can assess all the factors that make up a dive, and make a balanced judgement as to the safe and correct course of action. The diver must have the right temperament to know when the risks are unacceptable as well as the strength of character to call a halt when they are not. The temptation to go just that bit further and for longer, to reach the limits, is hard to resist and indeed, in certain cases, may be justified. Sometimes adverse conditions can be very stimulating. Drift diving in a fast tidal stream or riding through a rough sea are exhilarating and make the adrenalin flow !

Do remember, however, that divers must always consider their responsibilities and the safety of their companions, hence the sensible rule of always diving in pairs.

As a diver, you will be entering an alien environment in which everything is different and strange. For the first time you will be deprived of a lot of essentials normally taken for granted, such as unlimited air to breathe, and will have to manage with limited senses and some physical constraints. This demands training and practice, but when you experience the thrill of poising weightless over a vertical 'drop-off', you will know it was all worthwhile.

Man underwater

Adapting to the environment

Although all life began in and evolved from the oceans, humans have forgotten their watery origins and are now entirely land animals, adapted to having two feet firmly on the ground. For us to enter the sea and stay there for long periods makes great demands on both our bodies and the technical equipment required to supply all the necessary respiratory needs. The diver will have to cope with an underwater scenario which is completely alien to his physical and mental make up. Not only will this new environment affect all of the bodily functions but it can also cause physiological and psychological problems — all of which the diver must learn to overcome.

There are two ways to accomplish this. Firstly, the training course should ensure the diver develops the right reflexes and will respond correctly to any situation likely to arise. Secondly, an understanding of the physical nature of the undersea world helps the divers to stay safely within the margins of their own capabilities.

The senses
It comes as quite a shock when all the sensations we take for granted in our everyday life on land are suddenly changed, inverted or removed. All at once, the diver finds he cannot rely on fundamentals like the ground and the horizon — from which we normally judge posture and balance, and our relative position in the environment. In fact it is not uncommon for the underwater diver to have no idea what is up or down and in which direction the surface lies. Once, when disorientated in mid-water, one of the authors looked about desperately for a clue to his whereabouts. To his amazement he saw bubbles travelling 'down' between his legs. He was upside-down but was completely unaware of the fact !

There are five main senses on which we depend to maintain our relationship with the world around us; sight, hearing, touch, taste and smell. Of these, the last two are removed and hearing is an unreliable source of information because the direction of sounds is so difficult to determine. This means a far greater reliance must be placed on the two remaining senses — touch and vision. As every diver knows, the distance that can be seen underwater is by no means comparable to the distance visible on land, especially in temperate latitudes. Also, unless artificial light is introduced, colours merge into a general greyness, even at quite shallow depths. Added to this, refraction confuses the diver's judgement of both the size and distance of surrounding objects. Touch alone remains a powerful sense but its use without vision is rather more difficult to interpret, as on land in the dark; so only those who, like the blind, have a highly developed sense of touch, are able to cope with confidence.

Managing by touch alone can be very unnerving, especially to the imaginative mind so it is important that divers practise and develop the sense of touch during training. Then they will be able to cope with greater confidence should they lose their masks, find themselves in a cloud of stirred-up silt or have to operate a BC by feel alone.

The diver must also learn to be aware of and use 'kinesthesia', the sensations that are stimulated by movement, body posture, and the perception of weight. The 'vestibular' sensations will also be important. These relate to balance, rotation and dizziness, and are detected by sense organs in the inner ear. On land, man uses these senses to coordinate movement and maintain body posture. Vision normally contributes to this but even in the dark, the brain, guided by the position-sensing nerves, enables us to walk upright and perform quite complicated actions. Gravity is perceived by the vestibular position-sensing nerves and gives a sense of weight which helps us orientate ourselves.

However, once we descend underwater, few of these perceptions remain the same.

Environmental stresses

Weightlessness
One of the delights of diving is the sensation of being weightless, but it can sometimes be disconcerting. Until accustomed to it, the lack of stability robs divers of their control of movement and posture. Like astronauts, who appear to lumber about when performing even simple manoeuvres, divers have to develop new techniques to overcome this clumsiness. For instance, when using a hammer, the diver must hold on to the object with the other hand, or on impact, he will be

sent floating away. Hacksaw blades with teeth pointing backwards are fitted to saws because pulling is an easier action than pushing. On land we are aware of gravity and make allowances for the weight of things. Underwater, the effect of gravity is very much less − because of the greater density of water and the buoyancy − so objects, including ourselves, weigh much less.

Anxiety

Diving can be said to be an intrusion into a hostile environment, so it cannot be recommended for people with a high level of anxiety. A certain amount of anxiety is normal in any adventurous sport and is not altogether a bad thing because it makes the diver check the equipment carefully and be generally more cautious.

All divers experience moments of anxiety, often for no obvious reason, but some become over-aware of the potential hazards underwater and, however well they may conceal their fears initially, they are still liable to panic and become a danger to others.

Claustrophobia

The fear of being in a confined space can present itself at awkward moments. Some beginners feel a certain amount of claustrophobia when first putting their heads under the water; others on being encased in a diving suit, but this feeling rapidly passes as soon as the divers are underwater and there are other things to think about. This initial claustrophobia rarely reappears once it has been overcome.

Nevertheless, there are bound to be times when the diver will need to cope with the problem. We have seen experienced divers balk at

having to enter an underwater cave, but this is in no way surprising. The only cure we can recommend is to use torches to dispel the gloom and to carry a lifeline so as to be able to find the way out. Similarly, entering a decompression chamber can produce the same irrational fears.

Nitrogen narcosis

This is an insidious effect due to depth, of which the diver may not even be aware. It has been variously described as a sense of elation, over-confidence, or as an intoxication similar to that induced by alcohol. It is dangerous because it influences divers' behaviour, often rendering them unable to make rational judgements or react to emergencies.

Nitrogen narcosis is fully described in *Problem gases* on page 95 Watch out for the symptoms at depths around 28 metres (92 ft), especially in divers who have not dived for a long period. It is easily dealt with provided it is recognized.

Apprehension and panic

Apprehension is a negative conception of what might happen. It can be a reaction to a potentially hazardous adventure, such as diving into a cave, or it may just be uncertainty over whether one is able to cope with a new experience.

To the apprehensive mind, any shape that is dimly seen in poor visibility can take on the proportions of a sea monster.

This can be overcome by thorough planning and briefing, so that there is a good understanding of what will be involved in the dive. Best of all, the reassurance provided by a sympathetic dive leader will help to dispel most fears. Avoiding poor

diving conditions and building up experience will do wonders to maintain control of apprehension.

Panic is quite different. Unlike apprehension, its victims are aware that they are losing control and are unable to extricate themselves from the situation. Panic produces physiological changes which can have severe consequences, and is probably the cause of most accidents in underwater diving. Post-mortem evidence shows that victims are often found with all their equipment functioning perfectly, the air cylinder full, and the buoyancy compensator inflated.

Victims of panic usually breathe rapidly, leading to a reduction of carbon dioxide; they do not notice what is going on around them and seem unable to take the best way out of the predicament. Ignoring their training, they snatch at the most obvious, but invariably the wrong solution − such as making a free ascent or grabbing a companion's air supply.

It is difficult to know how to prevent panic as few people really know how they will act in a desperate situation. It takes great self-control to fight the desire to regain the surface. Instead take time to assess what is wrong and select the best solution to the problem. Experience tells of course, but so do physical fitness and sound training.

Again and again we return to the point that the diver's training is designed to teach the novice to be independent of the equipment and to be familiar with emergency drills.

Taking sensible precautions will help too; always wear a buoyancy compensator and never dive alone.

Cold

Cold is dangerous for divers. It reduces their efficiency, both mental and physical, and makes even simple tasks difficult. Divers in temperate latitudes are especially susceptible to cold as these seas are often no warmer than 15°C (59°F), and can drop as low as 4°C (38°F), whereas man's normal body temperature is about 38°C (98°F). To make matters worse, water is a good conductor of heat which means that unless the swimmer is well insulated with protective clothing or a diving suit, he or she will suffer a progressive heat loss to the surrounding water. As the swimmer grows colder he tries to increase body heat by muscular activity and by shivering.

If heat loss continues the body tries to protect itself by slowing down the blood flow to the skin and to the extremities so that the hands and feet become cold and numb. This reduction in surface blood flow allows the body heat to be conserved in 'the core' (the heart and the brain). Thus the amount of blood in the core is increased and blood pressure raised. It is vital that the core temperature is not allowed to drop below 35°C (95°F). If it does the diver will become hypothermic; metabolic, respiratory and heart rate, as well as blood pressure, all begin to fall. Unless this process is stopped the victim will become confused, disorientated and lethargic. He will lose concentration and 'switch off' to what is going on around him. The muscles will stiffen and this eventually leads to unconsciousness. Divers who suffer from heart disease or high blood pressure are particularly at risk when hypothermic. Body cooling (hypothermia) makes the victim unable to help himself and he becomes 'an accident waiting to happen'. Divers must be alert to the signs and symptoms.

Sports divers usually wear protective neoprene suits which reduce the rate at which heat is lost to the water. Wet suits are adequate for average length dives in relatively cool water, for example 21°C (70°F) down to 10°C (50°F). However, neoprene dry suits will be essential if temperatures are only a few degrees above freezing. Divers cannot survive an unlimited time in cold water, even in a suit. As experience grows they will learn to adjust the dive-time to weather conditions. This 'time window' should never be overrun unless circumstances allow no other option.

Neoprene will become compressed with depth and lose its insulating properties. At 20 metres (65 ft) both the thickness and insulating properties of a wet suit will be halved. A diver also loses heat internally. Air inhaled via the regulator will cool as it expands through the various internal orifices. Internal body heat warms up this air so exhalations are warmer. This is all heat lost from the body, and is often demonstrated in warm waters by a diver claiming his chest and lungs feel cold after leaving the water. The danger is usually well hidden. Strangely, a diver rarely seems to feel very cold during the dive itself. Once on the surface however, the cumulative effect is felt and divers can become exhausted if not picked up rapidly.

If the core temperature should fall below 30°C (86°F) the breathing rate and heartbeat become irregular and the danger of heart failure is considerably increased. A severely hypothermic victim may not show any detectable signs of life. The victim must be rewarmed very gradually and carefully. However, people who have been cooled very rapidly, such as those who fall into icy water, are sometimes resuscitated successfully. In these cases the metabolic rate of all the major organs is slowed right down and little hypoxic damage occurs. In severe cases raising the legs will help to improve the blood pressure. Always be ready to cope with shock.

Exposure

Even if the victim is removed from the water he or she may still be exposed to the cold because of wind chill and the cooling effect of the water evaporating away from within the suit. Wet suits do not protect from wind. The air temperature around northern European shores varies over a range of as much as 40°C (72°F) between winter and summer. However, the underwater temperature may vary by as little as 10°C (18°F). Always take windproof garments (such as an anorak) to put on immediately after diving. This is especially important if there is to be a long boat ride back to shore. A hot shower, a change into warm clothes and a bowl of hot soup are to be recommended — but not alcohol!

The effects of pressure

Units of measurement

It is easy to take for granted the physical requirements for our daily survival on land. When we enter the hostile underwater world, new forces will be experienced which we must learn to counteract. To help understand the nature of these forces, here is an explanation of the terms used:

Matter

The physical world is made up of elements which are collectively called matter. Elements are made up of atoms which are able to group together to form molecules. Two hydrogen atoms (H_2) combined with one of oxygen (O) will form water (H_2O).

There are three states of matter: gas, liquid and solid. Their molecules are held together by molecular attraction which will vary with the nature of the matter.

In a gas, the attraction is so low that the molecules move apart from each other; as a consequence the weight and density of a gas is low. In liquids and solids, the molecular attraction is higher and the molecules are held closer together; therefore the weight and the density are greater.

Energy

Energy is the capacity to do work, and work is defined as the application of a force through a distance. It is a force measured in kilograms or pounds which lifts, pulls or pushes an object through a specific distance such as metres or feet. Some examples of energy in our physical world are sound, waves, weather and tides.

Gravity

A gravitational attraction exists between any two bodies. Because of the immense mass of the earth, its attraction is far greater than that of any other gravitational force, so any weight is pulled down by gravity towards the centre of the earth.

Weight

The gravitational force of attraction on a body is called its weight and is measured in kiloNewtons (kN), or more conventionally in kilograms (kg) or pounds (lb).

Weight diminishes with the height above sea level because its gravitational attraction is less. Underwater, weight will be affected by buoyancy (see Archimedes' principle which is explained in the glossary).

Weight is determined by the density of an object multiplied by its volume. Lead is of sufficient density ($20m^3$ or 708 lb/ft^3), for example, that its weight is not affected significantly underwater — whereas

petrol with its density of 1.4 m^3 (50 lb/ft^3), most definitely is. Aluminium, on the other hand, will lose 38% of its weight underwater, having a density of 4.7 m^3 (168 lb/ft^3).

Mass

The terms mass and weight are often used interchangeably and mass is, in fact, measured in kilograms or pounds. Simply stated, mass tells us just how much matter there is in anything. For example, mass indicates that there is more matter in a 10 centimetre (4 in) cube of lead than in a cube of ice of the same size. Mass stays the same anywhere and is not subject to gravitational forces.

Density

Density is mass per unit volume of a substance. It is a measure of the degree of 'packing' of the molecules from which the substance is made. The greater the degree of packing, the higher the density. The density of a gas varies in accordance with its pressure.

On the surface, the volume of air in a diving bell has a specific mass. When it descends to only 10 metres (33 ft), the same mass is concentrated in half the volume and so its density is doubled. The increase of density with depth affects the flow of air and can reduce breathing capacity at 30 metres (100 ft) by as much as 50%. This increase means more effort is required to move air through the lungs than would be needed at the surface. Equipment design may also induce resistance to the passage of breathable gas. Density is measured in kg/m^3 or pounds. (Density with regards to liquids and solids is more fully discussed on pages 90 - 1.)

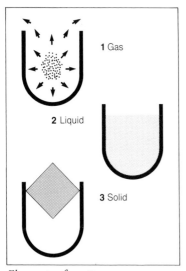

Elements of matter

1 Gas

2 Liquid

3 Solid

Physics of diving

Pressure

Pressure is defined as force per unit area of surface and it can be expressed in many forms: bar or ats, Pascals (pa), millimetres of mercury (mm/Hg), pounds per square inch (lb/in² or psi), kilograms per square centimetre (kg/cm²), or Newtons per square metre (N/m²) and so on.

Divers are affected by two types of pressure; atmospheric or air pressure, and hydrostatic pressure which is due to the weight of water. (Both of these are fully explained on this page and on page 75.)

The above definitions are precise enough for diving purposes. In this book it is assumed that gases are compressible and that liquids are not, even though this is not strictly true. (The special properties of gases will be explained on page 92 and those of fluids on page 74). It is also assumed that the tissues of the human body are an incompressible liquid, although it should be understood that the body's air spaces are not actually included in this category.

Volume

Volume is the measure of the internal space within a cylinder and is usually measured in either cubic metres (m³), cubic feet (ft³), gallons or litres. Cylinders are often marked with their water capacity (WC) which indicates precisely the volume of water they can hold.

Capacity

A cylinder's capacity, expressed in litres (l) or cubic feet (ft³) is the amount of air at atmospheric pressure that the cylinder can hold when charged to its pressure rating. Put another way, it is the volume of free air at atmospheric pressure which must be compressed into that particular cylinder to bring it up to its correct working pressure.

Buoyancy

This is the force that enables things to float. Any object immersed in a fluid is buoyed up by a force equal to the weight of the fluid displaced by that object. The buoyant force of a liquid depends upon its density (weight per unit volume). Salt water has a density of 1030 kg/m³ or 64 lb/ft³, fresh water 1000 kg/m3 (62 lb/ft³); so salt water is more buoyant than fresh.

Buoyancy is of great importance to the diver and is discussed in detail in *Volume Two.*

Atmospheric and hydrostatic pressures.

It has already been established that pressure is a force acting on a particular surface area. The diver will experience both the pressure of the surrounding water as well as the weight of the atmosphere over that water. This weight of air is called atmospheric pressure.

Atmospheric pressure

Air is basically composed of 21% oxygen and 79% nitrogen.

It is a colourless, odourless, tasteless but active gas which, like all gases, is compressible.

It may surprise some to know that air has a definite weight, having a density of 1.29gm/l or 0.081lb/ft³.

The earth is contained in an envelope of air called the atmosphere and everybody and everything within it is subjected to its weight.

Imagine a column of air stretching right up from sea level to the very top of the earth's atmosphere (the stratosphere) which is approximately 100 kilometres or 60 miles high. The pressure that is exerted by this column of air is equal to 1 kilogram on every square centimetre or to 14 pounds weight on every square inch.

Because of gravity, atmospheric pressure exerts a downward force towards the centre of the earth, being denser or heavier at sea level than higher up the column. It has been said that the human race lives submerged at the the bottom of an ocean of air — the ocean being the atmosphere !

The weight of the atmosphere can be measured by filling a dish full of sea water and immersing in it an open-ended test-tube. Atmospheric pressure acting on the surface of the water would be capable of forcing water up a tall tube to a height of 10 m (32.5 ft) !

The barometer does the same thing but mercury (Hg) is substituted for the water in order to keep the instrument to a more convenient manageable size. In a barometer the weight of the atmosphere will support a column of mercury 760 mm high. For the same reason it is impossible to pump fresh water out of a well, with a suction pump, if the well is deeper than 10.4 m (34 ft).

Pressure used to be measured in units called atmospheres (ats), one

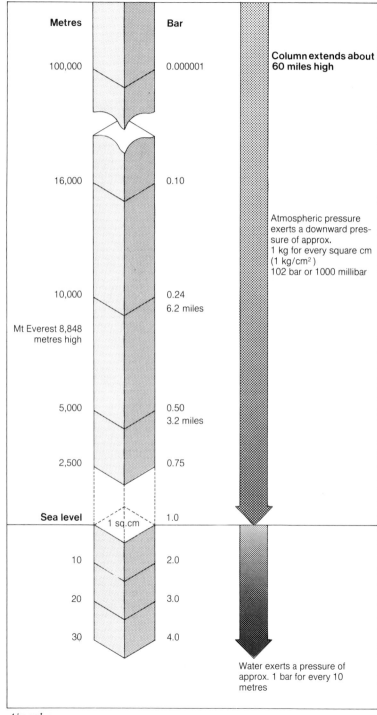

Metres	Bar
100,000	0.000001

Column extends about 60 miles high

16,000	0.10

Atmospheric pressure exerts a downward pressure of approx.
1 kg for every square cm (1 kg/cm²)
102 bar or 1000 millibar

10,000	0.24 6.2 miles

Mt Everest 8,848 metres high

5,000	0.50 3.2 miles
2,500	0.75

Sea level	1.0

1 sq.cm

10	2.0
20	3.0
30	4.0

Water exerts a pressure of approx. 1 bar for every 10 metres

Air column

'at' being equal to the weight of the atmosphere at sea level. The 'at' has been largely replaced by the bar, simply because it is a more convenient unit in calculation, but the difference between them is so small they are often interchanged:

1 bar = 0.98 ats
1 at = 1.02 bar

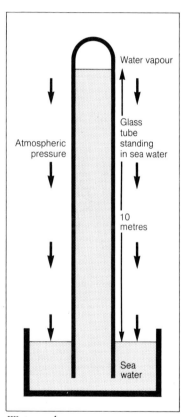

Water vapour

Atmospheric pressure

Glass tube standing in sea water

10 metres

Sea water

Water column

Although the atmospheric pressure does in fact fluctuate slightly with changes in the weather, the bar as a unit is sufficiently accurate for the purposes of diving.

Looking at the atmospheric column on the opposite page, it will be noticed that the change in the atmospheric pressure is only very gradual while ascending towards the stratosphere.

An aircraft flying at 5000 metres (3.1 miles) will be at a reduced pressure of only 0.5 of a bar. When a height of 100,000 metres (about 60 miles) is reached, the atmosphere has almost no pressure (0.000001 of a bar). Compare this rate of pressure change with that which takes place underwater (see *Hydrostatic pressure* below).

From the above it can be seen that a pressure gauge would read one bar at sea level; dive below the surface and this extra bar of pressure would show on the gauge, as well as the pressure of the water at depth. (Do not confuse this depth/pressure gauge with the pressure gauge which is fitted to a cylinder to indi-cate its contents.) Divers use the depth/pressure gauge to determine their depth below the surface.

For convenience these gauges are calibrated to zero at sea level and marked in metres or feet to measure the hydrostatic pressure. This cali-bration is referred to as gauge or ambient pressure.

Atm pressure + gauge pressure
  = absolute pressure

There are many ways of measuring atmospheric pressure. Here are some of the most commonly used equivalents:

1 bar = 0.98 atmospheres

  = 100,000 Pascal (Pa)

  = 1 kg per cm^2

  = 14.7 lb/inch^2 (psi)

  = 29.9 in. mercury (Hg)

  = 760 mmHg

  = 7000 millibar

  = 102 kN/m^2

  = 10 metres (33 ft) sea water (fsu)

  = 10.4 metres (34 ft) fresh water

Pascal measurements are used in science and technology; mercury millimetres or inches in meteorol-ogy; kilograms/cm^2 or lb/inch^2 in lifting calculations. All measure the same thing through different mediums. Divers use bar or ats.

Hydrostatic pressure

Water (H_2O) is a compound of oxy-gen and hydrogen. It is a colourless, odourless and tasteless liquid. For the purposes of diving, it is con-sidered to be incompressible.

Pure water weighs 1 kg/litre or 62 lb/ft^3. A column of water 10.4 metres produces on each square centimetre a weight of 1 kilogram (1000 gm). Other ways of measur-ing its weight are as follows:

1 m^3 of water, which is equal to:
 1000 litres (l)
 or 1000 kg
 or 1 tonne
 or 62.4 lb/ft^3
 or 1 gm/cc

Sea water is remarkably pure con-sidering the dreadful pollution of the oceans. Although it varies from sea to sea, basically sea water con-sists of 96% H_2O plus 1.9% chloride, 1% sodium, plus another seventy trace elements. Sea water is heavier than fresh water and freezes at a lower temperature; −1.91°C as opposed to 0°C. Sea water has a density of 1030 kg/m^3 (63 lb/ ft^3) and it is 800 times more dense than is the air.

Water pressure is called hydrostatic pressure. It has been shown that 10 metres of hydrostatic pressure is equal to 1 bar. This pressure, unlike the atmospheric pressure, increases very rapidly with depth, so that at only 30 metres (98 ft) there is a hydrostatic pressure of 4 bar abso-lute (3 bar ambient and 1 bar atmospheric pressure).

Whereas the atmospheric pressure exerts a downward force upon a body, hydrostatic pressure has the property of all fluids – that of exert-ing pressure in all directions. If a diver's body is considered as a liquid and therefore incompres-sible, the laws which apply to all liquids can be related to a diver underwater. These laws are:

1 If a pressure is applied to the sur-face of a liquid, it is transmitted to all parts of that liquid.

2 The pressure at any point in a liquid is the same in all directions, if the liquid is at rest.

3 In a liquid, the pressure at all points in the same horizontal plane is equal.

Pressure and volume changes

One might think the great pressures underwater would have a considerable effect on human tissues. In fact this is not so, because the body takes up the ambient hydrostatic pressure without any decrease in volume. The volume of water a body displaces is no more restricted than the surrounding volume of water; so it exerts equal and opposite pressures in all directions.

Any diver, at any depth, must be in pressure balance with the forces at that depth. The body can function properly only when the pressure

difference between the inside of the body and the forces outside is very small. In fact, the organs of the body function normally without restriction. The regulator will supply air at ambient pressure to the main air-space of the body (the lungs) so the pressure balance is maintained.

Because liquids exert an equal force in all directions, a diver in a cave at 30 metres (98 ft), with only a few metres of water immediately above the head, would be subject to the same hydrostatic pressure as a diver in open water at the same depth.

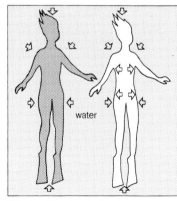

Effects of hydrostatic pressure on the body

Boyle's Law

All gases are compressible and pressure always increases with depth.

There is a relationship between a volume of gas and its pressure. This was first enunciated in 1660 by Robert Boyle, a 17th century physicist, whose law bears his name.

Boyle's Law states that at a constant temperature the volume of a gas varies inversely with its pressure.

Put another way, this means that when a gas is compressed its volume varies in inverse proportion to the absolute pressure (at a constant temperature).

As an object descends into the sea its pressure will increase. If the object is constructed with a rigid shell (a submarine for instance) any volume of air contained will remain at a constant pressure whatever the depth. This situation continues until the water pressure becomes greater than the strength of the shell which will then be crushed. If, on the other hand, the volume of air contained in the object is subject to

the ambient pressure of the surrounding water, such as in a balloon, the air volume will vary with the depth. Conversely, a balloon which is full of air at depth, say at 30 metres (100 ft), will on ascent expand its volume fourfold until it reaches the surface.

The principle of Boyle's Law, which is fundamental to diving, is illustrated on the following page.

The shape at the top represents an open-ended container, such as a bell or a bucket. It is shown lying upside down on the surface of the sea with a volume of air trapped inside it. Provided the air is not spilled out of it, it will float.

If this container is sufficiently weighted in order to force it down to a depth of 10 metres (33 ft), then the surrounding ambient pressure will compress the air inside it to $\frac{1}{2}$ of its volume.

At 20 metres (66 ft) the trapped air will be compressed to $\frac{1}{3}$ of its volume; and at 50 metres (164 ft) it

will be compressed to $\frac{1}{6}$ of the original volume.

The diagram shows how the volume changes with depth, but notice that these changes are comparatively small at greater depth:

* At 190 metres (623 ft) it reduces to $\frac{1}{20}$ of the original volume.

* At 200 metres (656 ft) it reduces to $\frac{1}{21}$. This is a reduction of only 4.8% of an additional bar, as compared to a reduction of 50% of a bar at 10 metres (33 ft).

If, however, air is pumped down to the bell at a pressure equal to that of the surrounding water, the whole volume of the trapped air will be maintained; the only change will be that the air pressure will be increased. The pressurized air will keep the water at bay, so to speak.

This explains how professional divers are able to leave or enter a diving bell underwater.

75

Boyle's Law

Air	Depth		Pressure		
	Feet	Metres	Bar	Psi	Millibars
	0ft	0m	1 bar	14.7 psi	1,000 mb
$\frac{1}{2}$	33ft	10m	2 bar	28.5 psi	2,000 mb
$\frac{1}{3}$	66ft	20m	3 bar	42.7 psi	3,000 mb
$\frac{1}{4}$	99ft	30m	4 bar	56.9 psi	4,000 mb
$\frac{1}{5}$	132ft	40m	5 bar	71.1 psi	5,000 mb
$\frac{1}{6}$	165ft	50m	6 bar	85.1 psi	6,000 mb
$\frac{1}{20}$	623ft	190m	19 bar	269.8 psi	20,000 mb
$\frac{1}{21}$	656ft	200m	20 bar	288 psi	21,000 mb

Boyle's Law

76

Compression and expansion problems

Descent

Breath-hold divers going down to a depth of, say, 10 metres (33 ft) have the air in their lungs compressed to one half of the original volume. They can then swim safely back to the surface as fast as they choose, with the same volume of air in the lungs as when they started out.

Aqualung divers are in a rather different situation. As they descend, the regulator supplies them with air at the same pressure as that of the surrounding water. Like the breath-hold divers, the actual mass of air in their lungs (the number of molecules of air) remains unchanged. Only the volume of air alters. Their lungs are not compressed like those of the breath-hold divers. Moreover, the fact that the pressurized air in the lungs is kept at the same pressure as the water outside, ensures that aqualung divers have full lungs of normal size, whatever the depth.

Ascent

Breath-hold divers will not be in any danger of damaging their lungs through expansion during the ascent. They retain only the original lungful of air at atmospheric pressure. For aqualung divers, however, it can be a very different story. If they neglect to vent the excess air as it expands on ascent they may well damage their lungs (see page 80).

What happens on ascent is particularly significant to the diver. The volume of the air will expand as the surrounding water pressure decreases, with the greatest rate of expansion in the shallows, from 10 metres (33 ft) to the surface, when the volume will be doubled.

For example, the volume doubles on ascent from 70 metres (230 ft) when it is $\frac{1}{8}$ surface volume to 30m (98 ft) when it is $\frac{1}{4}$ surface volume, over a depth range of 40 metres. The volume doubles again between there and 10m (33 ft) at $\frac{1}{2}$ surface volume, over a distance of 20 metres (66 ft), and again in the last 10m (33 ft) back to the surface.

But suppose a breath-hold diver is short of air at depth and 'borrows a breath' from a passing friendly aqualung diver! He or she would then have a lungful of pressurized air and will have the same problem as the aqualung diver – it will be necessary to vent the expanding air during the ascent.

Boyle's Law is of vital importance to the diver, whether breath-hold or aqualung diving. Mask squeeze, ear clearing, buoyancy, ascent risks, decompression and air consumption are all affected by this. The relationship between pressure and volume is of such fundamental importance that all divers really must thoroughly understand it. It will be referred to in many different places in this book.

Effects on the body

Having said that the body's tissues and skeleton are incompressible, we must now consider the effects of pressure on the body's air spaces – the lungs, airways, middle ear and sinuses; and, to a lesser extent, the stomach and the intestines. Externally, it must also be remembered that air can be trapped inside the mask and within a dry suit. During descent the pressure in these air spaces must be increased to balance the surrounding water pressure. This may not always be possible. On descent for instance, the volume of air in the lungs of the breath-hold diver is decreased as pressure on the lungs increases. The aqualung diver can increase the pressure in the body's air spaces by artificially supplying them with compressed air so that they will be at the same pressure as the surrounding water. The regulator will ensure a supply of air of the right pressure to the lungs and airways. From there the air must be allowed to enter those air spaces within rigid walls, such as the middle ear and the sinuses. If it does not, a pressure difference between the air in the cavity and its surrounding tissues will build up, eventually causing damage. A rupture of the eardrum is a typical example of this.

The opposite will take place on ascent; the air in these body air spaces will expand as the pressure decreases. Unless the excess air can be vented, it will exert pressure on the surrounding tissues and damage them. Air or gas may be present in small quantities in the stomach and intestines. This can lead to discomfort if there are any changes in pressure.

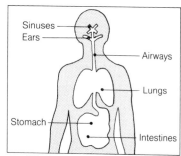

Air-filled spaces in the body

Pressure problems

Barotrauma

Any injury to the body's tissues caused by the effects of a pressure change is called a barotrauma (derived from the Greek word *baros* meaning a weight, and the Latin for wound, *trauma*). A barotrauma is the direct effect of gas-volume changes within the body's gas spaces (see Boyle's Law). It is most important not to confuse a barotrauma with other problems involving the respiratory gases, such as nitrogren narcosis, oxygen poisoning or decompression sickness; these are the indirect effects of pressure. The body will function normally if the pressure difference between the inside of the diver's body and the forces acting outside is very small.

All the gas spaces in the body, except the lungs, are surrounded by rigid bone and so pressure cannot be compensated for by a reduction in their volume. The result will be that as pressure increases on descent, the differential between the tissue pressures (the water ambient pressure) and the gas pressure in the air spaces will increase. Unless gas can be admitted to these spaces to equalize the pressure with that of the tissues, a barotrauma will result. The damage is usually a swelling of the tissue lining the bony cavities and bleeding caused by rupture of the blood vessels. Barotrauma is almost always painful and relieved only by decreasing the pressure or by an actual rupture taking place, similar to the bursting of a boil. There are two types of tissue damage — barotrauma due to descent and barotrauma due to ascent.

Barotrauma of descent

Where a barotrauma occurs on descent, divers call it a 'squeeze'. It is perhaps fortunate that often the effect of a squeeze can be felt on the way down, eventually causing some pain. It is controllable if the diver reacts to the pain instead of ignoring it. Squeeze affects mainly those spaces inside the body which have rigid walls. Gas in the stomach or intestines is not usually a problem as it is easily compressed and easily expelled. The first two barotraumas may occur outside the body.

Mask squeeze
During descent, air pressure within the mask must be equalized with the hydrostatic pressure outside by exhaling into it through the nose. Sometimes a novice feels the effect on a first dive and the instructor tells him or her how to cope with it (see page 23). The problem may persist when diving in deeper water.

The diver may still feel the effect and surface, but the minor capillaries rupturing outwards cause a condition known as 'red eye'. Fortunately it usually clears up in a few days without after-effects.

Suit squeeze
While dressing in a dry suit the diver is effectively sealed inside it with air at atmospheric pressure. This trapped air must be kept in balance with external hydrostatic pressure on descent by using a direct-feed equalization system (see page 60) or the diver will suffer a squeeze to the body. The effect is much the same as submerging a rubber-gloved hand into a bowl of water. The diver presents an enormous body surface area open to this squeeze effect. By 3 to 5 metres (10-16 ft) he or she will be aware that there is a problem — and on undressing afterwards may find underclothing seams 'embossed' on the body. Painful areas will occur where a suit fold traps and nips a layer of flesh.

The ears
During a descent, the increasing water pressure will cause the eardrums to bow inwards. This will cause pain and problems unless the procedure known as ear clearing is used to equalize the outside water pressure by air pressure from the back of the throat (see page 24). For air to reach the back of the eardrum, it must pass along the Eustachian tube which is restrictive enough to impede the flow. Ear clearing involves opening this tube. Three methods of clearing can be used underwater — the choice depends on individual response. Physically we are all different and the Eustachian tube may be open in some cases and almost closed in others. Individuals must find the method which suits them best.

1 Pinch the nose closed and blow against the restriction (Valsalva's manoeuvre) so that air is forced to move along the Eustachian tube (see following page).

2 Swallow while you are pinching your nose. This action will move the tissue which surrounds the tube's entrance and therefore allows the air to pass up.

3 Move the lower jaw, which also acts on the tissue surrounding the tube entrance. This method seems to work best for those divers whose tube entrances are relatively open.

Success in ear clearing will be rewarded with a characteristic click or pop. If a hiss is heard, this means that there is usually some restriction remaining in the tube.

Failure to clear can be due to a faulty clearing technique. Although Valsalva's manoeuvre should work every time, often its failure is because the diver has gone too deep before trying to clear. What happens is simply that air pressure in the throat pushes the tissue surrounding the Eustachian tube firmly shut, with a force greater than the muscle action trying to open it. All that can be done is to come up for a few metres, which lessens the air pressure in the throat and the force on the tissue, and then try again. The regulator action keeps air pressure inside the body equal to water pressure on the outside, so this should work. But two things can go wrong. Firstly, the delicate tissue around the Eustachian tube entrance may swell up due to the battering it has taken. If this occurs, it will be almost impossible to clear the ears. Secondly, if the diver goes too deep initially, the eardrum will be similarly aggravated as it is unequalized and distended inward by excessive water pressure.

In extreme cases the ear drum could rupture, or it might simply become reddened. Once this occurs the eardrum is in no condition to take any more pressure. Apart from the pain, a pressure imbalance in the middle ear will cause the tissues to swell into the space, leaving the diver vulnerable

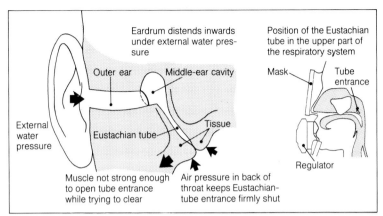

Ear clearing problems

to ear infection. Such infections can be very difficult to clear up.

A ruptured eardrum may allow cold water to enter the middle ear and cause vertigo. Many months out of the water may be necessary before this condition clears itself so always exercise considerable caution if you have an ear-clearing problem.

Avoiding such difficulties is really very easy. Clear the ears as soon as the water first closes over the head, then clear constantly during the first

4 metres of descent. If there are clearing difficulties, come up a little way and try again. Hopefully this will work and it will be possible to descend and continue as before. If it does not work, then either your clearing action is at fault or you have a definite restriction. In this case, abandon the dive and seek experienced advice. A ruptured eardrum will mean no diving for six months or more but will normally heal satisfactorily in a healthy adult. Ear problems can also occur on ascent.

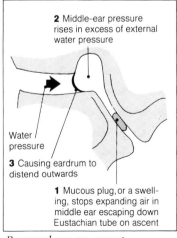

Reversed ear on ascent

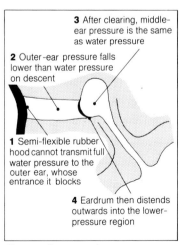

Reversed ear on descent

79

Pressure problems

Sinus barotrauma

The sinuses which may be affected by diving are shown in the accompanying illustrations. All these cavities are hollow air spaces surrounded by bone, and all open into the nose and throat space (the naso-pharynx). If the diver is in normal health, air is free to enter and exit through these spaces. If the sinus airways are blocked by mucus (such as produced by a cold) it will become impossible to equalize the air contained within them, with resulting swelling of the tissue linings and bleeding; this may partially equalize the pressure but will cause intense pain. On ascent the blood and mucus present in the sinus passages will be forcibly expelled as the gas re-expands. Ear and sinus squeeze can be avoided; never dive if suffering from a head cold or any nasal congestion.

Tooth squeeze

Occasionally a small pocket of trapped gas which has been produced by tooth decay can become isolated. When this happens the pulp can be squeezed into the space, causing considerable pain. Attention to the state of the teeth is the only way to avoid this.

Thoracic or lung squeeze

On descent, increasing hydrostatic pressure acts on the chest wall and diaphragm, trying to compress the air space within the lungs.

The lung volume of a breath-hold diver will be gradually compressed with depth. The maximum depth he or she could reach without a lung squeeze occurring depends upon a number of factors. The first of these is the diver's total lung capacity on full inhalation at the surface. The second factor is whether or not the diver takes a full breath before diving down, in which case there is a greater air volume to compress.

Problems may start occurring at depths where this volume is compressed to less than the lung's residual volume (that is, what would be left on full exhalation at the surface). Theoretically a breath-hold diver with a total lung capacity of 6 litres could not descend beyond 30 metres (98 ft) 4 bar.

Some Japanese and Korean women, however, the renowned 'Ama' pearl divers, actually go much deeper,

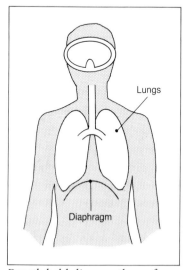

Breath-hold diver on the surface

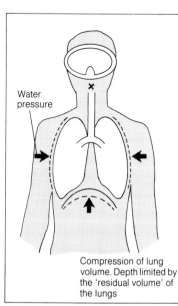

Breath-hold diver at depth

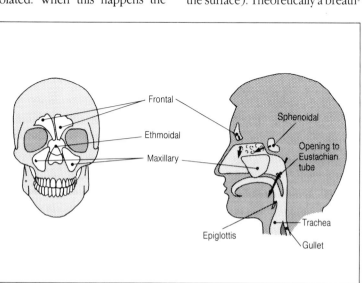

Front and side view of sinuses

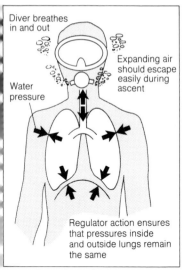

Diver breathes in and out

Expanding air should escape easily during ascent

Water pressure

Regulator action ensures that pressures inside and outside lungs remain the same

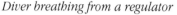

Diver breathing from a regulator

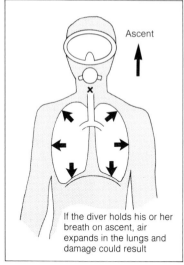

Ascent

If the diver holds his or her breath on ascent, air expands in the lungs and damage could result

Ascent

while those who attempt world record-breaking breath-hold dives actually dive down well in excess of 100 metres (305 ft). The mechanisms of the body which allow such depths to be reached are beyond the scope of this book. Novices should not expect to reach beyond 5 metres (16 ft) as a reasonable start, with practice working up to 10 to 15 metres (33-50 ft) maximum. On ascent, of course, lung volume returns to what it was originally. Compressed air apparatus (scuba) divers are supplied with air which is kept at the same pressure as the surrounding water by regulator action. Their lung volume will therefore remain the same, no matter what depth they reach.

Barotrauma of ascent

As a diver ascends, the gas within the body air spaces or the equipment will expand in accordance with Boyle's Law. If this expansion is not controlled, the diver may suffer from several serious disorders. By far the most important and potentially dangerous effects are sustained when pressure damage to the lungs is brought about by excess differential pressures. This can cause tearing of the lung tissue. It rarely occurs during compression; it is more likely to be a decompression injury.

This lung damage is called pulmonary barotrauma, from the Greek word *pulmos* which means pertaining to the lungs; it is sometimes referred to as burst lung. It can occur when a diver ascends through the water while holding the breath. This might happen, for instance, if a diver returns to the surface by a free ascent. It can even be caused by local retention of gas in a

diver who is exhaling perfectly correctly during ascent, but who is suffering from a chronic or recent chest illness. If for any reason the expanding air in the chest cannot escape, it will rupture the lung membranes and pass into the blood circulation or into the tissues between the lungs and the rib cage.

Once the lungs have passed their elastic limit, a pulmonary barotrauma will result. On surfacing, the victim may utter a high-pitched cry, due to the exhalation of expanding air. Pulmonary barotrauma is the cause of unconsciousness immediately following a too-rapid ascent.

Several things may have occurred, individually or simultaneously, and each one could be dangerous. There may be damage to the lung tissues, particularly the delicate aveoli, with air possibly entering between the loose tissue layers (emphysema). Should the lung

rupture, air might pass into the pleural cavity which separates the lung from the rib cage, and this could result in the collapse of the lung (pneumothorax) as it expands during the ascent. Air may move up into the tissues of the neck, causing them to swell up (subcutaneous emphysema) or, in more serious cases, it may gather between the lungs near the heart (mediastinal interstitial emphysema).

The most serious consequence occurs when air under pressure is forced back into the pulmonary veins and bubbles enter the arterial blood circulation − causing what is called 'arterial gas embolism'. If these bubbles in the bloodstream find their way into the brain circulation arteries, they will block the oxygen supply and cause brain damage. Occasionally the bubbles may create a blockage in the coronary arteries, causing heartbeat and breathing to stop suddenly.

Lung damage

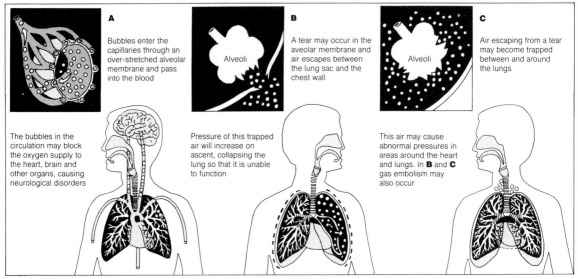

A
Bubbles enter the capillaries through an over-stretched alveolar membrane and pass into the blood

The bubbles in the circulation may block the oxygen supply to the heart, brain and other organs, causing neurological disorders

B
A tear may occur in the aveolar membrane and air escapes between the lung sac and the chest wall

Pressure of this trapped air will increase on ascent, collapsing the lung so that it is unable to function

C
Air escaping from a tear may become trapped between and around the lungs

This air may cause abnormal pressures in areas around the heart and lungs. In **B** and **C** gas embolism may also occur

Pulmonary barotrauma: **A** *Arterial gas embolism* **B** *Pneumothorax* **C** *Interstitial emphysema*

Signs and symptoms

Any diver who obtains a breath from any source at depth and becomes unconsious at the surface must be assumed to be suffering from a gas embolism. It is easy to confuse the symptoms of gas embolism with those of serious decompression sickness. Both are caused by gas bubbles. If in doubt, treat for gas embolism — a common symptom of this is chest pain.

Note: Any abnormal situation that starts within ten minutes of the accident should be treated as a gas embolism, no matter how shallow the depth. Any doubt about the correct diagnosis must be resolved in the best interests of the victim; so, if unsure, assume the worst and treat for gas embolism.

Arterial gas embolism
Chest pain
Visual disturbances, sometimes even blindness

Dizziness
Weakness or paralysis, which is usually one-sided
Numbness and tingling, usually one-sided
Headache
Sudden unconsciousness; often occurs on surfacing
Confusion and stupor
Cessation of breathing
Bloody frothy sputum (quite rare)
Respiratory distress (rare)

Pulmonary barotrauma without arterial gas embolism is quite rare and accounts for only 10% of pulmonary overinflation. None the less careful examination and observation are vital.

Pneumothorax
Bloody, frothy sputum
Shortness of breath; rapid shallow breathing
Pain anywhere in the chest (especially when breathing in) which is made worse by deep breathing
Coughing
Swelling of neck veins
Cyanosis (blueness of fingertips, lips and earlobes)
Irregular pulse

The pneumothorax that accompanies a pulmonary barotrauma is usually revealed by an X-ray and is seldom troublesome.

Interstitial emphysema
Pain under the breastbone, or elsewhere in the chest
Shortness of breath and difficulty in breathing
Feeling of fullness in neck area
Crackling sensation on skin, like crumpled cellophane, particularly near the front of the neck just above the collarbone
Change in the voice so that it sounds 'tinny'

Treatment

Arterial gas embolism

This is extremely urgent and very serious. Immediate recompression treatment is required. Victims are often 'near-drowned' so CPR may be needed. The chance of recovery decreases rapidly with each minute that is lost before the victim is placed under pressure.

Pneumothorax

If diagnosis is uncertain, recompress as though for a gas embolism.

Pneumothorax does not usually require recompression for itself. However, if recompression is needed for concurrent embolism, the symptoms of pneumothorax will be improved. Recompression is useful if symptoms are serious. If the victim is under pressure, stop any further decompression.

Treatment can include administration of oxygen-rich mixtures at appropriate depths. If breathing is badly impaired or further decompression is needed a suitably skilled person can withdraw most of the entrapped gas by inserting a hollow needle into the affected part.

Interstitial emphysema

If diagnosis is uncertain, recompress as for gas embolism. Treatment will be as for pneumothorax. The therapeutic decompression will be a slow procedure requiring very close medical supervision.

Symptoms and signs	Decompression sickness		Serious		Gas embolism — Serious		
	Skin	Pain-only	CNS symptoms	Chokes	CNS symptoms	Pneumo-thorax	Interstitial emphysema
Brain damage			▓		▓		
Pain-back			▓		▓		
neck							▓
chest			▓	▓	▓	▓	▓
head					▓		
stomach			▓				
arms/legs		▓					
shoulders		▓					
hips		▓					
Unconsciousness			▓		▓		
Shock			▓		▓		
Vertigo			▓		▓		
Visual difficulty			▓		▓		
Nausea/vomiting			▓		▓		
Hearing difficulty			▓		▓		
Speech difficulty			▓		▓		
Lack of balance			▓		▓		
Strange sensations			▓		▓		
Numbness	▓		▓		▓		
Weakness		▓	▓		▓		
Swollen neck							▓
Short of breath				▓	▓	▓	▓
Cyanosis				▓		▓	▓
Skin changes	▓						
'Cellophane' crackling							▓
Bloody frothy sputum				▓	▓	▓	
Paralysis			▓		▓		
Irregular pulse					▓		
Coughing/pain on breathing				▓		▓	

Diagnosis of gas embolism and decompression sickness (CNS = central nervous system involvement)

Vision

The human eye can focus properly only when in air. The lens in the eye will focus incoming light rays precisely on the back of the retina.

Light waves travel in straight lines when passing just one medium. When they pass between two different mediums, such as water and air, the rays will be bent due to the different densities. This phenomenon is called refraction.

Underwater, the light rays will not be bent as they enter the eye, but because the lens is focused to function in air, the rays will not converge at the correct focal point so vision will be blurred.

To compensate for this, divers wear a mask which puts an air space between the surrounding water and the eye, thereby allowing the eye to function normally. The left-hand diagram below illustrates the effects of refraction.

Effects of refraction

If an object underwater is viewed through a mask, and looked at straight on, no refraction will take place. When viewed at an angle, however, the object will then appear to be bent.

This occurs because light waves are slowed down when they have to pass through a denser medium.

Because water is denser than air, objects will appear larger than they actually are. Objects will appear one third larger than normal and seem to be closer (by about 25%) than they actually are.

The absorption of light

Light is absorbed and filtered by water and the constituent colours of daylight are absorbed in relation to the depth. The more water that the light has to penetrate, the more density the colour filter has and the greater will be the filtration effect.

Even when the diver descends by as little as 10 metres (33 ft), most colours will have been filtered out. The filtration will depend on several factors; the depth, the time of day and the angle of the light source (the sun), and the amount of suspended matter in the water.

The depths at which the various colours will be absorbed is shown in the diagram. An artificial light source, such as a torch, will restore the balance of the colours.

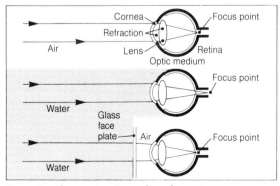

Focusing the eye in air and underwater

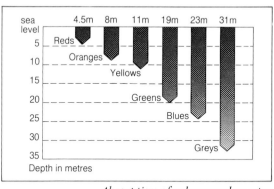

Absorption of colour underwater

Sound

Sound travels much faster underwater than on the surface; 1500 metres (4920 ft) per second as opposed to 300 metres (984 ft) per second. Although sounds will travel great distances, unfortunately it is difficult for the diver to locate the source because sound travels at an extraordinarily high speed. This means that when divers hear a particular sound, such as the noise of a boat's propeller, it can sound very close even though it might actually be a mile or two away.

On surfacing, divers must be careful to look all round to pin-point the sound. An interesting characteristic of sound waves is that underwater sounds will not pass through the surface, nor will sounds made in air penetrate into the water below.

Diving physiology

The release of energy

Metabolism is a word used to describe the chemical reactions which take place in the body. Every activity of a living thing depends on the process of converting food into energy and this release of energy is one form of metabolism. Human beings use the oxygen in the air they breathe as fuel for this process. Every living creature needs food in some form or other, firstly for the nourishment or replacement of body tissues and secondly as fuel to supply energy to the body. Simplified, this can be expressed as:

$$\text{Food and oxygen}$$
$$\downarrow$$
$$\text{Chemically burned to create}$$
$$=$$
$$\text{Energy and waste}$$
$$+$$
$$\text{Exhaust products}$$

This process is not unlike running a car with a mixture of petrol and air. Our digestive system reduces food into soluble material which is absorbed by the blood and carried to all the cells of the body by the circulation. The oxygen necessary for the slow burning (oxidation) of the food is brought to the lungs by the respiratory system from whence it too diffuses into the blood. Carbon dioxide is produced as a waste product and is carried from the cells to the lungs by the blood and passed out of the body by respiration.

When the demand for energy is increased by activity, the rate of metabolism increases as well. When the body is at rest, the metabolic rate is low and therefore so are the respiration and circulation. When activity is increased, respiration and circulation levels must increase to keep pace and maintain the supply of food and oxygen to the cells and remove waste products.

The body can tolerate a short interruption to most of its 'systems'. It is possible to live for several weeks without food because energy can be extracted from food materials stored in the body.

No one, however, can tolerate an interruption of the respiratory or circulatory systems. If deprived of a fresh supply of oxygen, cells will begin to die in only a few minutes. Hence the urgent need for expired air resuscitation (EAR). Even worse is the disruption of the circulatory system. If the heart stops beating, no oxygen-bearing blood will reach the cells, including those of the brain. Because the effects of a cardiac arrest are so catastrophic, every effort must be made to restart the heartbeat by external cardiac compression (ECC).

For these reasons the respiratory and circulatory systems must never be interrupted. The underwater environment by its very nature presents hazards to circulation and respiration.

In order to live, the body must:

1 Extract the oxygen from the air.

2 Supply this oxygen to all the tissues of the body.

To extract the oxygen from the air mixture (which is about 21% oxygen and 78% nitrogen) the body employs a respiratory system.

To carry the oxygen to the body's tissues, the body transports it via the circulatory system.

The respiratory system includes:

1 The act of breathing.

2 The absorption of oxygen by the blood in the lungs.

3 The transport of oxygen to the tissues by the circulation of oxygen-rich blood which is pumped there by the heart.

4 The absorption of the oxygen from the blood by the tissues.

5 The reverse process to carry away the waste product, carbon dioxide.

Very small simple creatures have no need for a respiratory system; oxygen is absorbed through the skin. But being large and with organs too great a distance from the oxygen source, man needs a more advanced system.

This consists basically of an air pump and two liquid pumps:

* The air pump is the diaphragm (a large sheet of muscle forming the bottom of the chest cavity) which, along with the muscles of the chest, draws air into the passive lungs and pushes it out again.

* The two liquid pumps are the ventricles of the heart. The right ventricle pumps the blood to the lungs in order to bring blood which is short of oxygen near to the air that contains the fresh oxygen.

* The left ventricle pumps the oxygen-rich blood to the tissues needing a fresh supply.

The diagram on page 89 illustrates this process.

Respiration and circulation

The mechanics of breathing

To be able to breathe is not simply a matter of letting air be sucked into the lungs via the mouth or nose. To draw in the air requires a vacuum to be created and this is achieved by the expansion of the lungs.

The lungs are elastic. The diaphragm pulls itself downwards as the rib muscles contract to enlarge the rib cage. This causes the chest wall to expand and pulls the lungs downwards and outward (see diagram on the right). Air rushes in to fill the vacuum. This is called inspiration. When the diaphragm and rib muscles are relaxed and the elastic lungs recoil, the volume of the chest decreases and the air is expelled. This is expiration.

The diaphragm can create considerable pressure on expiration. (This is used, for example, when inflating a life-jacket orally.)

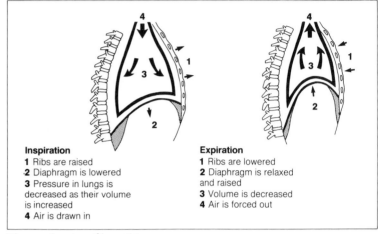

Inspiration
1 Ribs are raised
2 Diaphragm is lowered
3 Pressure in lungs is decreased as their volume is increased
4 Air is drawn in

Expiration
1 Ribs are lowered
2 Diaphragm is relaxed and raised
3 Volume is decreased
4 Air is forced out

The mechanics of breathing

A smaller pressure differential is involved when air is breathed in. We know, of course, that the pressure of water increases with depth, but when only 23 centimetres (9 in) below the surface, the pressure is sufficient to prevent breathing. This is why the length of a snorkel is limited. In order to be able to breathe, the pressure within the chest must be very nearly the same as that on the outside.

Lung capacity

The maximum amount of air a normal diver can hold in the lungs is about 6 litres (11 pts) and is called the total lung capacity. With the diver at rest and breathing normally, the amount of air moving in and out of the lungs might be only as much as $\frac{1}{2}$ a litre (nearly 1 pint), and this is called the 'tidal volume'.

With hard physical exertion, this tidal volume might be increased to around 3 litres ($5\frac{1}{4}$ pts).

The difference between a maximum expiration and a maximum inspiration will be about $4\frac{1}{2}$ litres (8 pts) and this is called the vital capacity. In other words, this is the maximum amount of air a diver

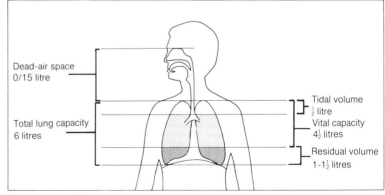

Dead-air space
0/15 litre

Total lung capacity
6 litres

Tidal volume
$\frac{1}{2}$ litre

Vital capacity
$4\frac{1}{2}$ litres

Residual volume
1–$1\frac{1}{2}$ litres

Lung capacities

could breathe in and out. The difference between this vital capacity and the total lung capacity is called the residual volume (about $1\frac{1}{2}$ litres or 2$\frac{1}{2}$ pts) and is the air that will always remain in the lungs and cannot be expelled, no matter how hard the diver might try to do this.

The effect of exercise

A relaxed diver at rest will breathe in and out ten to fourteen times a minute, each breath taking about 5 seconds. In each minute he or she will breathe in about 6 litres (11pts). If the diver should suddenly start doing violent physical exercise, the need for air will increase by fifteen to twenty times; some 90 litres (over 20 gallons) a minute may be used up in panting!

The body's reserves of oxygen are small and might be all used up in less than half a minute of such exertion, which means the diver's body could consúme more oxygen than he is able to inspire, building up an oxygen debt. If this should happen, the diver will have to take immediate action to reduce the debt by stopping all activity, in order to bring the oxygen level in the blood and tissues back to normal again.

The normal automatic control of the breathing rate depends mostly on the level of carbon dioxide in the blood. Mild exercise sends the breathing rate up without reducing the oxygen or increasing the carbon dioxide levels in the arteries.

However, violent physical exercise will reduce the oxygen and raise the carbon dioxide levels, as well as increasing the breathing rate; so it would seem that changing levels are linked with the change in breathing. The amount of air the diver must breathe in and out of the lungs is related to both oxygen consumption and carbon dioxide production. The breathing rate is determined by the need to eliminate excess carbon dioxide. By reducing the breathing rate, the diver would still obtain enough oxygen, but doing this might not expel enough carbon dioxide.

A normal inspiration will contain no carbon dioxide, whereas an expiration will have as much as 4%. Should the inspired air contain more than about 5%, the diver will quite likely lose consciousness, even though the normal 21% of oxygen is still present. (See also *Hyperventilation* and *Carbon dioxide* on pages 92 and 94.)

Thus, it is most important that the diver always makes sure that the lungs are ventilated with an adequate flow of fresh air.

The circulatory system

We have described how air is drawn into the lungs. The oxygen in this air will have to be brought as near as possible to the blood and diffused into it so that it can be carried to all the body's tissues. Interchange of the gases with the blood takes place in the lungs.

Blood may be described as the 'transport system' of the body. The average human body may contain about $5\frac{1}{2}$ litres (13 pints) of blood, about $\frac{1}{12}$ of the body weight.

Blood is slightly heavier than water, half plasma and half corpuscles (45% red cells and 5% white). The plasma is 92% water and is the medium that carries the red and white cells. The red corpuscles contain haemoglobin, the substance in blood which collects the oxygen from the lungs and carries it to the tissues. Blood-carrying oxygen is bright red; blood which does not contain oxygen is dark red. When victims are suffering from a lack of oxygen (cyanosis) they will be a strange blue colour.

The blood is circulated around a resting body once every minute. When a person suddenly starts doing hard physical exercise, the breathing rate will increase some fifteen to twenty times. To meet the demand for more oxygen, the heart will boost its blood delivery from 4 litres (1 gal) per minute to as much as 25 litres (5 gal) per minute.

This is the same as saying that the body's whole blood supply would be pumped around it approximately once every 12 seconds.

Different parts of the body need a greater supply of blood than others. The muscles receive eighteen times as much as other organs — such as the kidneys, the skin or the digestive system. The heart itself is a muscle and receives four times its normal supply of blood during heavy exertion.

Having brought air to the lungs, the oxygen in the air mixture will have to be transferred to the blood.

To achieve this, the heart needs to pump blood to the lungs. The heart is really two pumps side by side. One side pumps blood through the lungs and the other side pumps the blood through the body. The heart's right side pushes the blood through the lungs and back to the left side of the heart. Then the left

Circulation

side of the heart pumps the blood all round the body until it arrives at the right side again.

The heart beats about seventy times a minute, four times every breath. The beat quickens when increased demands are made on it, pumping more blood with each beat. A heart can pump five times more blood

when the body is active than when it is at rest.

Returning to the heart's right side, the blood is then carried away from the heart via the pulmonary artery.

This artery divides and subdivides into smaller and smaller arteries (arterioles) until it reaches the

capillaries, which are minute blood vessels covering each of the many alveoli in the walls of the lung where gas diffusion takes place.

Look at the diagram which shows how this system is arranged. Air is drawn down the windpipe during inspiration. The airways in the lungs resemble the branches of a tree.

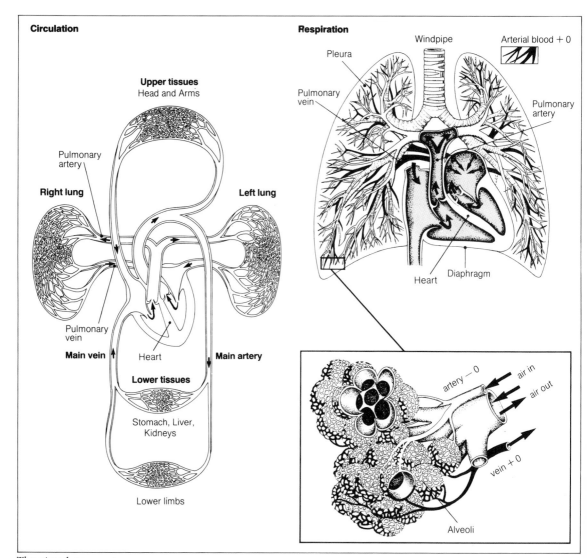

The circulatory system

These airways divide in two from the windpipe and these are called bronchi. The bronchi subdivide into smaller airways called bronchioles, on the end of which are the grape like air-containers called alveoli (little hollows). There are said to be about 500 million of these alveoli in a pair of lungs. This large number is necessary to maximize the surface area to be brought into contact with the blood.

The lungs are constructed so as to present an area for diffusion some forty to fifty times greater than the body's skin area, and are said to cover an area of about 90 square metres (1,000 sq ft) when flattened out. Each alveolus is surrounded by a network of minute capillaries, and it is here that the blood and gaseous exchange takes place. Each blood cell is pushed along these capillaries by the heart but stays for only $\frac{3}{4}$ of a second to collect oxygen atoms and to discharge carbon dioxide. The walls of the alveoli have to be incredibly thin, approximately $\frac{1}{25000}$ inch ($\frac{1}{1000}$ mm), in order to allow the gases to diffuse through them.

The inspired air will have been warmed and moistened by the mucous lining in the nasal passages. It passes into the lungs and then to the alveoli. Because of its high partial pressure, the oxygen is quickly dissolved by the alveoli's moist lining and diffuses through the membranes into the blood. The partial pressure of the oxygen in the blood which is returning to the lungs via the arterial capillaries is low because much of its dissolved oxygen has been taken up by the cells. However, the partial pressure of the carbon dioxide in this blood is relatively higher than that in the lungs; this means it will readily diffuse into the lower partial pressures in the alveoli.

This exchange of gases takes place rapidly because the partial pressures in alveolar air are almost the same as those in the blood leaving the lungs. The alveolar air mixed with any unused dead-space air will become expired air with an oxygen partial pressure of 116mm Hg, 17% of air. This is why expired air can be used for EAR.

The diver's atmosphere

Air is taken for granted; it is all around us and breathing presents no problem, even when 'out of breath'. Underwater, the air supply is mechanically metered to the divers, who must carry their own personal atmosphere around with them. The arrangement is completely unnatural, but the diver must adapt and learn to live within this limited environment. Respiratory requirements must still be satisfied without interruption, no matter what circumstances arise.

We shall deal here solely with divers who breathe normal air made up of a mixture of gases:

78% nitrogen (N)
21% oxygen (O)
0.04% carbon dioxide (CO_2)
0.93% argon

There will also be traces of neon, krypton, xenon, hydrogen, helium and radon, together with water vapour. (Chemical symbols for the common gases are shown above.)

On inhalation, this mixture will be brought into the diver's lungs, from whence the individual gases diffuse into the bloodstream by way of the lungs' aveoli. The blood then carries these gases to the body tissues.

The influence each gas has on the diver's system depends on two things; the gas's partial pressure, and its density.

Gas partial pressures

According to Dalton's Law, in any mixture of gases, each individual gas exerts its own partial pressure. This pressure is proportional to the percentage of gas present.

For example nitrogen partial pressure is 78% of whatever pressure air may be at, because (as shown above) it makes up that percentage of the mixture.

On descent, both the hydrostatic pressure and the pressure of the mixture being breathed rises, and so does the partial pressure of each gas in the mixture. When a gas has a noticeable effect on the diver, this effect will increase as the partial pressure of the gas rises — that is, the effect will increase with both the depth (which increases the pressure) and the concentration (or percentage) of the gas present.

The diver's atmosphere

Gas density

As the pressure of the gas increases, so does its density. Put another way, there is an increase in the number of gas molecules compressed into a given volume.

In theory, it should be more difficult to breathe this denser air at greater depths, though this is rarely apparent in practice because of efficient modern regulator designs.

However, as the body produces almost as much carbon dioxide as it consumes oxygen, this may present problems in extreme conditions if the carbon dioxide is not eliminated from the body on exhalation. For example, excessive work loads or extreme anxiety will produce a hopelessly inadequate fast and shallow breathing pattern. As the depth increases, very careful control of actions will be essential.

Solubility of gases

When a gas is in contact with a liquid, some of the gas molecules will dissolve in that liquid. Such a situation arises when the air being breathed is brought into contact with the blood.

The amount of gas that will dissolve and its rate of solution depends on four factors:

* The contact area between the gas and the liquid.

* The pressure of the gas.

* The temperature of the gas.

* The maximum solubility of the gas in the liquid.

There must be equilibrium between the air in the lungs and the air dissolved in the blood and tissues. Changes in pressure can disturb this balance.

Henry's Law states that 'the amount of gas that will dissolve in a liquid at a given temperature is directly proportional to the partial pressure of that gas over the liquid'.

In diving terms, the amount of oxygen and nitrogen in air that will dissolve in the bloodstream is in proportion to their partial pressures. Under increasing pressure, there comes a stage when no more gas will enter into solution in the blood (the saturation level).

No matter how much gas has been dissolved in the diver's body (at whatever depth and pressure), it will remain in solution so long as the pressure is sustained. If ambient pressure is reduced, the gas comes out of solution in the bloodstream.

The diver must be aware that as the ascent begins the ambient pressure will, in fact, be reduced, causing the dissolved gases to come out of solution. Enough time must be allowed for the oxygen and nitrogen to be released from the blood. If this pressure is decreased too rapidly, gas will leave the blood in the form of bubbles which may block the blood vessels and cause decompression sickness.

Oxygen (0)

Oxygen is the most important of all gases because it is the fuel for the body's metabolism and is therefore vital to support life. Oxygen exists in a free state in the atmosphere, where it is 21% by volume. It is a colourless, odourless, tasteless but chemically 'active' gas which readily combines with haemoglobin (the blood's red colouring pigment) to form oxyhaemoglobin. In this form it travels in the bloodstream to the tissues.

The concentration of the oxygen and the carbon dioxide in the arterial blood is constant, whether at rest or at work. If the body demands more oxygen because of increased work, the heart will beat faster to increase the circulation, and the respiratory rate will also increase to match it. To survive, the body requires a certain mass or number of oxygen molecules every minute. This requirement will increase with harder work; however it does not increase with depth for the same level of work.

At atmospheric pressure, a diver at rest might consume oxygen gas molecules equivalent to as little as 0.2 litres (0.007 cu ft) per minute, and from 1.3 to 1.9 litres (0.057 cu ft) per minute when swimming.

Hard exertion could raise this consumption up to 5 litres (0.18 cu ft) per minute.

Due to higher gas density at depth, with an increased number of gas molecules compressed into a given volume, these requirements represent only a fraction of the oxygen molecules available. Thus there will always be adequate oxygen available in the diver's air supply, and it is up to each individual to maintain a good breathing technique with adequate lung ventilation, in order to make full use of this oxygen.

Hypoxia and anoxia

A lack of oxygen (hypoxia) or its total absence (anoxia) in the diver's body will be highly detrimental!

Hypoxia can be due to many different causes:

1 Insufficient oxygen in the air being breathed.

2 A decreased capacity in the lungs because of some injury (collapsed lung).

3 Diseases such as asthma, bronchitis or emphysema.

4 Incapacity of the blood to take up oxygen such as carbon monoxide poisoning, anaemia or severe bleeding.

5 Heart failure, such as can happen with an embolism, when the body tissues are unable to receive sufficient blood.

Drowning, for instance, will cause death because the water enters the lungs and, in doing so, interferes with the transportation of oxygen to the body's tissues.

Always double-check everything.

For instance, in the early years of sports diving, when an incorrectly colour-coded cylinder was sent away for charging with air, it was returned filled with nitrous oxide (laughing gas), an anaesthetic. Just think what would have occurred if it had been used underwater!

Hypoxic situations

Chemoreceptors attached to the main body arteries are sensitive to the blood's oxygen level. If this falls, they send impulses to the brain's respiratory centre. This increases pulse rate, and then blood pressure, in an attempt to make up the deficit. If this is still not enough to provide the oxygen required, a state of mental confusion may follow. This can lead to a lack of response and finally unconsciousness.

This last may happen all too suddenly and will probably be the first sign to a companion that anything is amiss. The only other indication would be 'cyanosis', a blueness of the skin, nail-beds and lips. Normally, however, this would be noticeable only after the victim had been brought back to the surface.

Remember, a diver is primed for a possible hypoxic situation any time there is less oxygen than normal in his or her system.

Try to carry out these simple checks, bearing in mind that minor difficulties often combine with each other to create major problems.

1 Check your air supply

Contaminated sources are a danger. Be certain a compressor inlet sucks in clean air. Avoid paint fumes and cigarette smoke. In particular, do not allow the inlet to suck in exhaust fumes from a nearby car or the engine driving the compressor (see also *Volume Two*).

Exhaust fumes contain carbon monoxide (CO), a colourless and odourless gas which is denser than air. (This is why compressor inlets are set well above ground level.) Its effect on the body is very dramatic and often fatal. Carbon monoxide combines with the blood's haemoglobin about two hundred times more readily than with oxygen, which is therefore excluded.

This results in symptoms very similar to those of hypoxia; a persistent headache, tightness across the forehead, dizziness, muddled thinking and sudden unconsciousness. Carboxyhaemoglobin, the compound formed by carbon monoxide in the blood, has a bright cherry-red colour that shows up in the lips and may be noticed after a victim has been recovered to the surface.

2 Check your regulator

Badly maintained regulators could easily give a less than adequate flow-rate at depth. Worse, within the normal continuity of a dive, this reduced flow may pass unnoticed by the diver until he or she is called upon to perform some harder work demanding more air and then discovers the problem. So have your regulator serviced regularly and professionally — especially after a long period of non-use.

3 Check personal techniques

A diver may be affected by nervousness due to inexperience — or by overwork while finning. Both of these will induce fast shallow

Hypoxia

breathing which leads to inadequate lung ventilation. 'Beating the regulator' (when air is demanded faster than it can be delivered through a mechanical device) is an extreme case. Instructors will ensure that trainees do not undertake dives which are likely to induce a nervous response. Advanced divers, of course, have no excuse for overworking themselves – though in their case, problems are more likely to be due to carbon dioxide retention (see page 94).

Bad buoyancy trim

Negatively buoyant divers can easily overwork themselves on the final ascent by having to fin very hard. Unless the diver has been physically hit over the head, or some such accident has occurred, any unexplained unconsciousness underwater will always be due to an hypoxic, or at the very worst an anoxic situation. The victim must then be returned to the surface atmosphere as quickly as possible or the mouthpiece may slip from his relaxed lips and the victim could drown. Of the several cases of sudden unconsciousness known to the authors, the majority have taken place in mid-water.

For example, on a deep dive in a Swiss lake, a diver noted his companion venting air from his dry suit during the final ascent and immediately start finning hard. The diver continued watching, as it did not seem the right thing for his companion to be doing at the time, and he then saw his companion lose consciousness and start to sink. Obviously, the watcher had picked up the tail-end of some previously unnoticed drama. He quickly swam to his companion and carried out a rescue ascent, thereby saving the other diver's life.

The incident was caused initially by a faulty regulator. The diver was confused and vented his diving suit instead of inflating it to ensure an ascent. (He was not wearing a buoyancy compensator.) Fast nervous breathing and hard finning added to his problems. Other divers have been less fortunate. They have sunk and disappeared from sight unnoticed by their companions.

There is a reason why a diver primed for an hypoxic situation is more at risk and likely to pass out during the ascent.

As pressure is released, gases (including oxygen), move from the body tissues back into the bloodstream. If particular tissues then end up with less oxygen than they need, the resulting tissue hypoxia may cause unconsciousness. The situation will be further aggravated by finning, as this causes the tissues to use up the oxygen they contain even faster than before.

It must be emphasized that divers who follow the rules are at little risk to such events; all the same, be careful and make full use of an adjustable buoyancy compensator in awkward situations to ensure a full control of buoyancy.

Breath-hold diving

For their total time underwater, breath-hold divers must rely on one lungful of air. There can be no further ventilation until they surface again. They are a special case, with their own particular problems.

On descent, the gases continue to move from the lungs into the bloodstream and on into the tissues as normal. At depth, there is ample oxygen in the system due to its increased partial pressure and, with

normal-length submersions, carbon dioxide does not rise to an appreciable level (see page 94). This produces a relaxed feeling and a decrease in the desire to breathe, noticed by anyone familiar with the sport, even in shallow water.

But let us consider more extreme conditions, with greater depths and longer durations, as practised by many spearfishermen, who typically go down to 30 meters (99 feet) or more for 1½ to 2 minutes.

If they are well-practised, the decreased desire to breathe could cause them to stay down too long and use up too much oxygen from the unventilated system. They could pass out on the bottom but are more likely to do so during the final ascent, due to tissue hypoxia especially if they use up the little remaining oxygen by finning. The authors have lost at least two personal friends in this way and so have good reason to advise caution regarding both depth and duration.

Hyperventilation

Deep breathing prior to diving should be avoided. The intention is to flush any carbon dioxide from the diver's system and saturate it with extra oxygen. All it does, however, is lower the carbon dioxide level without significantly raising the amount of oxygen present. As carbon dioxide is the trigger to the desire to breathe, the diver can then stay underwater longer, but will stand a much greater chance of passing out on the final ascent.

This might occur while trying to swim the length of a swimming pool underwater and is then called 'shallow water black-out'. This term is also applied to situations when divers (usually military) who are using closed-circuit apparatus lose consciousness due to an hypoxic or anoxic state (see page 91).

How to breath-hold dive properly

Most divers breath-hold dive for pleasure and it is a safe sport if pursued under proper guidance. Simply follow a few rules.

The Snorkelling Manual by Lionel Blandford, published by the BSAC, will make particularly useful reading to anyone anticipating taking up this sport.

The ideal dive is to a depth compatible with the diver's experience and for a reasonable time, say for a minute. Do not hyperventilate prior to descent. When you feel you have to breathe, come up; do not stay a moment longer. Learn to glide and keep all your movements fluid by employing a good buoyancy trim. Remember, less finning means less use of oxygen. Always wear a buoyancy compensator, or at least a surface type of life-jacket, just in case of an emergency.

Oxygen toxicity and its dangers

Sports divers breathe air as a mixture of 21% oxygen and 78% nitrogen, which is perfectly safe to use to a limited depth of about 50 metres (163 ft).

Divers should be aware, however, of the dangers of using apparatus which utilize either pure oxygen or a high percentage of it as a mixture with inert gases.

Such apparatus is essential in clandestine military operations as it emits no bubbles, but its use demands special training. Sports divers should never be tempted to try out such equipment.

Pure oxygen, although used in recompression therapy for the treatment of decompression sickness, is not always beneficial. This is because breathing pure oxygen (or a high percentage mixture of it) over long periods can cause inflammation of the lungs. Moreover, when it is breathed at high pressure, the gas becomes toxic — as could happen, for instance, if it were breathed at depth underwater.

The depth threshold at which toxicity symptoms to begin to appear is generally accepted to be when the partial pressure of the oxygen breathed equals 1.6 bar.

If the diver is breathing pure oxygen, then this limit is equivalent to a depth of 8 metres (about 26 ft). Should he or she go down any deeper, then there is an increasing chance of sudden black-out. An associated epileptic-like convulsion may accompany this black-out.

It is generally thought that a greater danger at depth is posed by the effects of nitrogen narcosis. (This will be discussed in greater detail on page 95 .)

Obviously there is a depth where the partial pressure of the 21% oxygen in the breathing air equals 1.6 bar; this happens at 66 metres or 214 ft (see *Volume Two*). This, of course, is a great deal deeper than the diver could descend if breathing only pure oxygen.

It is not a well-defined limit and many divers, ourselves included, have gone deeper, being quite ignorant, in those early days, of the dangers involved.

What divers must be aware of is that at 66 metres they are entering the dangerous fringe area of depth while breathing air. Therefore the recommendation is that sports divers should stay within 50 metres (163 ft) maximum. This depth

should be reached only by divers with considerable experience.

Professional divers often make use of mixed gases in place of air. There can be various percentages of oxygen in nitrogen to maintain as high a safe partial pressure of oxygen as possible and to help avoid decompression problems.

Typical depth limits for such mixtures are:

8 metres (26 ft) is the limit for 100% oxygen (applicable only to military diving operations).

25 metres (82 ft) is the limit for 60% oxygen and 40% nitrogen.

42 metres (138 ft) is the limit for 40% oxygen and 60% nitrogen.

50 metres (163 ft) is the limit for 21% oxygen and 78% nitrogen.

Sometimes professional divers will be required to dive to much greater depths than the sports diver would ever expect to reach. Such dives may even reach depths well below 70 metres (227 ft).

In such cases, a reduced percentage of oxygen (in a mixture with helium) is used.

Problem gases

Carbon dioxide

This colourless, odourless and tasteless gas constitutes only 0.04% of the atmospheric air. However, depending on the level of activity being undertaken, it can make up between 4% and 5% of all exhalations as the waste product of the body's metabolic process. In the bloodstream carbon dioxide travels partly in solution, partly as a bicarbonate, and partly by combining with the blood haemoglobin.

Relative to other respiratory gases, it has a high density and is the cause of many problems in diving. However, the minor symptoms that it first produces can be of such an insignificant nature that they may very easily go unnoticed, with the diver remaining unaware of potential problems.

Carbon dioxide excess

In limited quantitites, carbon dioxide acts as a necessary stimulant to respiration, but in higher concentrations it becomes distinctly toxic. This excess is known as 'hypercapnia', and can cause muddled thinking, dizziness, blurred vision and eventual unconsciousness.

Victims recover quite quickly if returned to a well-ventilated atmosphere such as the surface, the only after-effects being some nausea and a persistent headache.

These are the classical symptoms and are similar to those of hypoxia, including the appearance of cyanosis. There may also be a marked increase in the rate of breathing, so that even light finning could prove to be exhausting.

Both of these symptoms can be difficult to spot in slight cases.

However, post-dive nausea or headaches must be attributable to some cause; if definitely not a sinus pain, chances are that a carbon dioxide excess is to blame. Something could have interfered with the elimination of carbon dioxide while underwater and the question must be, 'what was it?'

Carbon dioxide retention

The volume of air moved with each breath must not only ventilate the diver's lungs with adequate oxygen but should also eliminate any excess carbon dioxide, otherwise the gas may be reinhaled.

The chance of 'retention', as it is called, is in part dependent on the 'dead space' which can trap carbon dioxide, both within the equipment (the insides of the regulator and the mask) and within the respiratory tract (the nasal cavity, the mouth and the windpipe).

Respiratory dead space is something divers learn to live with; part of a diving medical examination is to ensure those taking part are fit

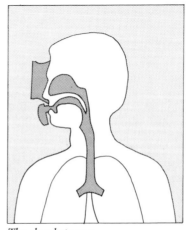

The dead spaces

enough to ventilate the lungs adequately, even at depth with increased gas density.

Diving regulators are specifically designed to limit the amount of dead space available.

Descent

A mild excess of carbon dioxide will be produced in the flurry of action that often precedes a descent. Normally, on the surface in the open air, this would be expelled in the next few breaths. However, it can happen that the diver goes underwater, trapping it in his or her own personal atmosphere. The gas is then difficult, if not impossible, to remove completely as its density increases during the descent. Its effect may not even be noticeable, but remember that problems are often due to cumulative effects.

Feet-first descents are best, using a controlled shift to negative buoyancy. (Swimming down will produce more carbon dioxide because finning is involved.) When mild cases of retention occur, due to this or to especially fast descents and ascents (even in a very shallow depth), a post-dive 'torpedo' headache may result.

A good breathing technique with adequate lung ventilation ensures that retention will not occur.

However, if an excess of carbon dioxide is present, no matter how slight, the diver will be less in control of the general situation although he may not be aware of this at the time. At greater depths the effect would be yet further increased by nitrogen narcosis (see also the following page).

Avoiding retention

Try to introduce a short period of inactivity just prior to making the descent. First take several, deep measured breaths – without hyperventilating. When you feel ready and at ease, commence the dive. This applies equally to aqualung and breath-hold divers.

Keep buoyancy well organized, so as to be able to make feet-first descents. Be wary of any buoyancy situations that will require excessive finning.

While on the bottom, avoid hard finning that cannot be matched with an adequate breathing cycle; that is, one that will properly ventilate the system. With difficult ascents, especially those from deep down, try to make sensible use of the adjustable buoyancy compensator in order to avoid an excess of hard finning.

Nitrogen

Nitrogen is the inert non-reactive gas in air and takes no part in the body's metabolic processes. It travels in solution in the bloodstream, its solubility increasing with the pressure at depth. Nitrogen has two important effects on the diver:

1 Nitrogen is absorbed by the body tissues during the time under pressure and must be eliminated during the ascent. This is accomplished by the procedure known as 'decompression'. (This is considered in detail in *Volume Two.*)

2 Nitrogen has a stupefying or narcotic effect on the diver as a result of its increased partial pressure. This effect is called 'nitrogen narcosis' and in many ways its 'symptoms' are very similar to those produced by alcohol intoxication.

Nitrogen narcosis

Inert gas narcosis is due to nitrogen being absorbed by the body. The feeling of intoxication this produces was noted by the early French free divers and was named, *l'ivresses des grandes profondeurs'* or 'the rapture of the deep' (as described in 1953 by Cousteau in his book *The Silent World*).

It impairs the diver's overall ability, powers of concentration and judgement, giving rise to euphoria, a false sense of well-being. Tunnel vision has been reported in some cases.

Although complete intoxication is likely to occur only when diving deeper than the suggested limit of 50 metres (165 ft) maximum, the moderate effects are serious enough to put a depth limitation on diving with compressed air. The danger from narcosis is that the diver has less control over his or her own actions. Symptoms disappear on ascent with no after-effects,

although in bad cases the individual may not remember everything that went on at depth. The effects will vary between individuals, having less effect on the regular practised diver. Narcosis will become more pronounced under such adverse psychological conditions as cold water, bad visibility and anxiety. As a guide, the 'Martini rule' was developed. This equates every 10 metres (33 ft) with the intoxication produced by one Martini !

For some, this at least brings the problem of narcosis into perspective. As a guideline, 20 metres (65 ft) would be recommended as a maximum limit for the less experienced, with 28 metres (91 ft) as the level where a certain amount of lightheadedness may be expected by more seasoned divers.

In the past many of the divers who surfaced after a dive in excess of 30 metres (99 ft) imagined that they

had not suffered from the intoxicating effect of nitrogen. However, this was not the case. During his commercial diver training, one of the authors made a dive to 65 metres (213 ft) in the Mediterranean to visit a wreck. This was the first time he had experienced breathing a mixture of 20% oxygen and 80% helium at these depths. This mixture contains about the same percentage mix as air but with the nitrogen content exchanged for helium, it is a much less intoxicating inert gas.

'The difference was enormous. I had never felt so clear-headed before – the fuzzy feeling an experienced diver comes to associate with greater depth was gone.

Instead we all experienced a sudden burst of confidence and the realization we had a new command over our immediate situation.'

Decompression

How our bodies absorb nitrogen

It has already been shown that the body tissues are absorbing nitrogen the whole time they are under pressure and this must be eliminated during the ascent back to the surface by the decompression process. The subject may appear complex at first, but it really is not difficult. It is of vital importance that the diver understands exactly what is happening to the body during the decompression, and is aware of the limits of depth and time entailed.

As discussed on page 85, after inhalation the gases in the breathing air are transported from the lungs to the tissues by the arterial blood. Here oxygen provides the fuel for the metabolic process and is used up; while nitrogen, the other major constituent of air and a chemically inert gas, plays no part at all. Such is the situation at atmospheric pressure on the surface, when the body's whole system is in a state of equilibrium.

During a descent, the pressure of air in the diver's lungs builds up, setting up a pressure gradient within the diver's system.

Blood now takes up this increased level of nitrogen (including the oxygen, of course) and transports this to the tissues, which begin to absorb it. The rate of absorption is relative to the pressure gradient; at first it is quite fast and then it progressively slows down (see the diagram on the right).

If a diver was able to stay at a constant depth, nitrogen tension in the blood and the tissues would eventually balance out into a stable equilibrium (at which point the tissues are said to be fully saturated). Should the diver go deeper still, then the whole process simply repeats itself.

The time taken for individual tissues to become fully saturated depends on their location in the body and their blood supply. A tissue's location is said to be well placed if it has a dense network of capillaries to supply it with nutrients at a fast rate. Vital organs such as the brain, heart, kidneys and liver are well placed; they receive a rich blood supply and saturate in a matter of minutes. At the other end of the scale, fatty tis-

sue and bone marrow have a poor blood supply and can take twelve hours or more to saturate. In between these two extremes are many other tissue 'compartments' (as they are called).

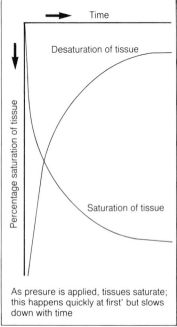

As presure is applied, tissues saturate; this happens quickly at first' but slows down with time

Percentage saturation of tissue

Elimination of nitrogen from the body

A reverse pressure gradient is set up as soon as an ascent is started and the gas pressure supplied to the lungs by the regulator is reduced, to conform with the surrounding hydrostatic pressure.

The venous return of the blood circulation now has to transport nitrogen back to the lungs, as the tissues desaturate to bring the system back into equilibrium. This is the process of decompression.

Should the speed of the ascent (the rate at which the pressure is released) be too fast, the blood will not have enough time to allow all the nitrogen to be released. Tissues which absorb gas slowly also release it slowly.

If during this time of desaturation a drop in pressure occurs, some of the gas remaining in the tissues forms bubbles. In extreme cases bubbles may form in the blood too.

It is these nitrogen bubbles in the tissues and the blood which are the cause of decompression sickness (DCS). Symptoms of DCS vary according to the size of the bubbles and their location in the body. Symptoms are grouped according to the organs involved.

Basically there are two kinds of decompression sickness. Firstly, there is the 'pain only' type such as joint pains, often referred to as 'the bends' which are the milder forms of DCS. Some cases may manifest themselves as an itch or rash on the skin, often on the fatty stomach tissue. These would be skin bends.

Secondly, there can be 'neurological manifestations' which effect the brain or spinal cord. In extreme circumstances other manifestations might present, such as paralysis, which could eventually result in death. Decompression sickness is

therefore not a subject to be ignored or handled carelessly. (See *Volume Two* for a fuller explanation of decompression sickness.)

DCS should not be confused with a gas embolism, which is another form of decompression 'illness'. Gas embolism also produces bubbles in the blood due to a too-rapid ascent, but its causes are not the same. With a gas embolism, lung rupture liberates gas into the lung

tissues as a result of overpressure. Fortunately the body has a natural tolerance level to nitrogen, before it reaches the point when bubbles are formed. Certain rules must be observed and then a safe return to the surface will be ensured — provided the diver does not allow too high a pressure gradient to develop by ascending too fast. It is essential to exercise control of nitrogen elimination by strict adherence to the decompression tables.

Compression, decompression and recompression

Earlier, on pages 77-8, it was shown how compression affects the diver's breathing gas, body air spaces and buoyancy. None of these need present problems if properly understood and dealt with. From the moment when a diver leaves the surface until the start of the ascent, the body will be under continuing pressure and the tissues will be absorbing nitrogen the whole time. This is the 'compression' phase.

Problems arise when the diver reduces the ambient pressure by beginning to ascend. This is the 'decompression' phase. Decompression is a drop in pressure which occurs while ascending to the surface after a dive. It also occurs when climbing to altitude in an aeroplane or up a mountain. The importance of decompression lies in the effect it has on the dissolved inert gases in the body, such as nitrogen. Decompression has a negligible effect on the body's oxygen because it is metabolized by the tissues.

Decompression sickness can occur if the elimination of nitrogen via the blood to the lungs is unequal to the rate of reduction of the ambient pressure, when the nitrogen may

come out of solution to form bubbles. So decompression is a necessary part of every dive, during which the return to the surface must be slow enough to ensure that any quantity of nitrogen left in the diver's body will be too small to cause trouble.

In the normal way, a diver must follow a decompression schedule which will govern the time he can safely stay at any given depth and return directly to the surface. If the diver spends longer periods of time at depth than this schedule allows, it will be necessary to pay certain penalties in the form of obligatory 'stops'. These are pauses of a given time and depth during the ascent which allow time for the process of nitrogen elimination. If the strictures of the schedule are not adhered to (such as overstaying time at depth and ascending without making the necessary properly-timed stops) then the diver may suffer from decompression sickness. The cure for DCS will be to put the diver into a specially equipped pressure chamber and then subject him or her to a 'recompression', the time and pressure of which is specified in an appropriate therapeutic

recompression table. The pressure can then be released slowly until all the schedule requirements have been satisfied and the symptoms of DCS relieved.

It has already been recommended that the diver should accept that every dive will necessitate decompression. In the shallows and for shorter underwater durations, this may mean simply maintaining a slow controlled return to the surface. Generally, the best advice is that if you have not had the required training in how to make stops, do not be talked into going too deep or staying down too long.

For instance, as a recently qualified diver, you may go on holiday and then find you are dealing with others trained to differing standards. These divers may well use techniques outside your immediate experience. Always keep within sensible limits and pay attention to the points on the following page.

There are several tables which sports divers commonly use. These include the RNPL/BSAC air diving tables and the US Navy Standard Air Decompression Tables.

Decompression

Make full use of the body's natural level of toleration to nitrogen without bubbles being formed. The trick is to adapt the body by making a series of progessively deeper dives. This holds true for inexperienced trainees, as well as for experienced divers entering the water after a 'lay-off' period without diving. Only those who have been diving regularly will have bodies that are fit enough to go to greater depths.

While it is best to stay well within the no-stop limit, deeper dives will narrow the time window available. A planned no-stop dive may then accidentally become one requiring stops. The more advanced trainees should be well aware of this possibility as the dives they undertake become deeper.

Note that the terminology used by experienced divers relates 'decompression dives' only to those where they know stops will have to be made, with all the extra preparation and tight management such dives demand. (See also *Volume Two*.)

Practical decompression for beginners

Under qualified instruction, novice divers initially make relatively shallow dives. As their experience grows, they then go deeper under the guidance of their instructor. This is a progressive approach, calculated to adapt them to the general format of deeper diving and decompression in particular. On all such training dives they should refer to and make use of decompression tables, with particular regard to the following:

* Rate of descent; 30 metres (98 ft) per minute, which is quite fast.

* Rate of ascent; 15 metres (48 ft) per minute — no faster, no slower.

* No-stop limit

Because of the body's nitrogen-level tolerance, provided that the pressure gradient is not unduly high (through too fast an ascent), there is an interval of time, at any particular depth, during which it is possible to make a direct ascent back to the surface. The residual nitrogen left in the body after surfacing would still be tolerable. These 'no-stop' dives represent a very safe way to dive.

The 'limiting line' or no-stop limit is clearly marked on decompression tables and should be used by sports divers whenever possible.

Tables usually put no time limit on very shallow dives, typically up to a depth of 8 metres (24 ft) for up to 8 hours in any 24-hour period.

Never commit yourself to any extended stay at shallow depth, as an endurance test for instance, because there may be some danger from decompression sickness attached to such a practice.

All references in this book are to the tables compiled by the Royal Naval Physiological laboratories for the BSAC (The BSAC/RNPL Decompression Table). If other sets of tables are used, for example the US Navy Standard Air Decompression Tables, then their interpretation and use must be thoroughly checked out.

To make proper use of no-stop limits, adapt the diving routine you have already learnt, as follows:

Depth and time
Carry a watch or dive timer and an accurate depth gauge on every dive. Decide the maximum depth you are going to reach (prior to entering the water) and make certain that you know the no-stop time which applies to it. Take this time from when you leave the surface, inclusive of descent, bottom and ascent time, until you reach the surface again. Go no deeper than planned and stay well within the no-stop time limit for that depth.

Decompression tables
Develop the habit of always carrying a decompression table which clearly lays out the no-stop limits for various depths, particularly on dives that will be deeper than 8 metres (24 ft). They can be purchased printed on plastic or rubberized fabric for gluing to the sleeve of a diving suit. The instructor will show you how to interpret the tables. (For layout and interpretation of tables see *Volume Two*.)

Trainees usually dive with more experienced companions and a table allows them to relate directly to what is going on and become familiar with the procedure and the reasons behind it.

Decompression tables have been calculated by recognized authorities in many countries; they are designed to give the following information to divers:

1 Times and depths from which a direct ascent may be made. This is called a no-stop dive.

2 Times and depths for pauses during the ascent to release nitrogen, if the no-stop times have been exceeded. These are called decompression stops.

3 Surface interval times required for repeat dives.

To keep within the no-stop limit, the diver will have to enter the decompression table with these two relevant factors:

* The interval between leaving the surface until the start of the ascent (called the 'bottom time').

* The deepest depth reached.

Provided that the diver does not exceeed the time or depth allowed in the tables, it is possible to return directly to the surface. In fact, the majority of sports divers practise no-stop diving.

Stage decompression

Should the diver for any reason stay longer or go deeper than the DC tables allow for a no-stop dive, it will then be necessary to carry out what is known as stage decompression, that is, to make stops.

The diver should always be aware that penalties have been incurred and stops are necessary as he will have kept a check on the bottom time (with a watch) and the maximum depth (with a depth gauge).

As discussed on the previous page, there are different ways of carrying a decompression table on a dive, but the important thing is that the information must be readily available. An even better idea is to learn the no-stop times and depths by heart — there are not many of them.

When you have confirmed that you must carry out stops, refer immediately to the decompression table. Move up to a pre-determined depth as shown on the table, at the correct rate of ascent; 15 metres (50 ft) per minute), and then stay there for the prescribed length of time before recommencing the ascent.

If a no-stop time has been accidently overstayed by just a minute or two, only one stop may be necessary for the nitrogen level in the body to drop to a point at which it will be safe to ascend further.

For example, if a diver descends to 20 metres (66 ft) then the no-stop time limit will be 46 minutes. If, however, he or she overstays this limit by a further 3 minutes, then it will be necessary to stop at 5 metres (16½ ft) for 5 minutes.

Deeper maximum depths would almost certainly require more than one stop. An example of this would be as follows:

* If a diver descends to 43 metres (141 ft) for 15 minutes, then the tables will prescribe a stop at 10 metres (33 ft) for 5 minutes and another stop at 5 metres (16½ ft) for 5 minutes.

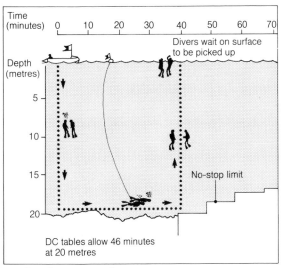

Profile of a no-stop dive

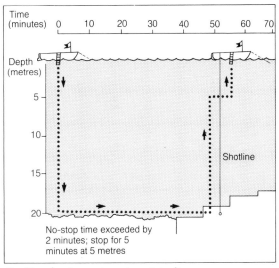

Profile of a decompression stop dive

The open water

Introduction

The time comes when the novice is sufficiently confident to move away from the safe controlled conditions of early training and make the first open-water dive. This could take place in fresh water or in the sea and will involve both greater depths and the hazards associated with later diving activities.

This section describes the preparations and procedures necessary before diving and then the actual conduct of a dive. Although diving practice obviously varies according to the country and type of group organizing it, the basics will be much the same.

The change from sheltered conditions to open water can come as a psychological jolt after having been trained in a warm, clear swimming pool. A diving suit will probably be worn, buoyancy control is more critical, visibility may be poor and the weather all important. It is a new experience in a hostile environment – but it is, at last, a real dive !

For their initial dives, novices will be paired with more experienced companions and at first will be very dependent on them. Usually this companion is an instructor who will be patient and sympathetic to the problems of a novice.

The intention is to gradually introduce the diver to the many new conditions he or she will be experiencing for the first time.

Ideally, each dive should impose progressively greater demands on the abilities of the novice diver and on the skills he will need in order to develop safety consciousness and self-sufficiency.

Conduct of a dive

The dive plan

All dives should follow a plan which should be decided upon before entering the water. Communication is limited underwater, making later changes of plan difficult to be understood. We shall consider the dive under three main headings:

* Pre-dive: The planning, organization, and equipment assembly; the checks and briefing.

* In-dive: Diving techniques in phases; the descent, the bottom time and the ascent.

* Post-dive: Record of the dive, equipment disassembly and, finally, the de-brief.

Collectively, the descent, bottom time and the ascent deal with the depth reached and the time spent underwater. These give any particular dive a unique profile which may be presented graphically (see diagrams on this page). Naturally, for the early dives these profiles are kept simple — to a limited depth and length of time, which will be increased as the novice becomes more confident.

Dives should not be undertaken in a haphazard way, especially in a training programme. It will probably come as a surprise to many to realize just how much planning has to be done. There must be a careful analysis of many factors, such as the nature of the location — called the dive site; the prevailing and the future weather; and the resources and equipment available — to name but a few.

In open-water training this planning is usually the task of a dive marshal, an experienced diver who

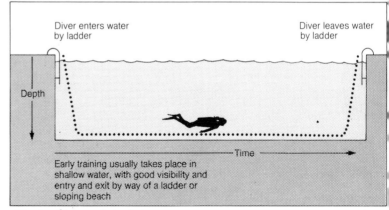

Dive profiles: early training

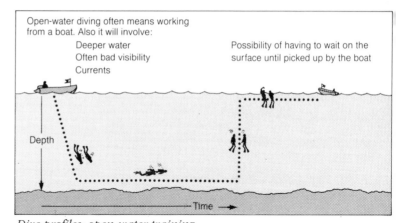

Dive profiles: open-water training

will have a back-up team of instructors and qualified divers. The dive marshal will have studied the weather forecasts and arranged for all the necessary equipment, such as boats (and their engines and fuel). The marshal will draw up a list showing who will dive with whom, and this must take into account the experience and capabilities of each diver as well as assigning a dive leader to each pair.

Diving can be a hazardous sport and if things start to go wrong,

immediate and correct action must be taken. Even if the divers are carrying out all the correct procedures, and even when the conditions are good, there are quite a few things that can happen accidentally which could not have been foreseen and avoided. The novice will not be expected to be able to recognize or cope with such accidents and will very properly be put in the care of someone who can.

It is usual for every dive to have an objective, such as an exploration or a wreck dive, or it may be just a training dive. Once the objective has been decided, the dive leader will study a chart of the dive site and, taking all the other factors such as weather into consideration, will formulate a dive plan. After this, the two most important factors will be; firstly, the maximum depth to be reached, and secondly, the projected time to be spent underwater.

Once there is a dive profile and a basic plan, these will be discussed with all the participants before entering the water. Every person concerned with the dive will need to know the details, so if an accident (or anything out of the ordinary) occurs, those in a position to initiate help will know what to do. (Many incidents have shown that when things go seriously wrong there have been gross deviations from an accepted dive plan.) It is very comforting to know that if things do go wrong, somebody will be aware that you are in trouble and will come to your assistance. This is not to suggest that divers are always meeting difficulties, but once things start to go wrong underwater, the situation must be checked before it is out of control. So we emphasize that the dive plan, once agreed, must be followed. George Skuse, in *Diving Incidents Report* (DOC 1981) formulated a golden rule: 'Plan the dive and dive the plan'. This applies particularly to dives involving training and beginners; it is probably less relevant to a dive made by really experienced people.

The brief

The dive leader will brief his or her companion before they are kitted up. The dive plan will be explained to the novice, along with any specific instructions for that particular dive. The brief will include reminders of the need for coping with ear clearing and mask squeeze; comments on the danger of holding the breath on ascending; as well as agreement on the action to be taken if separated.

Preparations for the dive

The dive leader will assist the novice to kit-up and check everything mechanical is in working order. It is essential to have an equipment list to look through rather than relying on memory! (This list should be checked over a few days before the dive. If this is left until the last minute and something is found to be damaged or missing, there will be no time to put this right.) The cylinder should have been filled as it may be difficult to obtain air on the dive site. It is also very useful to have a large strong bag that will keep all the diving gear together. Otherwise, it is all too easy to mislay an essential item of equipment, making the dive impossible. Ensure the BC emergency mini-cylinder is fully charged from a full cylinder. A partially filled emergency cylinder could mean the buoyancy of the BC is not enough to lift the diver to the surface. Never just assume it has been filled; do it before every dive, even if convinced it was not used on the last dive!

☑	**Cylinder**	(Filled to its working pressure Is the cylinder within its test date?)
☑	**Regulator**	(When was it last serviced?)
☑	**Diving suit**	Including hood, bootees and gloves
		Have any necessary repairs been done?
☑	**Buoyancy compensator**	Inflate compensator orally to test for leaks
		Has the emergency mini-cylinder been filled, and was it filled from a full cylinder?
		Is it within the test date?
☑	**Mask, fins and snorkel**	(Are the mask and snorkel fin retaining straps perished?)
☑	**Weightbelt**	(Plus a few spare weights)
☑	**Depth gauge**	(Has it ever been tested?)

A typical check-list

Preparations

Now you will need to fit the regulator to the pillar valve of the cylinder. When this has been done, turn on the air and test that everything is in good working order.

This is a good time to find out whether the cylinder has been properly filled with breathing air, and to check that it has not been contaminated with another gas, such as carbon monoxide.

Do not wait until you are underwater to find this out. The results could be disastrous!

Finally, you will need to check the pressure in the cylinder (typically 200 bar). Do not rely on your memory to tell you whether it is full or not. Always double check.

Allow a good twenty minutes for dressing and equipping yourself. Do not leave this to the last minute; it takes longer than you think and a diver who keeps others waiting about in their restrictive diving suits is acting anti-socially and will probably be promptly advised of the fact by his or her diving companions!

The order of dressing is important. Proceed as follows:

1 First put on the diving suit. Do this in a sheltered location to avoid losing body heat; do not let your body become chilled before entering the water.

2 Secondly, place the bootees on your feet.

3 Now put on the buoyancy compensator, with its straps kept loose about the body.

4 Watch, depth gauge and compass must be added next.

5 Strap on the knife and slip the snorkel into place.

6 Put on the aqualung with the regulator and pressure gauge.

7 Weightbelt; always put this on last so that it can be ditched freely.

8 When you are ready, don the hood, mask and gloves. (These are usually left off until the last moment before actually diving.)

Buoyancy check in a diving suit

If this is the very first dive, novices will have to do a buoyancy check with their dive leader. This is best done from a sheltered shore. With a companion, enter the water from the beach in full equipment and carry out a buoyancy check. You will need to adjust your weighting until it is neutral on the surface. (See also *Weighting technique* and *Buoyancy control* on pages 33-4 Carry some spare weights with you ready for this. Once weighting has been organized, your next dive will be much simpler!

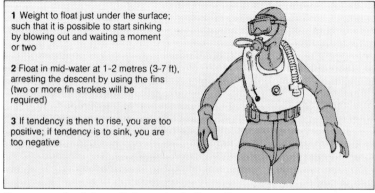

1 Weight to float just under the surface; such that it is possible to start sinking by blowing out and waiting a moment or two

2 Float in mid-water at 1-2 metres (3-7 ft), arresting the descent by using the fins (two or more fin strokes will be required)

3 If tendency is then to rise, you are too positive; if tendency is to sink, you are too negative

Buoyancy check in a diving suit: shallow dives

Blow out to start a descent. You will notice that it is now rather more difficult to arrest the descent by using mid-water fin strokes than it was previously. This is because extra weights are worn to offset diving-suit buoyancy and overall buoyancy is in a more critical balance.

Consult the instructor or a more experienced companion, if slightly less than this weighting is required, according to the planned depth of the dive to come.

Weighting technique will be stabilized by the second or third dive.

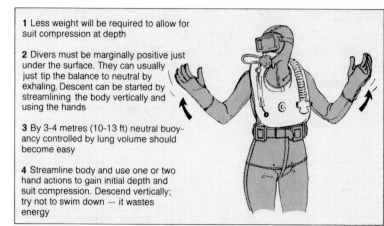

1 Less weight will be required to allow for suit compression at depth

2 Divers must be marginally positive just under the surface. They can usually just tip the balance to neutral by exhaling. Descent can be started by streamlining the body vertically and using the hands

3 By 3-4 metres (10-13 ft) neutral buoyancy controlled by lung volume should become easy

4 Streamline body and use one or two hand actions to gain initial depth and suit compression. Descend vertically; try not to swim down — it wastes energy

Buoyancy check in a diving suit: deeper dives

The buddy system

This is a simple system that ensures safety while underwater. Dives are made by pairs of divers, with each of the two companions looking after the other.

Never dive alone; many unfortunate incidents or accidents are attributable to divers 'going solo'. It is simply not worth the inherent extra risks involved.

Even if your companion is more experienced, from the first moment of a dive and throughout its duration, you have the responsibility of looking after him or her.

* Discuss all aspects of the dive with your companion diver.

* If trained in different places or countries, check the hand signals to be used, particularly the 'I am out of air' signal, which may be different.

* Compare the physical capacity of his (or her) cylinder. Does his cylinder contain a greater volume of air than yours?

* Check the other diver's contents gauge. The total dive time will be decided according to the contents of the cylinder with the least air.

* Could you easily release your companion from his equipment if this was required?

* Good divers have all their equipment well organized and then put it on in a well-practised manner. Watch how other divers handle the apparatus; it will tell you a lot about their competence.

* It is not what divers say that matters: it is what they do and the way that they do it — on the surface and under the water.

* When all is checked and ready, unless diving from the shore, the novice should go down to the boat with his or her companion.

The boat might be a large 'hard' boat with its professional skipper or, more usually, it will be an inflatable. The boathandler will direct

the divers as to when and how to launch and board the boat. (See *Volume Two*.)

* Each pair should sit facing each other so that they can monitor each other's equipment and actions.

* They will have to equip themselves with an SMB (surface marker buoy) which will mark their position when underwater.

* If the actual place where the divers will descend is not far from the launch point, it is customary to sit in the boat fully kitted except for mask, fins and gloves.

If the journey will be long, or the sea rough, the breathing sets may be stowed in the bottom of the boat and donned on arrival.

* While travelling out to the dive site, take the opportunity to check each other out. Always remain seated and hold on to the beckets (the looped ropes secured along the top of the inflation tubes).

Check-out

Talk and check

The equipment you are now wearing may be different from that with which you trained — so make sure you are familiar with it.

Remember also, you may have to render assistance to a companion so it is important you know how his or her equipment all works. If unclear, ask him to show you how it operates; it is in your companion's interests to do so.

In particular, discuss together the dive plan, the maximum depth and the approximate dive time.

Be extra wary of new diving companions, especially those from a different training background. It is equally important that you do not take your regular diving companions for granted. Check them out just as carefully. Do they look fit to dive? Are they seasick or anxious?

Even at this late stage, do not hesitate to abort a dive if you or your companion are unwell or feel very anxious or seasick — or if you simply do not feel like diving. An experienced sensible diver would always prefer to stop at this

point, rather than risk having an accident which would almost certainly involve other people. After all, amateur divers do not have to dive unless they want to. There are no professional obligations; the idea is simply to enjoy yourself — so if it is no longer fun, stop !

We present here two typical sports-diver rigs, each using different combinations of equipment. The first illustration, Diver A, shows a diver wearing a wet suit and buoyancy compensator. He appears ready to dive, but is he?

Diver A

Because he is wearing a wet suit, he is unlikely to have the buoyancy control problems which might be involved if he had been in a dry suit. Also, you will notice that his regulator is of the less common twin-hose type.

Look at him very closely and check every item of equipment before you enter the water together. Should an emergency arise there will be no time to fumble around, finding out where everything is and how it works.

Ask yourself the following questions:

1 Are you familiar with the action of twin-hose regulators?

2 Do you know the drill for air-sharing with a twin-hose?

3 From which side would you approach this diver to effect a rescue underwater? Does it matter?

4 Do you know where his buoyancy-compensator emergency cylinder is, and on which side the tap is located?

5 Has he checked if his emergency cylinder is full?

6 When he put on his aqualung set, did he make sure that the straps were clear of the BC? If he has not done this, the straps may prevent the bag from inflating

7 Are the BC dump valve and oral-inflation tube accessible for operation?

8 The BC has no direct-feed inflation system so that any buoyancy adjustment will have to be done orally

9 Could you release him from his aqualung set in an emergency?

10 Does he have a snorkel tube ready to hand? Is he carrying a watch, a depth gauge and a compass?

11 Does he use the same sort of hand signals as you? If not, are you familiar with the alternatives?

12 Is his air turned on?

Diver B

You will note that this diver is wearing a dry suit. Are you familiar with the buoyancy control of dry suits? Visually check and question your companion on all the following points:

1 Do you know where the inflation controls on his dry suit are to be found? Are they accessible under the buoyancy compensator?

More importantly, where is the vent valve located and do you know how it operates?

2 Is the entry zip to his dry suit properly done up?

3 How is his buoyancy compensator inflated? You should note that he has a direct-feed system which allows him to adjust his buoyancy by BC inflation as well as by suit inflation. Do you know how to bleed air from it?

Where is the emergency cylinder located and on which side is the tap to be found? Is this emergency cylinder full?

4 Has he checked that his regulator works properly? Where is his cylinder contents gauge located? Is his cylinder tap turned on?

5 You may have noticed that your companion has his weightbelt fastened incorrectly, underneath the buoyancy compensator support strap. Chances are

that it is the same at the back. If released, the weightbelt would end up dangling from the support harness. Also, check if you can release all the harnessing buckles with ease?

6 This diver has his mask strap underneath his hood. This means he would have to take off his hood should he need to remove the mask for any reason

7 Do you know where he carries his watch? Where are his compass and his depth gauge located?

8 Check that you both use the same set of hand signals

9 Has your diving companion checked you (and all your equipment) equally thoroughly?

Entering the water

If shore diving without a boat always follow this rule:

* Before entering the water, decide how and where you will come out again, and make provision for this.

Surface conditions may change during the course of a dive. In the Mediterranean we have often surfaced to find the sheltered rocky ledge from which we entered now buried in a foaming maelstrom due to a wind change. Good divers must have alternative exits available.

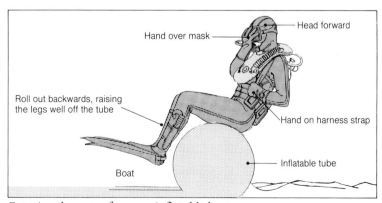

Entering the water from an inflatable boat

The dive

All the normal modes of entry into the water from above have been covered in early training (see page 35). For entries from a beach, see *Volume Two*.

In open water, small boats are often used as tenders to follow the course of a dive or to anchor over a fixed dive site. Rubber inflatables are particularly suitable for this purpose, as they have a low freeboard over which it is easy to exit or to enter.

The procedure will be as follows:

* Sit on the inflatable tube facing inwards. By this time you should be fully dressed and ready for the dive.

* Stabilize the equipment. Check that your air has been turned on.

* Place one hand over the mask to keep it from being dislodged, and put the other hand on the harnessing in order to prevent the cylinder riding up and striking the back of the head (see page 107).

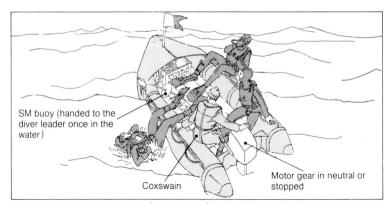

Divers entering the water from an inflatable boat

SM buoy (handed to the diver leader once in the water)

Coxswain

Motor gear in neutral or stopped

* When ordered by the boathandler to proceed, having first checked that the water below is unobstructed, tuck your head forward on to your chest and roll backwards into the water.

Confirm a safe entry

Once in the water, surface briefly and give the 'I am all right' hand signal to those watching. One of the two divers will have entered the water with the SMB (surface marker buoy). For the first few dives the leader will probably take this.

Close up to your companion, signal to descend, and then make a feet-first descent. Experienced divers use the initial few metres of their descent to check that their buoyancy is correct. Trainees making their first open-water dive will take much longer to do this and so they should try to complete these checks before the dive.

Words of guidance

Here are a few suggestions to those who are about to make their first open-water dives:

* Take your time underwater. Make a slow descent, and if you have ear problems, start coming up again very slowly. An experienced com-panion should notice and respond to your situation immediately.

* Once on the bottom, stay close together but be careful you do not overswim your companion's fins.

* Signal all your intentions clearly.

* Use physical contact to attract the other diver's attention if necessary. If you are not happy, then indicate this by the appropriate signal.

* Make a slow final ascent, alongside your companion. Be sure not to separate in the water.

Descent, ascent and maximum depth

Diving in open-water conditions will demand a rigid personal discipline, and so it is important that the trainee should assimilate all the essential routines as quickly and as thoroughly as possible.

Make any descent slowly, up to a maximum of 30 metres (100 ft) per minute. Ascent rates are more critical as decompression requirements must be adhered to, and a rate of 15 metres (50 ft) per minute is correct.

Maintain this by constant reference to your watch and the depth gauge.

Early open-water training should take place in shallow water — no deeper than 10 metres (33 ft).

At the instructor's discretion, visits may later be made down to 20 metres (66 ft). Only towards the end of the training period should a deeper dive be made. Then plan to reach a maximum depth of no more than 30 metres (100 ft).

Remember, depth will be the one condition you will need to become used to; most of the necessary skills should have been learnt equally well in the shallows.

While the divers are below, the cover boat will not anchor but will remain underway with the motor running and just circle around the divers SMB's. The boat will be ready to go to the divers' aid immediately. If diving on a wreck or carrying out a search (or any type of dive where the divers will stay in one fixed position), the boat will probably anchor and buoy the anchor warp, which the divers will use as a shotline for descent and ascent.

The gentle purring sound of the cover boat's motor as it circles the divers' SMB's overhead is very reassuring to those below. It gives them the comfortable feeling that should something go wrong, there is somebody up there who will take the necessary action.

Most boathandlers are experienced divers who should have an appreciation of what will be happening to the divers in the water below.

Visual contact

Underwater, divers rely heavily on vision to maintain contact with a companion. The small unconscious sounds that betray someone's presence on land are missing. A new set of rules must be learnt:

* Efficiency diminishes with distance. Stay close together or it becomes all too easy to stray outside the visibility range.

* Maintain visual contact at regular intervals, exchanging the 'Are you OK?' signal.

* Glance at your companion at frequent intervals to check your relative positions. Move closer together if necessary. Failure to narrow the gap between you may allow the other diver to fin out of visibility within just a few seconds.

* Masks blinker vision, making it directional. Learn to look from side to side and up and down; a great deal happens just outside your peripheral vision.

* When watching your companion note if there is anything wrong. Look at the exhaust-bubble pattern. Is the other diver breathing heavily?

Take a quick glance every ½ minute or so

Glance quickly at companion

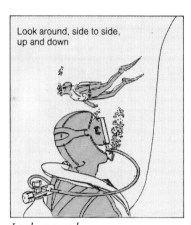

Look around, side to side, up and down

Look around

In low visibility stay closer together

Do not separate - stay together all the time

Stay together

Danger zone - just under surface. During ascent, exhaust bubbles join up and a companion can disappear because the bubbles are bright and reflecting.

Danger zone

The dive

If you are not happy with either your own or your companion's situation, close up to the other diver as quickly as possible.

In bad visibility keep close together. Similarly, keep close during the ascent, a time when it is easy to part company, particularly in the bubble mass just under the surface. Water visibility is a limiting factor. When it is bad, companions may be roped together for safety.

On well-defined dive sites (alongside a jetty perhaps) diving alone is permissable while tended by rope from the surface. In effect the buddy is on the surface above — and this is the only allowable deviation to the 'never dive alone' rule.

We must emphasize the safety value of visual contact and monitoring each other's actions, but would point out two problems typically present in those who are new to open-water techniques:

* Newcomers will often swim straight ahead, scarcely ever looking at their companion divers.

* They will frequently become totally absorbed in whatever holds their immediate interest, to the exclusion of all else.

From hard-won experience, we offer a finding common to all levels of diving expertise:

* Whenever something starts going wrong, you can guarantee your companion will be looking the other way !

* The closer you are, the easier it will be to make physical contact.

Separation drill

You look around for your companion and cannot locate him (or her). What action should you take ?

* Stay exactly where you are for the moment. Your companion may find you, or reappear within seconds.

* Turn through 360° — he or she may be behind you.

* Look up and down while turning. He may be above or below your visual field. He will often be located behind and above, a sector we do not visually scan very often on land.

* Do all this quickly; you may catch a glimpse of the other diver before he disappears out of visual range. If your companion cannot be located at all, assume he or she has started upwards. Commence an immediate ascent yourself as your assistance may be required. At this moment in time you do not know his situation and he does not know yours.

When separation occurs, start an ascent. Do not wait around longer than is necessary.

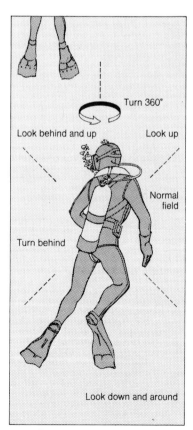

Turn 360°

Look behind and up

Look up

Normal field

Turn behind

Look down and around

Search

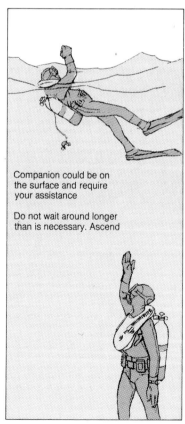

Companion could be on the surface and require your assistance

Do not wait around longer than is necessary. Ascend

Ascend

The ascent

When the planned dive has come to its scheduled time limit, or if the air remaining in the diver's cylinders has fallen to one quarter of its total capacity, the ascent will begin. If the no-stop time for the maximum depth reached has been exceeded, it will be necessary to allow some reserve air for carrying out the required stops.

The dive leader will give the 'go-up' signal, and begin winding in the SMB line as both divers begin the ascent. During the dive they may have inflated their buoyancy compensators or dry suits to adjust their

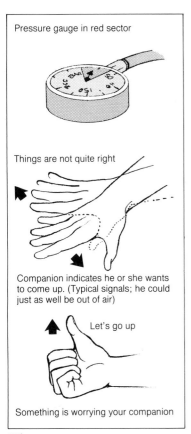

Pressure gauge in red sector

Things are not quite right

Companion indicates he or she wants to come up. (Typical signals; he could just as well be out of air)

Let's go up

Something is worrying your companion

When to come up

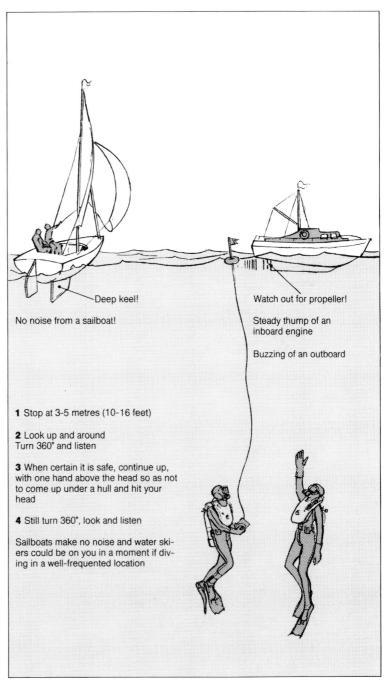

Deep keel!

No noise from a sailboat!

Watch out for propeller!

Steady thump of an inboard engine

Buzzing of an outboard

1 Stop at 3-5 metres (10-16 feet)

2 Look up and around
Turn 360° and listen

3 When certain it is safe, continue up, with one hand above the head so as not to come up under a hull and hit your head

4 Still turn 360°, look and listen

Sailboats make no noise and water ski-ers could be on you in a moment if diving in a well-frequented location

Surfacing drill

On the surface

buoyancy at depth. This additional buoyancy may help to overcome the inertia of beginning the ascent, so do not dump it too soon.

Care will have to be taken to control this extra lift during the diver's ascent, in order to avoid his rising too rapidly.

Be sure that the dump valve or oral inflation tube is to hand, especially when approaching the shallows — from a depth of 10 metres (33 ft) to the surface. The volume of trapped air will then be doubled.

* Face your companion, keeping an eye on his or her rate of ascent (and your own) by glancing at your depth gauge and watch.

In practice, many divers control their speed simply by ensuring that they do not overtake the ascending small bubbles which will be streaming past the mask faceplate.

* Maintain a normal ascent rate of about 15 metres (50 ft) per minute, by referring frequently to your watch and the depth gauge.

* Breathe normally; do not hold your breath. This is very important (see page 81).

* Stop at 3 to 5 metres (10-16 ft) depth. Look upwards and about; and listen.

If a boat's engine can be heard locally, the sound either growing louder as it approaches or fainter as it moves away, you will have to wait until it is clear.

* Proceed upwards with caution. Turn through 360° and look up. Remember that sailing boats make no noise and have deep keels. (For instance, a boat once ignored our diving flag and nearly ran us down from behind, while we were coming up our own anchor line!)

* In bad visibility, proceed with extra caution, ascending with one hand above your head to ward off any unexpected impact with a keel.

* Stay together, do not drift apart; it is easier to spot two heads in the waves than one!

On the surface

Once you are on the surface, proceed as follows:

* First inflate the buoyancy compensator to ensure that you have some stability and to keep your head out of the water.

* Now identify the direction of the cover boat or the shore.

* Immediately give the boathandler the 'I am all right' hand signal, or the distress signal, if necessary. Wait and repeat until they respond.

* Either start swimming toward the exit point or wait until picked up by the boat.

* The dive leader will wind in any loose line on the SMB. Unless the sea state is calm and smooth, it is best to keep the mask and regulator in place until the boat arrives. Stay close together.

Give the 'I am all right' hand signal

It should be returned by the watchers on the cover boat

On the surface

A diver is in a vulnerable position between surfacing and leaving the water. The air supply is usually all but finished and he or she sits very low in the water due to the weight of the equipment.

This position leaves the diver open to the effect of 'wave slap', even in mildly choppy surface conditions. At best, it is a demoralizing situation, and one which can eventually lead to exhaustion.

When waiting to climb a ladder or board a boat, avoid wave slap by staying just under the surface in the calmer and more controlled conditions there. Do ensure, however, that your position there is safe.

Picking up divers

The cover boat will approach the divers on the surface from a down-wind direction.

Boats are more controllable when they are heading into the wind and this is especially true of inflatables which have high freeboards and keels so small that they are barely capable of gripping the water.

There are two techniques for picking up divers. If an instructor is taking a novice on one of his or her first few dives, both of them will stay close together and be picked up by the boat on the same side.

More experienced divers will move about 3 metres (10 ft) apart and the boat will gently nose in between

them, with the motor put out of gear to stop the propeller. Whichever technique is adopted, all divers must hold on to the boat's grab lines, called beckets, so as not to be swept away. Remember a boat will drift in the wind, whereas an almost totally submerged diver will drift only in the direction of the tidal stream and not the wind.

Leaving the water

Divers are still vulnerable to wave action even when out of the water, before they can move themselves and their heavy apparatus clear of the water's influence. It is all too easy to be smashed against a rock, bowled over by surf, or washed off a boat's ladder. Securing the diver with a spare rope will ensure that he or she is not lost or swept away. A rope can make lifting a diver over a high gunwhale much easier.

The power of waves must never be underestimated. Therefore, when landing on a beach, appraise the chosen point of exit from the water from some distance away, noting wave action and indications of a surface current. Never commit yourself to a landing until you are certain it is safe.

If landing on to a beach through surf, bide your time and follow in behind a smaller breaker, so as to be washed up in its after-surge.

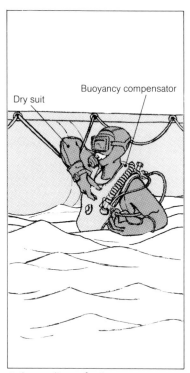

Release direct-feed systems

Pass up the weightbelt

Out of the water

Quickly pick yourself up, remove fins, and move well clear before the next breaker arrives. In locations where surf is commonly encountered, such in in California, these landings are taught and practised as part of the training sessions. Avoid heavy surf and rocky locations in anything but calm conditions.

When leaving deeper water, to clamber on to a boat or up jetty steps, for instance, it is often possible to remove the apparatus in the water and pass it up to those already out. In a swell this makes the final exit less encumbered, although often the removal of apparatus is best effected just below the surface where conditions are calmer. Adapt the action already practised in the shallow-water training sessions:

* Hold on to something, such as the boat's beckets, to avoid being swept away.

* Leave the mouthpiece in place.

* Release the direct-feed quick-fit connector to the BC.

* When in a dry suit, reach under the compensator and similarly release the direct-feed to the suit.

* Remove and pass up weightbelt.

* Slip out of the cylinder harness with the mouthpiece still in place. Remove it on the surface just prior to handing the apparatus upwards.

* Leave BC in position, although while you are finally pulling yourself out of the water it can prove a hindrance if inflated to any degree.

Every diver should know how to board the two types of boat that are commonly used in diving.

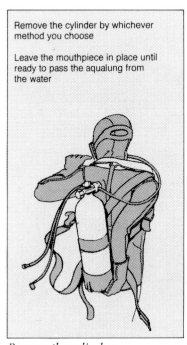
Remove the cylinder by whichever method you choose

Leave the mouthpiece in place until ready to pass the aqualung from the water

Remove the cylinder

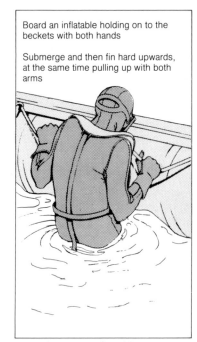
Board an inflatable holding on to the beckets with both hands

Submerge and then fin hard upwards, at the same time pulling up with both arms

Boarding an inflatable

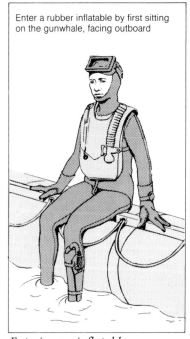
Enter a rubber inflatable by first sitting on the gunwhale, facing outboard

Entering an inflatable

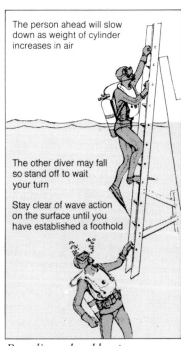
The person ahead will slow down as weight of cylinder increases in air

The other diver may fall so stand off to wait your turn

Stay clear of wave action on the surface until you have established a foothold

Boarding a hard boat

Boarding an inflatable boat

Rubber inflatable boats have a low freeboard and provide stable diving platforms which do not roll appreciably in a swell. To enter these boats, do the following:

* Grasp the boat's looped side rope (the beckets) with both hands, submerge briefly at arm's length, then pull and fin upwards to end up lying on the float.

* Having pulled yourself up on to the boat's side (which in the case of an inflatable will consist of an air tube) turn and sit facing outwards on it, then swing inwards. Do not enter directly over the tube head-first. Items of equipment can be caught in the beckets and it is diffi-

cult to bring the legs inboard, especially with fins on.

Boarding a 'hard' boat

Larger diving boats have high gunwhales requiring a ladder. Often these are so high it is impossible to pass the equipment up first and you must continue wearing it. Be careful on the ladder as such vessels are susceptible to rolling in a swell.

Approach the ladder and wait your turn to exit; either stay on the surface or, if the sea is choppy, hang on to the lowest rung of the ladder.

The person ahead will slow down as soon as they surface and have to take the full weight of their equipment, or as the boat rolls. Stay off to

one side until they are well clear, in case they should fall.

Establish a foothold on the lowest rung and grasp both sides of the ladder. Commit yourself to the surface only when your position is well established and you are ready.

It is a good rule to leave your fins on until well clear of the water. If you should fall or be washed back in, you would need them.

There is a fresh invigorating feeling associated with the first few breaths in the open air. Savour this briefly, then move on — in order to make room for those following behind and to take yourself well away from the wave action.

Post-dive actions

Although the novice will probably be feeling a sense of satisfied elation after such an exciting new experience, there are still some routine matters that must be attended to at the end of the dive.

* Check cylinder is turned off and the buoyancy-compensator emergency mini-cylinder tap is closed.

* Make sure the set is safely and securely stowed so that it cannot

roll about and there is no risk of damage to the regulator.

* Check all your equipment is together. If landing on a beach, assist with the boat.

Debriefing and records

The dive leader may want to debrief you on the conduct of the dive. A record must be kept of the maximum depth reached, the time spent underwater, as well as any 'out of the ordinary' or significant events which occurred.

This must be accomplished as soon as possible after leaving the water, for the mind has a habit of reviewing matters and forgetting or muddling detail. When working in a group it is usual for one person to be appointed as record keeper to keep a note of such information,

which wiil be necessary when calculating repeat-dive intervals and if decompression sickness occurs.

As trainees, the things that will remain in the mind are the faults made. Do not be ashamed of them: discuss the mistakes with your companion. Talk things over with a number of more experienced divers to obtain different viewpoints, and in this way you will be able to remedy matters next time.

Learn from your mistakes. Question others as to the circumstances

surrounding theirs. This analysis is an important part of the dive and vital to the learning process.

Make certain that your personal diving log is maintained and up to date.

Equipment maintenance

Wash all the equipment in fresh water as soon as possible, but do not allow any water to enter the first stage of the regulator. Dry and store the equipment.

If a fault is found, attend to it immediately or it may well be forgotten.

Emergency ascents and rescues

Introduction

There are many ways to effect rescues and while all of them may be successful, the rescuer will probably adopt the one remembered from training sessions. In an emergency the whole predicament is so critical that clearly this is no time for rescuers to consider the rival merits of this or that method. So much depends on the sea state and the weather, on the type of equipment worn and the skill of the rescuer, that it would be unrealistic to formulate a series of rules. Moreover, remember panic, fear and exhaustion also play their part. Only those divers who have experienced this can know what it is really like. Our hope is that the situations described here will be studied carefully, so that if and when such an emergency happens, the diver will remember these ideas and be able to respond to what is happening both automatically and competently.

A word of warning; remember, free and buoyant ascents are emergency procedures and expose the participants to some risk of lung damage and decompression sickness. Practising these drills in open water is not therefore recommended, unless under close supervision and with recompression facilities immediately available. However, assisted ascents can be safely practised if both divers are sufficiently trained and adequately supervised; and there are many aspects of rescuing that are safe to be taught in pools, such as familiarization with the operation of BCs, direct-feed and weightbelt release. (It is assumed divers will be wearing wet suits and the overhead type of buoyancy compensators. Most beginners will train and dive first in wet suits as their buoyancy is easy to manage.)

117

Emergency ascents and rescues

Because diving may be hazardous, the diver must constantly ask the question, 'If something went wrong now, could I deal with the situation?' A consistent 'yes' is either the mark of good technique or over-confidence, so be on your guard against the latter!

No matter how careful the diver is, emergencies can occur and usually the best course of action is a direct controlled ascent back to the surface. It is important to practise making some of these emergency ascents, but there are often unpredictable factors.

Here are some typical panic reactions which can impede a rescue attempt – be aware of them:

* There may be an overwhelming desire to start for the surface. With beginners this is known as a 'wild break', which can be brought under control only with a more competent companion's help and intervention. This inclination becomes less acute with experience.

* Forgetting the emergency procedures, divers of limited experience tend to tackle problems by the most direct means. A diver may start to fin upward, forgetting that he or she is wearing a buoyancy compensation device. Or, for instance, a diver who is wearing an 'octopus rig' (see also page 124), may forget that there is a spare regulator and instead offer his own mouthpiece to a companion for air sharing !

* There is always the danger of becoming overwhelmed by stress due to the situation, or from the physical effort required to maintain a finned ascent. Rescuers are as vulnerable as victims. There may also be after-effects on the surface.

The overall success of the ascent may depend on two things:

* Having clear water overhead. Inside a wreck or a cave some horizontal movement is necessary before a vertical ascent can be tackled. Ropes, lines and the hulls of vessels may pose similar problems.

* Whether or not decompression stops are necessary.

Although most situations will be straightforward, the distance back to the surface matters a great deal. There are two basic divisions:

* The shallows: from the surface down to a maximum depth of 10 metres (33 ft).

* Deep water: from 10 metres (33 ft) down to 40 metres (130 ft) or more.

Here we shall concentrate on techniques for self-rescue, but later in this section we shall also discuss the problems of rescuing a companion who has become incapacitated or unconscious.

If the diver makes an extra fast ascent or fails to control an emergency ascent in mid-water, this can increase the chance of a traumatic arrival on the surface and also adds to the risk of possible lung damage (see page 81).

Methods of self-rescue

Diving alone without a lifeline, or becoming separated from a companion during a dive exposes the diver to risk so there is a very strong case for proficiency in self-rescue. Emergency ascent techniques will involve buoyancy use and control as well as the need to obtain a sufficient air supply. It is impossible to fully anticipate what complications may arise, so some flexibility of approach is required. Here are two basic self-rescue methods:

Starting an ascent
Before doing anything, the diver must regain composure after the

shock of realizing that this is an emergency. Having re-established control, the first thing to do is to try and assess the situation properly.

Act early, as soon as the problem is recognized. (Do not forget to signal your intention to your partner.) The action of moving up will in fact provide some measure of relief in the diver's mind – once the initial shock has worn off ! Wait around, and you will find that the situation may all too easily deteriorate.

This can be called a 'near-normal' emergency ascent.

Dropping the weightbelt
In a normal ascent, the weightbelt will be essential to control the rate of ascent to the surface.

However, dropping the weightbelt is an acceptable way to help an emergency ascent when close to the surface, as it tips buoyancy in favour of the victim.

Deeper down, diving-suit buoyancy becomes more negative and dropping the belt has less immediate effect. By about 40 metres (130 ft) or so, it will be hardly any use at all (see also page 58).

Advanced divers should ditch the weightbelt only when they feel this will help turn an emergency more to their advantage – the weightbelt will ensure a stable and safe face-up, legs-down attitude when the diver arrives on the surface.

However, trainees should be taught not to hesitate to ditch it when they are alone and need some extra buoyancy in an emergency. It is surprising, but the records show that in most diving fatalities, the victim did not drop the weightbelt.

Having made the decision to ditch, hold on to one side of the belt, undo the quick-release and lift it well clear of the body before letting go. Do not stop to reconsider; it is better to over-react than to let the situation deteriorate.

Ascents from depth

Compensation devices have often been referred to as 'underwater parachutes' but it is unwise to rely on them as a solution to all ascent problems. It is worth considering the following situations:

* An emergency might occur just after the diver has vented the air buoyancy and is descending with considerable momentum.

* Part of dealing with an emergency may involve venting air buoyancy, prior to starting an ascent.

* Divers caught in a strong current or tide race, may find themselves swept horizontally, not upwards, if the compensator is inflated.

* When the compensator is inflated from a static position, there is a time

lag before its buoyancy has any effect. Also, on occasions when a diver is carrying a heavy weight at depth, the compensator seems to have no effect at all. Both of these can prove to be rather alarming experiences.

* Worst of all, there may be no air available with which to inflate the compensator!

Negative buoyancy

If a buoyancy compensator is not available, or cannot be inflated, the victim must fin up to a point where at least his (or her) diving-suit buoyancy starts to be regained. Whatever the depth, such ascents will always require considerable sustained effort.

Deeper down, at 30 to 40 metres (100-130 ft), negative buoyancy due to suit compression might be acceptable – until something goes wrong. Then, even dropping the weightbelt has little or no immediate effect.

It takes a very fit person to fin up under these circumstances. Extra effort is required well into the mid-water phase of the ascent, until suit buoyancy partly returns. Practice sessions show these difficulties to be increased when rescuing a companion, with the ascent coming to a

complete stop unless the rescuer can maintain a very strong impetus.

The rules for deeper dives, with emergencies in mind, are simple, but often ignored:

* Use a good buoyancy trim which requires a minimal compensation at depth. Remember that you will need to use slightly less lead weighting on deeper dives.

* Do not pick up heavy objects on the bottom and try to bring them up. As little as 2 kilograms (4 lbs) can swing the balance and make an ascent very difficult. We have seen divers who start to sink again in mid-water without realizing it.

* If you are going to lift heavy objects, use a spare BC or lifting bag, or better still, attach a rope to the object and have it pulled up.

* If one is available, use a shot line, or stay near to the anchor cable; so it is possible to pull yourself up. Cliff faces can also be used.

* Just after reaching depth, when the cylinders are still heavy with air, the diver will be at the most negatively buoyant stage of the dive and therefore particularly susceptible in an emergency.

* Stay fit; this is the only way to be able to tackle heavy finning.

Ideally, aim to be neutrally buoyant. Otherwise, if neutral at the surface, the extra weight at depth (due to loss of wet-suit buoyancy) may be more than you can lift.

Remember that when you are in deeper water many suits will lose their insulation properties because they are compressed.

Emergency ascents

Buoyant ascents

Given clear water above, sufficient buoyancy ensures that a diver will rise to the surface from any depth. Buoyant ascents are the standard way to tackle an emergency, particularly from depth, but they will always be faster than normal. Therefore practice must take place under controlled conditions from a maximum of 20 metres (65 ft) and should always terminate at about 10 metres (33 ft).

There are three essential elements to such ascents, although the exact procedure used will need to be varied in order to suit different kinds of equipment:

Initiating the ascent

To help the diver leave the bottom in a hurry, air can be added to the buoyancy compensator to effect a prompt 'lift-off'. This can either be done quickly from the compensator's emergency air cylinder, or more slowly using the direct-feed system. At the same time, the venting device must be ready to hand.

It is important to remember these following points:

* The diver should know by experience when enough air volume has been added to tip the buoyancy to positive. When at depth, the diver may well find that the bag must be almost filled before any effect will be noticed.

* The diver does not ascend immediately — there is a definite time-lag of several seconds before the buoyancy takes effect. Help things along by pushing off from the bottom. The time-lag is minimized by a good weighting procedure (the addition of the minimum amount of air).

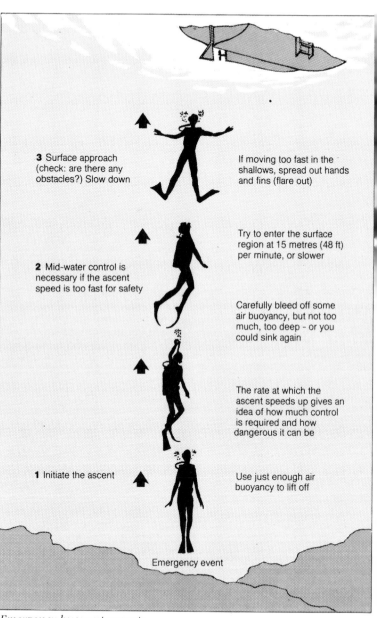

3 Surface approach (check: are there any obstacles?) Slow down

If moving too fast in the shallows, spread out hands and fins (flare out)

Try to enter the surface region at 15 metres (48 ft) per minute, or slower

2 Mid-water control is necessary if the ascent speed is too fast for safety

Carefully bleed off some air buoyancy, but not too much, too deep - or you could sink again

The rate at which the ascent speeds up gives an idea of how much control is required and how dangerous it can be

1 Initiate the ascent

Use just enough air buoyancy to lift off

Emergency event

Emergency buoyant ascents

* In an emergency the tendency is to keep on adding air until the ascent is forcibly started. Circumstances permitting, a better method is to add just enough air to initiate the lift-off. The time-lag will be only marginally longer and the ascent much more controllable.

Mid-water control

Once clear of the bottom, the ascent soon speeds up. Hopefully the diver will sense when the ascent needs to be brought under control and how much air must be vented to slow things down. Do not use the venting device too soon if rising from depth. It is easy to vent too much air too fast, which will retard upward motion and make the diver sink again. The knack of knowing when to vent and just how much air to lose comes with practice.

For safety's sake, these practice sessions must be carefully supervised by the instructor. Develop a feel for your buoyancy and ascent speeds during normal dives and practice sessions; this is the only way to appreciate what might be involved in an emergency. Watch your rate of ascent, using your small exhaust bubbles as a gauge of the speed; keep an eye on your depth gauge, and learn how to slow down.

Approaching the surface

Divers are very aware of the surface approaching: there is more light around and their bubbles start expanding furiously. Even when the air may be totally vented, the upward exhaust-bubble stream will often help to maintain the victim's momentum. To allow expanding air in the lungs to escape, the diver must keep the head back and consciously blow out. Divers must be aware that they are most susceptible to lung damage due to breath holding when approaching the surface. If the speed is excessive, it is possible to spread out the hands and fins as a brake. Or, if the buoyancy device is only partly inflated at this stage, lean right back and present a large chest area to the water, parallel to the surface. An amusing variation, recounted by a submariner, was to open the top of the swimming trunks and use them as a drogue while practising in a tank!

Trying this in the open sea with the trousers of a wet suit could be a very cold undertaking!

Extend one hand above the head, as the exhaust bubbles may obscure the vision. The head may even disappear inside one large bubble!

Divers' free ascent

The normal diving procedure is always to keep some air in reserve as a contingency. However, an emergency ascent back to the surface may become necessary should a diver find that he or she has no air available from any source. There are two main occasions when such an ascent might be required:

1 When the air supply abruptly runs out due to bad management; everyone may be guilty of this at one time or another.

2 If there is regulator malfunction. This may be depth-related, sometimes rectifying itself in shallower waters during the ascent.

If a companion can move in very quickly, a shared ascent may be started (see page 124). However, if for any reason the diver is alone, the only option is to perform what is called a free ascent back to the surface. On the way up the diver makes use of whatever residual air remains in the lungs. As the air expands there will be more than enough available for his requirements, though this must be constantly exhaled. If the diver holds his breath, lung damage will result. Obviously this technique is potentially dangerous, and must only be attempted when there is no other option available. Anxiety is an added problem. The realization that there is no air to breathe can be rather frightening.

The drill for any attempted free ascent is as follows:

* Keep the mouthpiece in place at all times; this at least prevents the diver from inhaling water! Moreover, the apparently empty cylinder may still yield one or two extra breaths in the shallows as the pressure decreases and the air expands. The mouthpiece holds the mouth open; do not consciously block it with the tongue.

* Attempt to follow the normal inhalation and exhalation breathing cycle – in and out. This is the best way of avoiding lung damage from internal overpressure.

Put the head back, look up and keep the airways as open as possible. You must exhale the expanding air consciously so hold nothing back. Maintain a steady controlled rate of ascent, as near to 15 metres (50 ft) per minute as the circumstances will allow.

The only safe way to practise the points covered above is during the course of making normal open-water ascents. In these circumstances you will have plenty of air but try to imagine what it would be like if no air was available !

Partial free ascent

Those who have made a free ascent all the way to the surface will agree that it is an alarming experience. Because there is almost certain to be some fear, even panic, it will not be the best moment to decide what action to take. The success of a free ascent will therefore depend on the diver performing all the right procedures automatically. This book has already included warnings of the dangers of practising such drills, so in the end the diver's survival will depend on his acquaintance with each type of ascent procedure.

The number of people who have experienced a completely free ascent are perhaps less than those who, in the event, make a partial free ascent. This is because it is quite a common occurrence for a diver carrying out a free ascent to obtain air from one source or another while on the way up. For instance, in the middle of a free ascent, a faulty regulator may well start to function again as the pressure decreases in the shallows. The diver will be able to bring the situation under control and continue normally to the surface.

Also, hopefully, other divers may be able to intercept and help the victim in mid-water.

Breathing from a buoyancy compensator

In northern Europe, buoyancy compensators are usually fitted with a mouthpiece which not only makes oral inflation possible, but also allows air inside the bag to be breathed. Exhaled air passes into the surrounding water via a one-way valve. Practising the technique of breathing from the buoyancy compensator will train the diver to be able to use this as a last resort in an air-failure emergency. The diver has to be able to add just enough air into the bag to satisfy one or two breaths without upsetting his buoyancy. To breathe air by this method demands careful training and considerable coolness. The average diver will, under stress in an emergency situation, probably be quite incapable of performing such a complicated manoeuvre.

This method should be used only if no other air supply is available. (A word of warning: some life-jackets use CO_2 cylinders for their emergency inflation. On no account must breathing from such cylinders be attempted.) Here are two examples of real situations when breathing from the buoyancy compensator has been successfully applied:

A controlled buoyant ascent
A diver who was well trained in this technique made such an ascent under full control from 46 metres (140 ft), breathing from his buoyancy compensator bag after his regulator had started to deliver water. During a decompression stop, he found the regulator fault had almost rectified itself and he could tolerate the small amount of water in the air it delivered. His other option would have been a free ascent. But how would he have managed the decompression stop?

Draining the mouthpiece

His companion, who had taken no active part in this crisis, was afterwards heard to query what all the fuss had been about!

Horizontal movement
Diving off the coast of North Africa, a diver disturbed the silt on a cave floor. This silt promptly welled up and reduced visibility to zero. The diver did not have a distance line and when he tried to return the way he had come, his air supply ran out. He had to breathe from his buoyancy compensator until rescued.

Breathing from the bag

Helping a companion

Introduction

With the 'buddy' system of diving, there is an obligation on each diver to look after his (or her) companion, in case assistance is required. So always note how your companion puts on the equipment, and check the venting (dump) valve positions, inflation-tube locations, the position and type of weightbelt release, and over which shoulder the regulator hose passes. Query arrangements you do not understand. If something goes wrong and your companion is unable to help or co-operate, you will at least be able to cope with the diving gear.

Ensure your companion knows all about your equipment too; you may be the one who requires assistance!

These are the pre-dive requisites. The key to handling such problems is to have an awareness of your companion's diving state by regular observation. If something happens, you will then have a good idea of what has gone wrong and, through your training, should know how to handle matters.

Of course, the victim may not be another diver. He could be an ordinary swimmer or someone who has fallen overboard, and who will not therefore be wearing a buoyancy compensator. If the victim has sunk to the bottom, the rescuer will first have the difficult task of locating him. Unless the accident has occurred very recently, the rescue will probably be instead the recovery of a body. As the body will have no

buoyancy, the rescuer will have to make a buoyant ascent for an unconscious victim (as described on page 125).

The practicalities of being able to help a companion are influenced by four factors:

1 Whether the victim is conscious or unconscious.

2 The victim's buoyancy state, and whether or not this is favourable.

3 The depth.

4 Complications of the incident.

All of these are important, but it is the first point that will be the prime consideration.

A conscious victim

This is the most likely rescue a diver may be called upon to perform; it can also be one of the most hazardous. Unless a conscious victim is co-operative he or she can create a progressively complicated situation through panic.

There are two basic techniques for dealing with the more straightforward problems.

1 The helping hand
When you notice that something is amiss with a companion, move into the victim's visual field and swim towards him or her. When the person in trouble sees that you are there and that you are closing in, this often helps resolve some of the difficulties. Once you are alongside, a hand on the arm will help to restore your companion's confidence, and this is also the first stage in an assisted ascent.

Move into line of sight

Experienced divers always watch beginners who are having even the most minor problems to see if the situation deteriorates. There are two classic signs which indicate that the beginner is about to start up to the surface. The first sign is when his movements begin to slow down. The second is when his physical attitude changes and he appears to direct himself upwards.

The alert dive leader will step in at this moment and take charge. If the experienced diver swims towards the beginner on an upward angle, the chances are that the two divers will meet soon after they leave the bottom and some control may be retained. If the attempt at interception is left too late, it will merely result in the two divers disappearing from each other's view.

If the victim starts to make an ascent meet him in mid-water

Rescue ascents

2 Assisted ascents

At some time or another a diver may be faced with a companion who has run out of air, or had a regulator malfunction. For the victim, there are two possible courses – to move towards a companion and share his or her air; or if the divers are too far away from each other, the victim will have to start upwards independently. An assisted ascent can take place if the divers do manage to come together.

The technique to employ should have been learnt in early training. It starts with the rescuer taking the initiative; the victim must not be allowed to take control for obvious reasons. Actions must be well ordered and precise. Proceed as described here:

* Approach the victim and, on contact, angle yourself to one side so that your fins will not clash.

* Catch hold of the victim's harness or equipment immediately. At this moment it may be difficult to appreciate the full circumstances of the situation and, if contact is lost, the victim may drift off and sink, so do not let go. Moreover a tight secure hold will transmit confidence to the victim, thereby assuring him or her

Positioning for air sharing

that you have the situation fully under control.

Probably the safest assisted ascent is when the rescuer is equipped with an octopus rig (as shown below). The rescuer passes one of his two mouthpieces – whichever is immediately to hand, to the victim who will have dropped his own mouthpiece. He should be allowed time to recover his equilibrium before an ascent begins.

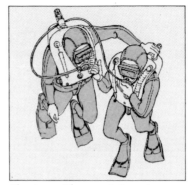

Sharing with an octopus rig

If the rescuer is not wearing an octopus rig and only one mouthpiece is being shared, try to establish a combined breathing cycle. (This is when past practice helps!) Usually this breathing pattern is comprised of two breaths each, out-in, out-in, then pass. Notice that, on receiving the mouthpiece, it is essential to exhale in order to clear the mouthpiece of water. The rescuer takes a breath from his or her own mouthpiece, and then passes it across to the victim who will remove his own. The rescuer always retains a hold on the mouthpiece when the victim is breathing from it, so as to remain in control of the air supply. As to whether the rescuer should purge the mouthpiece on presenting it to the victim's mouth – if purging is necessary, it is probably better to

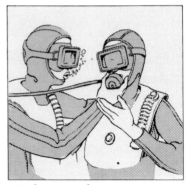

Air-sharing technique

leave the victim to do this for himself whenever possible. However, if the victim is in an uncontrolled distressed state it may be advisable for the rescuer to purge the valve. But this should be done only until a calmer state has been restored and the victim is once again able to control his own breathing.

Do not delay! Once a breathing rhythm has been stabilized and the victim's confidence has returned, start finning upwards. If the buoyancy is unfavourable, use the buoyancy compensator. Once the divers are off the bottom and moving, assess the combined buoyancy and try to slow the ascent rate down to about half the normal rate – to about 7 metres (23 ft) per minute. Watch the depth gauge and the small bubbles. Breathe in and out quite normally when you have the mouthpiece. When the victim has the mouthpiece (if ascending), the rescuer should blow air out slowly; look on it as a lengthy exhalation. This is important in order to avoid lung damage as the outside pressure decreases. Judge matters so that there is a little air in reserve by the time the mouthpiece is returned. Be wary – the victim may try to keep the mouthpiece longer than two breaths.

Whilst the rescuer has the mouth-piece, the victim will have to be discouraged from breath-holding (see page 80). A push on the diaphragm area is usually enough to control this so do not punch his stomach. It is not necessary to do anything this violent !

A frontal approach is the best because it enables you to keep the victim's eyes in view, so that you can be ready for any unexpected move that he or she might make.

Always try to keep the diver slightly above you, never lower. Be careful you do not release your hold on the regulator or the victim's harness.

Past experience has shown that the worst cases to deal with are those that occur when the rescuer has to approach a victim when he is in mid-water. The diver in trouble will be well into a full emergency ascent and so offering the mouthpiece to him will be little more than a gesture of assistance.

If the victim does take the mouth-piece, do not expect to have it returned for a little while, and resign yourself to doing a partial free ascent, maybe receiving only a breath now and then. Providing you keep control and remember your training, this will work. Realize that it is one thing to practise air sharing in shallow and controlled condi-tions, but quite another to deal with an emergency at depth. Be patient and considerate to a victim short of air; it is a most unnerving situation.

Unconscious victim

Sometimes an accident victim may become unconscious, so that a res-cuer has the task of raising an inert body back to the surface. The victim could pass out on the bottom or during the ascent or, most likely, soon after surfacing.

Rescues from the bottom
Every diver must be competent in a variety of techniques as no rescue is going to be straightforward. Two or more techniques may have to be welded together to suit the circum-stances of an accident. However, you should always use the same initial approach.

If you find the apparently lifeless body of a diver, do not assume he or she has already drowned. Immedi-ate action is required. Swim toward the victim and start appraising the situation, so that you can swing into the best rescue sequence as soon as possible. Decide quickly on the order of priorities for dealing with the problems concerned.

1 Air to breathe
First, it is essential to ensure that there is air to breathe; without it the victim will drown for sure.

Rescuer finding a body

Rescue ascents

Now check the following:

* Is victim unconscious?

* Is the victim breathing? Look for exhaust bubbles. The diver may still be semi-conscious.

* Is the victim's mouthpiece in or out? If mouthpiece is out, it must be purged and replaced.

As soon as you reach the victim, use the regulator purge button to feed him with some air. Hold the mouthpiece in place whenever practical.

2 Secondary problems
Move the victim into open water. If entangled, he or she must be freed. It may be necessary to cut the victim loose from a rope, net or kelp.

3 Buoyancy for an ascent
All methods of lifting a victim back to the surface are dependent on available buoyancy.

Does the buoyancy look favourable? If victim is lying on the bottom appraise his or her attitude. An unconscious diver could be found partly floating.

Is the victim wearing a buoyancy compensator or some other buoyancy aid? Is it the direct-feed type and is it connected? Note location of emergency inflation cylinder.

All lifts back to the surface become much more difficult with increasing depth, though in rescue terms it is impossible to place a clear demarcation between shallow and deep water. Practise and develop different techniques and remember to have alternatives available (if only held in reserve) as the situation can deteriorate further.

Deadweight lifts

If neither victim nor rescuer are wearing a BC or there is no air available to fill it, the rescuer must fin a deadweight back to the surface. This will involve great effort and even a fit rescuer will begin to tire in mid-water. Therefore it is a hazardous rescue attempt from great depths. On first reaching the victim:

* Replace his mouthpiece and/or feed the victim some air.

* Buoyancy must be made favourable, so slip the victim's weightbelt. Slip your own if this is the only way to start the ascent; otherwise drop it in mid-water, but only if you do not appear to be ascending.

* Square yourself on the bottom. Take firm hold of the victim's equipment so that the unconscious diver can be lifted up and above you in one continuous action.

* Retain your hold on the victim and use the bottom to kick off. The victim now has upward momentum of which you must try to take advantage. See if you can manage one or

two good full fin strokes now, to continue the lift, as you will have to take the full weight of the victim once the initial momentum lessens.

* Try to keep the victim's head back and face up during the ascent in order to keep his airways clear.

* You may or may not have been able to hold the victim's mouthpiece in place during the initial flurry of action. If, once off the bottom, the ascent seems to be starting, angle yourself behind and to one side of the victim (the side that the regulator hose passes over his

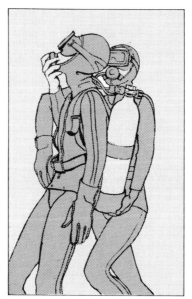

Making a deadweight lift without any buoyancy aids

shoulder). Do this before taking the victim's weight.

* One hand goes under the victim's armpit to hold the mouthpiece in place, while the rescuer's arm supports the body's weight. The other hand goes under the victim's cylinder, supporting its bottom or taking hold of adjacent harnessing so that it will be possible to complete a two-point lift.

* Use full measured fin strokes. Should the other diver become a deadweight, you will be effecting the lift from slightly above and the victim's body will interfere with your fin movement. This has to be ignored. Such a rescue will work if you are fit and well practised.

If the victim's buoyancy is positive, the trick is to keep him or her slightly above and over you, so that the centre lines of both your bodies are as close together as possible.

Buoyancy rescues

If a buoyancy compensator is available, use it to help lift the victim. Although this section will deal with only one type of buoyancy aid, obviously the techniques described can be adapted to suit any other.

It is preferable that, of the two divers, the victim be the one made buoyant. This ensures that the diver who is in difficulties will continue to rise should contact be lost.

Meanwhile, the rescuer should keep his or her own buoyancy compensator deflated and make sure that its emergency air supply is intact against any further eventualities.

Very shallow rescues
If the rescue takes place in shallow water, from 2 to 4 metres (6-13 ft) maximum, and in favourable conditions, move the victim quickly back to the surface, as follows:

* Replace the victim's mouthpiece and/or feed the victim some air.

* Inflate the victim's BC, using the emergency cylinder. Two hands may be required to gain a purchase on the tap.

* It saves time if you do not fully inflate the BC. Shut the tap as soon as you sense that buoyancy has been regained. Now act quickly.

* Square yourself on the bottom. Grasp the yoke on the victim's BC, and use it to pull him up and above you in one continuous movement.

* Use the bottom to push off and follow. The ascent is now under way and the surface should be gained after a few fin strokes. Continue to hold the victim's mouthpiece in position and his head back.

Shallow rescues
When the rescue is initiated in slightly deeper water, from 4 to 9 metres (13-30 ft) a buoyant ascent may noticeably speed up as it approaches the surface. This is due to the expansion of air trapped in the BC and diving suit.

In this situation, it is entirely possible for the ascent to speed up uncontrollably, or for a rescuer to over-vent the victim's compensator on nearing the surface and so lose both buoyancy and the upward momentum. Therefore, for rescues from deeper water, more time must be taken to ensure you have complete control before attempting to leave the bottom.

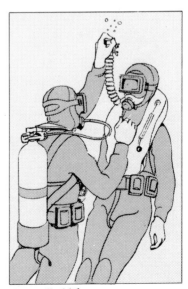

Establishing buoyancy   *Controlled lift*

Alternative rescues

Add more air than before to the BC, so the victim's buoyancy becomes noticeably more positive. Use the time while this added buoyancy takes effect to check the BC's venting device is freely available.

Face the victim and lift him up, using the bottom to gain momentum and start the ascent. Slip one arm up and under the BC so that the hand projects from the yoke and can hold the mouthpiece in position. This keeps both parties close together and allows the other hand to be used for operating the venting device on the BC, for adding more air to the BC from the direct feed or the emergency cylinder and, finally, for taking hold of harnessing to apply a deadweight lift, should this become necessary.

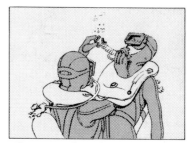

Alternative front buoyant lift

Deep rescues

If the victim is considered to be truly negative, particularly at the beginning of a dive when the cylinders are still full of air, the BC will have to be fully inflated to start a rescue ascent. Due to the full inflation of the BC, ascents from depth will be faster than normal; that is faster than 15 metres (48 ft) per minute — and therefore difficult to control.

Try to save energy and mentally stabilize yourself for the problems of the ascent proper. It takes time — about five seconds — for the BC to inflate and the victim's buoyancy to swing towards positive so an ascent can start. Put this time to good use. Make certain that both the victim's and your own BC venting devices are freely available. Shut off the victim's BC inflation tap once he or she has started to lift. Take a firm grip on the victim.

During the ascent the victim is buoyant, the rescuer is not. Unless they stay very close together from the beginning, this difference in buoyancy will pull them apart. If separation occurs, usually near the surface, it should be possible to still hang on to both of the victim's shoulder harness straps. Sometimes the ensuing turning movement may cause the victim to arch overhead and actually slow down the ascent as a large body area is presented to the water.

One of the knacks that can be gained only through practice, is knowing how much air to vent from a victim's BC, and when. This is not easy, as the ascent must neither speed up uncontrollably nor slow down to the extent that it loses upward momentum.

Victim has buoyancy

Once the victim is moving up, pull him very close to you and lean across to place one arm firmly between his cylinder and his back. The other hand can be placed over his shoulder and both divers will be pulled closer together. Once off the bottom, wrap both legs around one or both of the victim's legs. The intention is to use the victim's buoyancy and ride 'piggy-back' upward. You will need to hold the harnessing securely, keep the mouthpiece in place, and vent, or add air to, the BC. Try to keep both body centre lines close together.

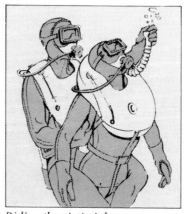

Riding the victim's buoyancy

Venting a dry suit

Victim has no buoyancy

Here the rescuer must provide the buoyancy and use it to lift a dead-weight. In practice, the physical strain of holding on to an unconscious diver is enormous. Such rescues are very difficult — but not impossible.

Slip off the victim's weightbelt. If at depth, he or she will still stay on the bottom. Pull the victim up off the bottom and jockey him around so that your knee slips up between his cylinder and back. Inflate your BC and just as you feel you are lifting from the bottom, close the inflation tap. Now you must act quickly.

Reach over between his cylinder and neck, so that your hand holds his harnessing under his armpit. Pull both bodies close together. Hang on tightly while the lift gets

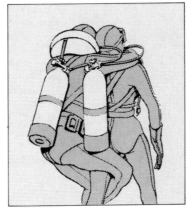

Lifting a non-buoyant victim

underway. Once off the bottom, wrap both legs around the victim's body; just one leg will do if this is all that can be managed. You must both ascend as one. Releasing one hand to vent the BC during ascent

(without being pulled apart from the victim) is quite tricky. However, provided that such venting can be achieved, matters become much easier towards the surface when the diving-suit buoyancy returns.

Such rescues are very much a matter of hanging on as tightly as possible. This is not easy for the rescuer because, as the compensator bag fills with air, the rescuer's head all but disappears inside it and he or she is forced chin up.

If separation does occur, the victim will sink and the rescuer will continue soaring upwards.

The reason why rescuers should retain their weight-belts is so that they can make a second descent if this proves necessary.

Descent to a rescue

It could be that the diver must descend prior to lifting the victim back to the surface. There have been cases, for instance, when a victim passed out on arrival at the surface and sank out of sight.

Rescues in such circumstances must be adapted from the techniques already suggested, though they will have added difficulties.

In mid-water the victim's downward momentum must be arrested before a lift can be attempted.

Should a victim sink unnoticed, he or she must be located. Hopefully the victim will still be within a well-defined area, provided that there is no current. With luck, a few tell-tale bubbles, or perhaps the diver's marker buoy, will pin-point the

exact location even when the water is not very clear.

To have to descend to a victim, knowing a rescue is necessary but not yet knowing all its difficulties, puts the rescuer at a psychological disadvantage.

The rescue will seem far better once you know you are rising.

Rescues wearing a dry suit

If the victim is wearing a dry suit, it will be necessary to adapt the rescue techniques already described.

Up till now it has been assumed that both divers will be wearing wet suits, as these are commonly used

by beginners and have easily controlled buoyancy characteristics.

However, as their buoyancy is difficult to control underwater, dry suits can themselves be the cause of problems requiring a rescue.

Weighting

If the diver is badly weighted, under adverse conditions there can be an excessive swing towards negative at depth, particularly with the membrane type of dry suit. The tendency then is to introduce an excess of air

129

Completing the rescue

into the suit to compensate for this. To keep the ascent speed under control, air must be ditched as it expands on the way to the surface. Ditch too little too late and the diver may continue soaring upwards. Ditch too much too early in the ascent and the diver may become negative again and sink, even if he or she has dropped the weightbelt. Good weighting leads to minimal suit compensation and venting on the ascent, and allows normal rescue methods to be used.

Buoyancy compensators
These should always be worn with a dry suit as they offer a separate source of controllable buoyancy. They are useful because if a suit is ripped or a zip accidently bursts open, the suit will lose most (if not all) of its internal buoyancy. This is particularly true of the membrane type of suit. To avoid the problem of having to control two volumes of air — one in the suit, the other in the BC, it is recommended that air is put in to one only. This will most likely be the dry suit, as it will already have some air in it to avoid suit squeeze.

If for some reason the BC cannot be inflated, then enough buoyancy to initiate an ascent should be sought by inflating the dry suit. A dry suit has the same air inflation and venting facilities as the BC so, with practice, it is possible to use one for a controlled buoyancy ascent.

Even a ripped suit may trap enough air to help an ascent.

On the surface

Even after a traumatic arrival on the surface, both the victim and rescuer are usually still far from safety. The shore or the covering boat may be a long way off. The course of action will be as follows:

1 Immediately inflate both BCs to act as life-jackets and keep heads clear of the water. This inflation may have to be done orally if all the available air has been used up during the ascent. It is possible, even at this stage, for one of the divers to pass out, so hold on to each other and do not drift apart. If they are still being worn, do not drop either weighbelt.

Always use the BC, as it is designed to put lift on the upper chest so that a victim who is wearing a weightbelt adopts the correct attitude with the head well out of the water. If the dry suit is inflated instead of the BC, air gathers in the shoulders but is free to move around inside the suit. Although the victim will still be in a vertical position, he or she will lie very low in the water with the head encompassed by the inflated suit.

2 Draw attention by shouting and using the 'Come and get me' signal.

Inflate buoyancy compensator

3 The next action is to remove the victim's mask and mouthpiece. The victim will have retained the mouth-

Signal 'Come and get me !'

piece during the ascent to prevent the inhalation of water, but now it will no longer be required. If the rescuer tilts the victim's head back to clear the natural airways, with luck this will be sufficient to restart breathing if this has stopped.

4 This will be the first opportunity the rescuer will have to make a more thorough assessment of the victim's condition and he should now check the following:

* Is the victim conscious and able to assist, or unconscious?

* Is the victim breathing or not?

The rescuer will have formed some idea of the state of the victim during the ascent. It should now be possible to confirm whether a conscious victim is helpless because of some other accident, such as a flooded dry suit, or perhaps because of a physical disorder such as decompression sickness. As long as the victim is breathing, all the rescuer can do is to keep the other diver's head clear of the water and support him or her until help arrives.

If the victim is unconscious, the rescuer must suspect there has been a cardiac arrest (which is the sudden unexpected cessation of the circulation). Unconsciousness could be due to at least fifteen causes, but this is not the time or place to start trying to make a specific diagnosis. Unfortunately the victim's diving suit, hood and gloves will prevent the obtaining of a pulse – the sign that the heart is still beating. To make matters worse, there will be no possibility of giving the necessary treatment for a cardiac arrest, external cardiac compression (or ECC), whilst still in the water.

If there is no circulation, the ventilation of the lungs by expired air resuscitation (EAR) will be of little use. The air breathed into the victim's lungs will simply stay there instead of carrying the vital oxygen to the tissues. However, drowning victims usually suffer from respiratory arrest before cardiac arrest (which is quite opposite to what happens in most other kinds of death). In many immersion victims, the heart will continue to beat although the breathing may have stopped, making ECC unnecessary. Giving expired air resuscitation (EAR) to an unconscious victim as soon as possible is of prime importance even whilst still in the water.

This prompt action of giving EAR may just be sufficient to sustain the victim in the brief interval between a respiratory arrest and a subsequent cardiac arrest. To be frank, there are no other alternatives. So, this means that the immediate treatment for an unconscious victim who is not breathing is always EAR.

5 To give EAR effectively, the victim's mouth and throat must first be cleared of any obstacles. Most drowning victims vomit and there has been at least one case where the victim's dental plate lodged in his throat. Drowning victims will often

EAR in water

clench their teeth, so be prepared to force the mouth open.

It is essential that EAR is commenced at once. If the brain is deprived of oxygen for any more than thirty seconds, unconsciousness will result. A total deprivation (called 'anoxia') for more than three minutes may result in brain damage and possibly in death.

In the anxiety of a real emergency it is not difficult to overlook the most obvious things. A heaving chest and the usual sounds of the breath moving in and out are not easy to detect against the noise of the wind and waves, especially with the the rescuer's own laboured breathing. Divers may try to give EAR to a victim who is still breathing for no other reason than that they were taught to do so in training.

The technique is shown stage by stage on page 135. All divers should be proficient in cardiopulmonary resuscitation (called 'CPR'), and it is a good idea for even the more experienced divers to practise the drills at least once a year.

To save but a single life would compensate for the extra effort.

Decide quickly in which direction safety lies, and start towing the victim towards safety, either to a boat or to the shore. Stop only to give one cycle of EAR about every half-minute or so.

6 Make an appraisal of the effects of wind and current. Are you drifting? If so, in which direction? Do not attempt to swim against wind or tide. If it is necessary to move at all, swim across the current.

Once legs are raised victim moves easily
Use your momentum to jerk victim into a towing position and initiate movement

Towing a victim to safety

7 The decision of whether to retain or to remove masks and mouthpieces depends on the sea state and whether there is still air in the cylinder. With a co-operative conscious victim in relatively calm sea, both might be removed. In a choppy sea there is the discomfort of 'wave slap' in which case the victim's mask only should be removed.

With an unconscious diver (as has already been said) both his mask and mouthpiece must be removed to facilitate breathing and to allow the rescuer to give EAR. The rescuer should always retain both if he still has air available, in order to deal with any difficulties — such as a struggling or unmanageable victim. If the rescuer's air supply has finished, a snorkel should be used.

8 There is also the question of whether or not to ditch the breathing sets. If the condition of the victim looks at all unstable, it will be best to ditch his or her set. As to

whether or not rescuers should retain their own sets — this will depend largely on two factors:

* Will the tow be lengthy?

* Will the air supply be sufficient to last the journey?

If the answer to the first question is yes and to the second is no, then rescuers would be advised to jettison their breathing sets, as they are an encumbrance and will make the rescue more difficult and tiring.

9 Attract attention by whatever means are available — whistle, flares, arm signals or even just shouting. A shout carries well over water when there is little wind. Normally the cover boat will be quite nearby because it has been following the surface marker buoy. When using a large boat, it is good practice to post a look-out whose responsibility will be to watch out for the surfacing divers.

10 One form of surface rescue not yet mentioned is that of an aqualung diver by a breath-hold diver. Some diving groups always have a fully-kitted stand-by ready to go to the assistance of a diver who might surface in distress. A breath-hold diver in basic equipment and who is wearing a BC is probably better able to effect a surface rescue than a fully-kitted aqualung diver. The breath-hold diver will reach a victim faster on the surface and, without any encumbrances, will be better able to handle the other diver.

11 Finally, do remember that life-saving is very demanding, both physically and emotionally. Rescuers will have to watch out that they don't become victims themselves through over-exertion. They will have so many things to do that they may find themselves acting automatically without time to think. For this reason, the importance of sound training and practice cannot be too highly stressed.

Landing the victim

Sometime after reaching the surface, possibly during the towing period, the rescuer as well might suffer from shock. At best, the rescuer may be psychologically, if not physically, exhausted, and then the handling of the victim can become increasingly difficult. Whenever circumstances allow, help should be summoned and waited for, with the responsibility for lifting the victim clear of the water left to someone who is fresh and clear thinking.

The removal of a victim from out of the water is most easily accomplished if this can take place from alongside the soft rubber pontoon of an inflatable cover boat. Because

of its low freeboard, on-board assistance is readily available.

With a larger vessel, a rear-mounted diving stage makes picking up a helpless victim much easier. With a diving ladder, the rescuer has to physically hold the victim in place until those on board can position themselves and accept the transfer of weight out of the water. The best way is for the rescuer to hold on to both sides of the ladder and keep the victim in between. Weight support can be given by putting one leg on the ladder and sitting the victim on or astride it. The important thing is to make sure the victim is not washed away by a wave. The whole

Hoisting the victim on to an inflatable boat

Resuscitation

Raising a victim up a rope ladder

operation will be a great deal easier if the victim's aqualung set can be removed first. Even when firmly secured alongside the boat, it may still be difficult to manoeuvre the victim safely aboard. If cold, shocked or injured, the victim will be unable to help. If there is no landing stage or boarding ladder, face the victim outboard and haul him aboard by the armpits. A line secured to the harness may help.

When the landing has to be made through surf, then rescuers must consider the relative dangers of the particular foreshore. Is it rocky, shingle or sandy?

When you are ready to start, proceed as follows:

* Choose a calm period in the wave action, and then follow a breaker.

* If it is necessary to go through the surf, first trim both of the buoyancy compensators right down so that they do not act like corks.

* Once in the surf, move clear of the next breaker as quickly as you possibly can.

* It will be easier to carry or drag a victim through the undertow if you first abandon your fins.

Resuscitation

The basic technique for rescue from drowning is called cardiopulmonary resuscitation (CPR). It differs from other methods of restoring circulation and breathing on dry land only in detail. The treatment is always the same, although the technique may vary with the rather special circumstances which attend drowning and with the skill of the rescuer concerned. CPR is dealt with in three phases.

Phase 1: Basic life support
This is the immediate on-site treatment given by the rescuer as soon as the victim is safely out of the water. The intention is to restore blood circulation in a victim who has suffered a cardiac arrest, and this will be the first possible opportunity to do so. The cause of the arrest is not nearly as important as the need to mechanically reproduce the heartbeat.

Phase 2: Advanced life support
The stabilizing of the cardiopulmonary system and the restoration of a near-normal blood flow.

Phase 3: Prolonged life support
Long-term resuscitation by intensive care in a hospital.

The only treatment which can be administered by a non-medical rescuer is *Phase 1: Basic life support.*

Basic life support

As stated before, this is no time to diagnose the cause of the accident. The rescuer must be concerned with only the most urgent and vital life-saving actions.

Resuscitation can begin in earnest only when the victim has been brought into the boat or on to the shore. Proceed as follows:

1 Send for help — preferably the coastguard or an ambulance. Do

not forget you may be able to summon their help by radio.

2 Lie victim down. Then remove his hood and unzip the suit jacket.

3 Check for respiratory arrest by the 'feel and listen' method. First extend the victim's airway, then place your cheek over the victim's open mouth to check if he or she is breathing. If not, expired air resuscitation (EAR) must be given imme-

diately. If the victim is breathing, EAR will not be necessary but the victim must be watched carefully in case the breathing stops.

4 Check carotid artery for a pulse; this is usually weak, erratic and hard to find in a drowning victim. A pulse means that there has been no cardiac arrest. If, however, no pulse can be found external cardiac compressions (ECC) must be applied to restart the heart.

5 Although CPR can be carried out by only one operator, it will be much less exhausting and more likely to be successful if there are two operators — especially when the victim has no pulse and is not breathing. This technique is shown on the opposite page.

Accept help with the actual giving of CPR only from people who have been trained to do this. Any other offers of assistance can be diverted to the summoning of aid and the provision of transport.

6 EAR is effective only if done properly. Avoid these pitfalls:

* Air will not be able to pass into the victim's lungs unless the airways are extended. The air passes into the stomach instead and the rescuer will be able to see the stomach bulging — watch for vomiting !

* If rescuers give EAR too fast they may make themselves dizzy. Do not exceed the recommended rate of 18 breaths per minute.

* If there are two operators (one giving EAR and the other ECC), they should maintain a steady uninterrupted rhythm — one breath with every 5 compressions, at a rate of 60 compressions per minute — without interrupting the rhythm of the compressions. When there is only one operator, he or she should try to maintain 2 breaths to every 15 compressions.

7 The treatment of any wounds must take second place to resuscitation, except perhaps in the case of a very severe haemorrhage. Several injuries may have to be dealt with at the same time, and it should not be forgotten that one symptom may mask that of another injury.

8 If the CPR has been successful, the victim should be put into the recovery position which is shown in the diagram on the following page.

During recovery, the victim must be kept under constant observation in case his breathing or pulse stops unexpectedly. Also there is always the danger of a victim vomiting and this vomit may go down the air passages to the lungs.

The victim must be taken to hospital, accompanied by a companion who will be able to furnish the medical staff with the necessary details of the accident. It would be sensible to send the most experienced and knowledgeable diver who may be able to advise.

Do not expect the duty casualty staff of a small coastal hospital to include doctors experienced in dealing with diving accidents.

If water has entered the lungs, the victim may drown even after a successful rescue. The hospital will need to keep the victim until Phase 2 (Advanced life support), and Phase 3 (Prolonged life support) have been completed. CPR can be a lengthy treatment.

Four vital rules for resuscitation:

1 It is important to start CPR at the earliest possible moment.

2 Keep the victim's airways clear.

3 Apply ECC to maintain circulation if the heart stops.

4 Continue with EAR until breathing is restored.

The question is often asked 'How long should CPR be maintained?'

The rescuers should set themselves a half-hour minimum target to re-establish breathing. In a genuine emergency it would be difficult to continue beyond this target without serious risk of the rescuers themselves becoming victims.

Most authorities side-step the issue by referring the decision to stop resuscitation to a qualified person, but of course, in remote places, it is unlikely that such a qualified person will be available.

Modern diving medical opinion seems to say that efforts at CPR may reasonably be discontinued after a minimum of half an hour if the victim remains 'pulseless'.

However, do not give up resuscitative efforts too readily since, in some cases, recovery from near-drowning has been successful after long periods of submersion, especially if hypothermia has been induced by cold water.

Not all diving accidents involve drowning with respiratory and cardiac arrest. Many problems will manifest themselves only after the ascent to the surface, some even several hours after that. Pulmonary barotrauma (or burst lung) and decompression sickness are but two examples of this.

The treatment for such accidents will not require EAR or ECC, but may still need urgent action, such as transporting the victim rapidly to a recompression chamber.

So divers must never respond with a stereotyped reaction to an emergency; and it is very important that the diver should become familiar with all the drills for life-saving. (See also *Volume Two.*)

Cardiopulmonary resuscitation (CPR)

Basic life support — the **ABC** of lifesaving

A **Airways:** clear the airways of any obstruction

Check for respiratory arrest by the 'feel and listen' method

Obstruction by the tongue

Lift neck and tilt head

B **Breathing:** blowing air into the victim by expired air resuscitation (EAR)

In the water — mouth to nose method; when static, about 15 breaths/minute, when towing, a rhythmic cycle of 2 breaths every $\frac{1}{4}$ minute

Out of the water — mouth to mouth; 18 breaths a minute

Check that the chest rises with every breath

Inhalation

Exhalation

C **Circulation:** restarting the heart by external cardiac compression (ECC)

Technique of ECC

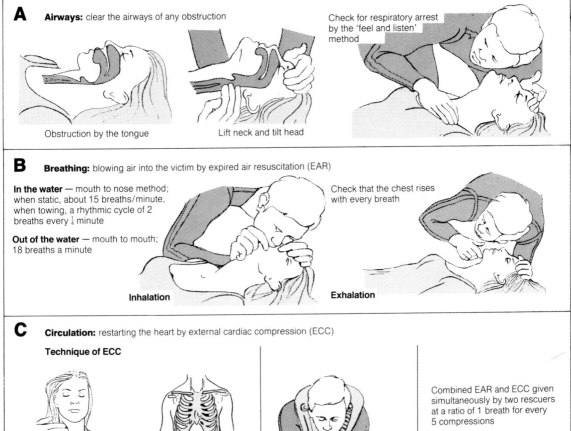

Feeling for a pulse

The pressure point

Compression

Release

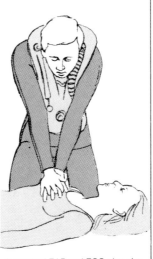

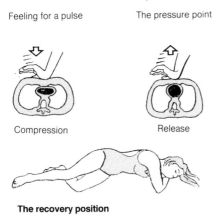

The recovery position

Combined EAR and ECC given by a solo rescuer, 2 breaths for every 15 compressions, at a rate of 60 compressions a minute

Combined EAR and ECC given simultaneously by two rescuers at a ratio of 1 breath for every 5 compressions

Conversion tables

To convert	Into	Multiply by
atmospheres	cm of mercury	76.0
	ft of water (4°C)	33.9
	fsw	33.072
	in of mercury (0°C)	29.92
	kg/cm²	1.0333
	kg/m²	10332
	pounds/in² (psi)	14.7
	tons/ft²	1.058
bar	atmospheres	0.9869
	kg/m²	10200
	kg/cm²	1.02
	pounds/ft²	2089
centigrade	Fahrenheit	(°Cx9/5)+32
centimetres	inches	0.3937
	feet	0.0328
	yards	0.01094
centimetres of mercury	atmospheres	0.01316
	ft of water (4°C)	0.4461
	kg/m²	136
	pounds/ft²	27.85
	pounds/in² (psi)	0.1934
centimetres/sec	feet/min	1.9685
	feet/sec	0.03281
	km/hr	0.036
	knots	0.01943
	metres/min	0.6
	miles/hr	0.02237
	miles/min	0.0003728
cubic centimetres	cu. inches (in³)	0.06102
	cu. feet (ft³)	0.00003531
	cu. yards (yd³)	0.000001308
	gallons (US liquid)	0.0002642
	litres	0.01
	ounces	0.03381
cubic feet	cu. cm (cc)	28320
	cu. inches (in³)	1728
	cu. metres (m³)	0.02832
	cu. yards (yd³)	0.03704
	gallons (US liquid)	7.48052
	litres	28.32
cubic feet/min	cu. cm/sec (cc/sec)	472
	gallons/sec	0.472
cubic feet/sec	gallons/min	448.831
cubic inches	cu. cm (cc)	16.39
	cu. feet (ft³)	0.0005787
	cu. metres (m³)	0.00001639
	cu. yards (yd³)	0.00002143
	gallons (US liquid)	0.004329
	litres	0.01639
cubic metres	cu. inches (in³)	61023
	cu. feet (ft³)	35.31
	cu yards (yd³)	1.308
	gallons (US liquid)	264.2
	litres	1000
feet	millimetres	304.8
	centimetres	30.48
	metres	0.3048
	miles (naut.)	0.0001645
	miles (stat.)	0.0001894
feet of water (fsw)	atmospheres	0.0295
	in of mercury	0.8826
	kg/cm²	0.03048
	kg/m²	304.8
	pounds/ft²	62.43
	pounds/in² (psi)	0.4335
feet/min	cm/sec	0.5080
	feet/sec	0.01667
	km/hr	0.01829
	metres/min	0.3048
	miles/hr	0.01136
feet/sec	cm/sec	30.48
	km/hr	1.097
	knots	0.5921
	metres/min	18.29
	miles/hr	0.6818
	miles/min	0.01136
gallons (Br. Imperial)	cu. cm (cc)	3785
	cu. feet (ft³)	0.1337
	cu. inches (in³)	231
	cu. metres (m³)	0.003785
	cu. yards (yd³)	0.004951
	litres	3.785
	pounds of water	8.33
	gallons (US)	1.20095
gallons (US)	gallons (Br. Imp.)	0.83267
inches	millimetres	25.4
	centimetres	2.54
	feet	0.08333
	metres	0.0254
	yards	0.02778
kilograms	grams	1000
	pounds	2.205
	tons (long)	0.0009842
	tons (short)	0.001102
kilometres	feet	3281
	miles	0.6214
	yards	1094
kilometres/hr	cm/sec	27.78
	feet/min	54.68
	feet/sec	0.9113
	knots	0.5396
	metres/min	16.67
	miles/hr	0.6214
knots	feet/hr	6080.2
	kilometres/hr	1.8532
	metres/sec	0.5144
	statute miles/hr	1.1516
	yards/hr	2027
	feet/sec	1.689
litres	cu. cm (cc)	1000
	cu. metres (m³)	0.001
	cu. inches (in³)	61.02
	cu. ft (ft³)	0.03531
	cu. yards (yd³)	0.001308
	gallons (US liquid)	0.2642
metres	inches	39.37
	feet	3.281
	miles (naut.)	0.0005396
	miles (stat.)	0.0006214
	yards	1.094
metres/min	cm/sec	1.667
	feet/min	3.281
	feet/sec	0.05468
	km/hr	0.06
	knots	0.03238
	miles/hr	0.03728
metres/sec	feet/min	196.8
	feet/sec	3.281
	km/hr	3.6
	km/min	0.06
	miles/hr	2.237
	miles/min	0.03728
miles (nautical)	metres	1853.248
	kilometres	1.853248
	feet	6080
	yards	2025.4
	miles (stat.)	1.1516
miles (statute)	centimetres	160900
	metres	1609
	kilometres	1.609
	feet	5280
	yards	1760
	miles (naut.)	0.8684
miles/hr	cm/sec	44.7
	feet/min	88
	feet/sec	1.467
	miles/min	0.1667
	km/hr	1.609
	km/min	0.02682
	knots	0.8684
	metres/min	26.82
	metres/sec	0.447
millimetres	inches	0.3937
	feet	0.003281
	yards	0.001094
ounces	pounds	0.0625
	cu. inches (in³)	1.805
	litres	0.02957
ounces/in²	pounds/in²	0.0625
pounds	kilograms	0.4536
	ounces	16
pounds/ft³	kg/m³	16.02
pounds/in³	pounds/ft³	1728
pounds/ft	kg/m	1.488
pounds/in	gm/cm	178.6
pounds/ft²	atmospheres	0.0004725
	kg/m²	4.882
	pounds/in² (psi)	0.006944
pounds/in² (psi)	atmospheres	0.06804
	feet seawater	2.250482
	kg/m²	703.1
	pounds/ft²	144
pounds of water	gallons	0.12004
square feet	sq. mm (mm²)	92900
	sq. cm (cm²)	929
	sq. metres (m²)	0.0929
	sq. inches (in²)	144
	sq. yards (yd²)	0.111
square inches	sq. mm (mm²)	645.2
	sq. cm (cm²)	6.452
	sq. feet (ft²)	0.006944
square kilometres	sq. miles	0.3861
square metres	sq. feet (ft²)	10.76
	sq. inches (in²)	1550
	sq. yards (yd²)	1.196
square miles	sq. kilometres	2.590
square millimetres (mm²)	sq. inches	0.00155
square yards	sq. metres (m²)	0.8361
temperature (°C) + 273	absolute temperature (°K)	1
temperature (°C) + 17.78	temperature (°F)	1.8
temperature (°F) + 460	absolute temperature	1
temperature (°F) −32	temperature (°C)	5/9
tons (long)	kilograms	1016
	pounds	2240
	tons (short)	1.12
tons (short)	kilograms	907.1848
	ounces	32000
	pounds	2000
	tons (long)	0.89287
yards	centimetres	91.44
	metres	0.9144

Comparison of cylinder pressures			
lbf/sq. in	MN/sq. m	ats	bar
1800	12.4	122	124
2000	13.8	136	138
2250	15.5	153	155
2500	17.2	170	172
2650	18.2	180	183
3000	20.7	204	207

From	To	Multiply by
fsw	msw	0.3048
psi	fsw	2.250482
bar	psi	14.503774
atmospheres	psi	14.696
atmospheres	fsw	33.072

1 bar = 100kN/sq.m=100 kPa

Comparison of cylinder capacities and mass of air contained				
Capacity of cylinder			Mass of air	
cu. feet	litres	cu. metres	lb	kg
40	1133	1.133	3.1	1.39
45	1274	1.274	3.4	1.56
50	1416	1.416	3.8	1.74
55	1557	1.557	4.2	1.91
60	1699	1.699	4.6	2.08
65	1841	1.841	5.0	2.26
70	1982	1.982	5.4	2.43
75	2124	2.124	5.7	2.60
80	2265	2.265	6.1	2.78
85	2407	2.407	6.6	2.99
90	2549	2.549	6.8	3.08
95	2690	2.690	7.2	3.27
100	2832	2.832	7.6	3.45

Beaufort wind scale (Numbers 1 to 6 only)

For an effective height of 10 metres above sea level.
* This table is only a rough guide as to what may be expected in the open sea. Small boats may be unsafe in conditions of Force 4 upwards and should **never** venture out to sea above Force 6. In enclosed waters of when near land with an offshore wind, wave heights will be smaller and the waves steeper. Figures in brackets indicate the probable maximum height of waves.

Beaufort number	Descriptive term	Mean wind speed equivalent in knots	Deep sea criterion	Probable mean wave height* in metres
0	Calm	<1	Sea like a mirror	—
1	Light air	1-3	Ripples with the appearance of scales are formed, but without foam crests	0.1(0.1)
2	Light breeze	4-6	Small wavelets, still short but more pronounced; crests have a glassy appearance and do not break	0.2(0.3)
3	Gentle breeze	7-10	Large wavelets; crests begin to break; foam of glassy appearance; scattered white horses	0.6(1)
4	Moderate breeze	11-16	Small waves, becoming longer; fairly frequent white horses	1(1.5)
5	Fresh breeze	17-21	Moderate waves, taking a more pronounced long form; many white horses are formed (chance of some spray)	2(2.5)
6	Strong breeze	22-27	Large waves begin to form; the white foam crests are more extensive everywhere (probably some spray)	3(4)

Feet to metres, metres to feet

The central columns of figures in bold type can be referred to in either direction. To the left to convert metres into feet, or to the right to convert feet into metres. For example, five lines down: 5 feet = 1.52 metres, and 5 metres = 16.40 feet.

Feet	Metres	Feet	Metres
3.28	**1**	88.58	**27**	8.23
6.56	**2**	91.86	**28**	8.53
9.84	**3**	95.14	**29**	8.84
13.12	**4**	98.43	**30**	9.14
16.40	**5**	101.71	**31**	9.45
19.69	**6**	104.99	**32**	9.75
22.97	**7**	108.27	**33**	10.06
26.25	**8**	111.55	**34**	10.36
29.53	**9**	114.83	**35**	10.67
32.81	**10**	118.11	**36**	10.97
36.09	**11**	121.39	**37**	11.28
39.37	**12**	124.67	**38**	11.58
42.65	**13**	127.95	**39**	11.89
45.93	**14**	131.23	**40**	12.19
49.21	**15**	134.51	**41**	12.50
52.49	**16**	137.80	**42**	12.80
55.77	**17**	141.08	**43**	13.11
59.06	**18**	144.36	**44**	13.41
62.34	**19**	147.64	**45**	13.72
65.62	**20**	150.92	**46**	14.02
68.90	**21**	154.20	**47**	14.33
72.18	**22**	157.48	**48**	14.63
75.46	**23**	160.76	**49**	14.94
78.74	**24**	164.04	**50**	15.24
82.02	**25**	328.08	**100**	30.48
85.30	**26**	3280.80	**1000**	304.8

1 nautical mile = approx. 1.853 km (6080 ft)
1 statute mile = 1.609 km (5280 ft)

Glossary

Airways
The air passages within the nose, mouth, pharynx, larynx and trachea through which the air breathed in passes to the lungs

Alveoli
Air sacs in lungs where gaseous exchange takes place

Ambient pressure
The pressure that immediately surrounds a diver

Anoxia
Total lack of oxygen which will, unless immediately rectified, result in unconsciousness and ultimately death

Archimedes' principle
When a body is wholly or partially immersed in a fluid it experiences an apparent up-thrust equal to the weight of the fluid displaced

Assisted ascent
An ascent when two divers share one aqualung

Ats
'Atmospheres'; units of pressure

Atmospheric pressure
Pressure of the atmosphere measured in ats or bars

Bar
Unit of pressure, about one 'atmosphere'

Barotrauma
Damage to body due to expanding or contracting air

Basic equipment
Mask, fins and snorkel — the minimum equipment needed for breath-hold diving

BC (buoyancy compensator)
A bag or life-jacket which can be inflated to make the diver more buoyant and help an ascent

NB: Can be called an ABLJ (adjustable buoyancy life-jacket)

Bends
A form of decompression sickness; so-called because assuming a bent position relieves the pain

Bottom time
Time lapse between the descent and the ascent

Breath-hold dive
Diving without any breathing apparatus. This may be called skin diving, or snorkelling if a snorkel is used

BSAC
British Sub-Aqua Club

Buddy
A companion diver

Buoyancy
The floating ability of a diver or an object. Positive buoyancy means a tendency to float up; negative buoyancy means a tendency to sink; neutral buoyancy lies between the two

Buoyancy trim
Adjusting buoyancy with weights to suit diver and depth of dive

Buoyant ascent
An ascent made with extra buoyancy — from a compensator or dry-suit inflation

Cardiac arrest
When heart stops beating

Carotid
Main arteries supplying oxygenated blood to brain

Capillaries
Minute blood vessels

Compressed air
The breathing gas normally used by sports divers. It consists of 78% nitrogen and 21% oxygen highly compressed, typically to about 3,000 psi or 200 bar

Contents gauge
Gauge indicating pressure of air inside cylinder

CPR
Cardiopulmonary resuscitation

Cracking
Opening cylinder tap or valve carefully to allow a short burst of air to escape

Cyanosis
Blueness of skin caused by large quantities of de-oxygenated blood in its minute vessels

Cylinder pressure
Pressure to which air in cylinder must be compressed to effect maximum capacity

Cylinder testing
Legally required every five years in Britain but a hydraulic check every two years and a visual inspection annually is to be recommended

DCC
Decompression chamber

DCS
(Decompression sickness)
Crippling (sometimes fatal)

affliction caused by incorrect decompression which results in nitrogen bubbles forming in blood, tissues and joints

Dead air space
Air spaces in respiratory system, such as the trachea, nasal passages and pharynx which take no part in gaseous exchange

Decompression
Escape of dissolved gases from the body tissues due to a drop in the pressure. Therapeutic decompression is planned and controlled recompression of a diver suffering from decompression sickness

Decompression meter
Instrument which measures times and depths and indicates absorption of nitrogen and necessary stops

Decompression stops
Specified time spent at certain depths to allow nitrogen to be eliminated from body

Decompression tables
Details of stages required for decompression showing a large range of depth/time combinations

Deep water
From 20 metres (66 ft) down

Depth gauge
An instrument which measures and indicates depth

Direct-feed system
System by which buoyancy compensator bag is inflated with air directly from the aqualung

Ditching
Abandoning equipment or weights to gain buoyancy

Drift diving
A dive when the tidal stream or current carries the diver along underwater

Dry suit
Diving suit which does not allow water to enter so diver stays dry

DV
The demand valve or a regulator

EAR
Expired air resuscitation (the 'kiss of life')

Ear clearing
Equalizing air pressure in middle ear with ambient pressure

ECC
External cardiac compression

Embolism
Blockage of blood vessel — may be caused by a bubble of gas

Emphysema
The escape of air bubbles into the body tissues due to a 'burst lung'

Equalization
Equalizing the air pressure in two spaces, as when ear clearing

Eustachian tube
Narrow tube which connects the middle ear to the throat

Free ascent
Ascent with air in lungs but without use of aqualung — usually in an emergency situation

Freeboard
Height of a ship's side above the surface of the sea

Gunwhale
Upper edge of a vessel's side

Hard-hat divers
Professional divers in standard dress who wear copper helmets

Hydrostatic pressure
Water pressure, which increases with depth

Hyperventilation
This is over-deep breathing which can be dangerous because it flushes carbon dioxide (needed to stimulate respiration) out of the lungs

Hypothermia
Body heat loss, when the body core temperature drops below 35°C (95°F)

Hypoxia
A shortage of oxygen in the body; this may be attributable to faulty apparatus, medical problems or to over-exertion

Inflatable
A boat, usually made of rubberized material, which can be inflated by air and which can be deflated for transport

Marker buoy
A surface buoy which is attached to the diver so as to indicate his position to those on the surface

Mid-water
The half-way point between the deepest part of a dive and the surface, when you cannot see the bottom or the top!

Near-drowned victim
A victim who appears to be drowned but whom it is possible to resuscitate

Negative buoyancy
Being heavier than water and therefore sinking

Neoprene
A synthetic cellular material used for making wet suits

Nitrogen narcosis
Effect on body of nitrogen under pressure — symptoms similar to drunkenness

No-stop dive
Dive where depth and length of time mean no stops for stage decompression are required

Octopus rig
A second 'take off' from the first stage of a regulator which can be used as a spare or emergency regulator

Open water
Naturally-occurring water such as sea or lake, rather than a swimming pool or tank

O-ring
Circular sealing ring which forms an efficient seal on apparatus used underwater

Partial pressure
In a mixture of gases, this refers to the pressure exerted by one gas only

Pulmonary barotrauma
Damage to the lungs caused by expanding air

Purge button
Button which when depressed allows a free flow of air to 'purge' water from the mouthpiece

Quick-release
A means of being able to jettison weightbelts and harnesses immediately if an emergency situation demands this

Recompression
Repressurizing a diver, as in a compression chamber

Regulator
Demand valve which automatically adjusts the pressure of air from cylinder with depth; air flows only on inhalation

Repeat-dive interval
Time which must elapse between a first and second dive depending on the depth of the first, to allow nitrogen to be eliminated

Reversed ear
Damage to ear caused by excess pressure within middle ear

RNPL
Royal Naval Physiological Laboratory

Shallow water
From surface down to depth of 10 metres (33 ft)

Skindiving
Underwater 'breath-hold' diving without any breathing apparatus

SMB
Surface marker buoy

Sports diving
Diving purely for pleasure or sport, as opposed to a professional undertaking

Squeeze
Increased pressure of air reduces the volume of mask, hood or dry suit, causing these to press on to or 'squeeze' the diver

Stage decompression
Stopping at set times and depths to allow excess nitrogen to escape from body

Tender
A diving assistant or support vessel usually linked to the underwater diver by a lifeline

Valsalva manoeuvre
Pressurizing the nose, lungs and ears by exhaling with the nose and mouth closed (ear clearing)

Venting
Removing air or allowing it to escape, usually from a dry suit or a buoyancy compensator

Weighting
Selecting the correct weights for the degree of buoyancy required

Weightbelt
Means of attaching chosen lead weights to diver. Can be jettisoned for extra buoyancy in emergency situations

Wet suit
Insulating diving suit which traps a thin film of water and keeps this at body temperature

Index

A

ABLJ *see* Buoyancy compensators
Air 89
composition 72
contamination 91
embolism 82-3
running out of 47
sharing 45, 124
see also Pressure
Ancillary equipment 31, 63-64
Anoxia 91
Aqualung
assembly 30
dismantling 41
function and operation 25
kitting up 31
removing 43
sharing 45
snorkelling with 46
Ascents
assisted buoyant 55, 124
assisted, with an octopus rig 124
barotrauma 81
buoyant 120-21
controlled buoyant 55, 122
emergency 116-129
free 121
normal 41, 77, 111-12
partial free 122
rate of 108
rescue 123-9
starting 118, 120
Atmospheric pressure (ats)
11, 72-4

B

Bar 11
Barotrauma 78-82
ascent 77, 81
descent 77, 78-80
pulmonary 81-2
Basic equipment 16-24
using 20-23
practise with 24
Basic life support 133

Blood composition 89
Boarding hard boats and inflatables 114-15
Bourdon gauge 63-4
Boyle's Law 75-6
Breath compression 77, 81
Breath-hold diving 13, 16-24, 92, 93
Breathing
from a compensator 56, 122
mechanics of 86
rhythm 32
sensitivity 48
without a mask 38
Brief 103
Buddy system 105
Buoyancy 33, 34, 50, 72, 92
check 104
compensation 54
control 34, 50
correction 54
for an ascent 120, 126
negative 119
rescues 127-8
see also Weighting
Buoyancy compensator (BC) 50, 54
breathing from 56, 122
deflation 52, 53
direct-feed 51-2
fitting 53
inflation 51, 53
maintenance 56
Burst lung 80-82

C

Capacity 72
Carbon dioxide 94-5
excess 94
in metabolism 85
percentage of 89
production of 87
retention 94
Carbon monoxide 91
Cardiac arrest 85, 130-1, 134
Claustrophobia 69
Circulatory system 87-8
Cold and exposure 70

Compression 75, 77-9, 97
Conscious victim 123
Contents gauge 63
CPR 134-35
Cylinder, emergency 52, 55
Cylinders and harness 25

D

Deadweight lifts 126-7
Debriefing and records 41, 115
Decompression 96-99
illness — signs and symptoms 83
sickness 83, 96-7
stops 99
tables 98-99
Density 71
Depth
gauge 63, 64, 74
Descent 77, 95, 108-9
to a rescue 129
vertical 39
Diaphragm gauge 63
Ditch and recovery 44
Dive
marshal 102
plan 102
preparation for 103
profile 102-3
surface 22-3
Diving
brief 103
downwards 22
physiology 85-97
time 98
Diving suit 57-62
compensation and venting 59, 60
seals 59
squeeze 78
see also Dry suit and Wet suit
Dressing 31, 59, 104
Drowning 91, 131
Dry suit 58-62
blow up 62
buoyancy 61
compensation 59-60
dressing 59
flooding 62

inflation 60
inversion 62
over-inflation 61
rescues with 129
weighting 61

E

EAR 89, 131
Ear
clearing 24,39,78-9
reversal 79
see also Valsalva's manoeuvre
ECC 131, 134, 135
Emergency
ascents and rescue 116-35
cylinder 52, 55
Emphysema, interstitial 82-3
Energy 71
Entries into water 35-6, 107-8
Environmental stresses 68-9
Equipment, ancillary 63-4
Exercise effect of 87
Exits *see* Leaving the water
Eyes *see* Vision

F

Facemask *see* Mask
Finning, technique 22, 24
on the back 46
Fins
choosing 20
swimming with 21
types of 18
First dive 50, 101-8
Fitness 15
Free
ascent 121
swimming 14

G

Gas
density 90

embolism 81, 82-3
exchange 89
partial pressures 89, 93
solubility 90
Gravity 71

H

Hand signals 34-5, 65
Hydrostatic pressure 74
Hyperventilation 92-93
Hypothermia 70
Hypoxia 91-2

K

Knives 64

L

Landing a victim 132
Leaving the water 44, 113-15
Life-jacket *see* Buoyancy compensator
Lung 86-9
capacity 86
pressure damage 80-2
squeeze 80-1

M

Mask 16-17
clearing 21,38,42
fitting 20
flanges 17
leaking and clearing 21,32
squeeze 23,78
Mass 71
Matter 71
Medical examination 15
Medical fitness 15
Mouthpiece 27, 33,49
recovering the 37

removing 37
replacing the 37, 49
twin-hose 49

N

Nitrogen 95
absorption and elimination 96-7
narcosis 69, 95
No-stop limit 97, 98-9

O

Octopus rig 124
Oxygen 90-1
intake of 85, 87, 89
toxicity 93

P

Picking up divers 113-15
Pneumothorax 82-3
Post-dive actions 115
Pre-dive checks and assembly 52, 103-7
Pressure 27, 72
absolute 11
ambient 11
at depth 23
atmospheric 72-4
hydrostatic 74
partial 89
problems 78-81
volume changes 75
Pulmonary barotrauma 81-2

R

Red eye 78
Regulator 26-7
assembling and testing 28, 91
fitting to the cylinder 28-9
function check 30

twin-hose 48-9
Rescues 117-35
buoyancy 127-8
deadweight 126-7
deep 125, 128
dry-suit 129-30
from the bottom 125
of a companion 123
on the surface 130-32
removal from water 132
self rescue 118
shallow 127
without buoyancy 120, 129
Respiratory system 85-9
Resuscitation 133-5

S

Self-rescue 118-122
Senses 68
Separation drill 110
Shallow-water blackout 93
Sharing an aqualung 45
Sharing an ascent 40,123-5
Signs and symptoms of decompression illness 82-3
Single hose *see* Regulator
Sinuses 80
Snorkel diving *see* Breath-hold diving
Snorkel fitting 19
Snorkelling with the aqualung 46-7
Snorkel tubes 19
Sound 84
Stage decompression 99
Stress 69
Suit *see* Diving suit
Surface dive 22
Surfacing 111-12
drill 22
see also Ascents

T

Talk and check 106
Tooth squeeze 80

Terminology, abbreviations and symbols 11
Twin hose
tube clearing 49
see also Regulator

U

Unconscious victim 125-6
Underwater movement 39-41
Units of measurement 11, 71

V

Valsalva's manoeuvre 15,79
Vertical descents 39
Vision 16, 84
Visual contact 109
Volume 72

W

Water column 73
Weight 71
Weightbelt 31,33,107
dropping the 118-9
Weighting 33,50,54
check 33
dry-suit weighting 58
overweighting 54
technique 33
wet-suit weighting 57-8
Weightlessness 68
Wet suit 57-8
weighting procedures 58

Acknowledgements

The authors have learnt so much from so many people it is difficult to know who to single out for special acknowledgement.

For our own early diving experience we are indebted to Mike Maloney, Ken Vaughan and the senior instructors at Holborn, No 130 Branch, British Sub Aqua Club.

For early ideas we should like to express special thanks to Tim Glover and Geoff Harwood; also to the following, our diving companions in Malta: Edward Arrigo, Brian Cudmore-Dixon, Anthony Cassar Desain, Charles Grech, Stephen Halliday, Joe Carvana Huber, Gunther Koppel, Winfrid Loffler, Joe Navarro, Malcolm Palmer, Joe Debono, John Stansby, and the late Tony Micallef Borg and Vincent Micallef Desesare.

We are grateful for advice and encouragement from Len Charlton, Jon Parlour and Peter Sieniewicz of the Sub Aqua Association.

We should like to express our gratitude to Peter Edmead, Martin Judd, and Keith and Jean Nicholson of London, No 1 Branch, British Sub Aqua Club.

Our thanks are also due to Walter Bain, Judy Hubbard, Dr David Thomsett, Dr J.J. Sammutt and Dr Peter Wilmshurst for their advice on diving medicine and physiology.

Lt. Cdr. Alan Bax RN of Fort Bovisand Underwater Centre, Lionel Blandford of the NSC, Mike Busuttili, Vice-chairman of the British Sub Aqua Club, Brian Hesketh, Martin Parker of A P Valves, Lorenzo Ricciardi, John Stubbs, Reg Vallintine of the London Underwater Centre, Sgt. Kevin Pitt, Cleveland Police Underwater Search Unit and Peter Zelepuken have also been very helpful — we thank them for their assistance.

We hope we have not forgotten to include any of our early mentors. The truth is that we have learnt something from almost every experienced diver we have met.

We should like to express our thanks to Fred English for his excellent drawings of gauges.

Finally we are most grateful to Ian Irvine, Chairman of the British Sub Aqua Club, and to Tony Hunt, Chairman of the Sub Aqua Association, for writing the foreword to our book.

The following books have been consulted:

The British Sub Aqua Club Diving Manual 10th Edition, 5th Revision

The Emergency Book by Smith and Stevens (Penguin)

Emergency Care 2nd Edition, by Grant and Murray (Brady)

Cardiopulmonary Cerebral Resuscitation by Peter Safar (Saunders Laerdal)

The Professional Diver's Handbook by David Sisman (Submex)

US Navy Diving Manual Change 2

Underwater Swimming (Connaisana et Techniques du Plonger) by Guy Poulet (Newnes)

Disabled Divers by David Royston (BSAC)

Diver's Handbook of Underwater Calculations by Wayne C. Tucker (Cornell Maritime Press)

Underwater Medicine 4th Edition, by Miles and MacKay (Adlard Coles, Granada)

The Body 1985 Revision, by Anthony Smith (Allen and Unwin)

The Diver's Medical Companion by Thomas and McKenzie (Diving Medical Centre Publications)

Diving and Subaquatic Medicine by Edmonds, Lowry and Pennyfather (Diving Medical Centre Publications)

World Underwater Book edited by Kendal MacDonald (1973)